Birds of Hedgerow and Garden

The Orbis Encyclopedia of Birds of
Britain and Europe
Volume Five

Birds of Hedgerow and Garden

Edited by John Gooders

ORBIS PUBLISHING
London

©1979 Orbis Publishing Ltd., London
©1971 Rizzoli Editore, Milan
Printed in Great Britain
ISBN 0 85613 390 6

Frontispiece: Nuthatch (J. A. Bailey/Ardea)

Contents

Editor's Preface

The world of birds is so remarkable, in many instances so almost unbelievable, that it is perhaps not surprising that ornithologists of previous generations were more prone to accept what to them were more reasonable explanations than the truth itself. The mystery of migration, of the regular comings and goings of birds season by season, seemed too far-fetched to the eighteenth-century world which accepted instead the idea of Swallows hibernating at the bottom of ponds. The idea of Arctic Terns flying 50,000 kilometres a year was equally unacceptable to a generation that had no railways, let alone any ambition to fly. Yet what we have since discovered makes even these 'startling facts' seem rather tame. Great Shearwaters journey over the whole of the Atlantic in a great looping migration and still find their way back to a tiny island in the Tristan group surrounded by thousands of miles of featureless ocean. The tiny Bee-Hummingbird beats its wings 200 times per minute to produce its characteristic sound and, incidentally, keep airborne. The female hornbill is cemented into its nest chamber with its eggs and young and remains imprisoned for weeks at a time. The White-throated Spinetail Swift flies at up to 200 kilometres per hour and is the fastest living animal. Other swifts find their way around darkened caves by a form of echo-location similar to that used by bats. The Malleefowl of Australia lays its eggs in a natural incubator and regulates the temperature by scratching earth on to, or off, the mound of the nest. When the young hatch under the ground they dig upwards and walk away on their own completely independent and capable of flying. One could go on and on describing the amazing things that birds do, but it should be quite obvious that much of this 'gee-whizardry' is concerned with their remarkable and enviable flying ability.

Man has always wanted to fly free like the birds. A few, just a very few, have managed to enjoy the life of a bird either in a light aeroplane or in a glider. But all that most of us have managed is to encapsulate ourselves along with a few hundred like-minded souls and skim from one place to another with barely a glimpse out of the window. Some years ago a prize was offered for the first man-powered flight over a given course. Years later the prize was claimed by a lightweight human who had furiously pedalled his huge, fragile machine around the short course and completed it exhausted. Man may be possessed of many and various talents, but as a creature he was obviously not designed to leave the ground!

Birds are remarkable machines. Their design is all centred around the ability to fly. Everything about them is constructed with weight in mind. Their bones are hollow and thin and maintain their rigidity and strength by being honeycombed like a popular chocolate bar or a mousse. 'As light as a feather' is a by-word for lightness, and with good reason, for the flexible strength of a bird's flight feather is remarkable. Yet feathers are only highly adapted reptilian scales. So feathers provide large surfaces for little weight, and honeycombed bones act as a lightweight structured support. How about fuel? Birds have a remarkably fast digestive system that enables them to extract nutrients and void the waste in a matter of minutes rather than hours. This means that they are never full of heavy food. Everything about a bird is lightweight except for one major item – the muscles that sustain flight itself. These are the muscles on the chest that form the breast of a chicken. In birds that spend less time walking and scratching and more time in the air, these breast muscles form an even larger percentage of total weight than in the chicken.

The purposes of flight are many and various. The earliest of birds, a creature called Archaeopteryx, was merely a feather-covered reptile that could just about manage to glide from one tree to the next. In the jungles of South America lives the Hoatzin, a bird that, though still alive and well today, does little more than its ancestor of several million years ago. In contrast, the hummingbirds can fly backwards, forwards, sideways and, one could almost imagine, upside down if there was a reason to do so. Hummers fly because they need to to feed, Hoatzins mainly because they do not swim very well as adults. Most birds fly to escape danger, but some have overcome danger by growing large enough to run away or defend themselves like the Ostrich or Emu, or have chosen to live in regions where flight from danger is unnecessary, like the Kiwi. Terns fly to feed and penguins 'fly' underwater for the same reason. But penguins also fly fast enough underwater to escape the danger of Leopard Seals, and terns fly to get from one part of the world to another and thus enjoy twelve months of summer. Vultures, those rather grotesque but highly efficient garbage collectors, fly to spot food, not to consume it. High in the sky they circle on broad wings letting the air currents keep them aloft just like a human-piloted glider. From over a thousand metres up other scavengers can be seen as they descend to gather round a food source. Then the vultures glide down to join in the feast on the ground.

The ability to fly is not unique to birds, but they are the largest and most obvious and numerous of the world's aviators. To us earthbound souls flight is a symbol of immense freedom, but to see birds as the epitome of liberty is misleading. Flight is just one of a bird's weapons in the continual struggle for survival, their lives being, in our terms at least, routine and very dangerous.

John Gooders

Introduction

For most of us the birds of hedgerow and garden are inevitably the most familiar. Whether we live in city, town, village or the countryside, there are a number of birds that we have in common – these are the birds that have learned to live alongside man and benefit from his presence. In Britain there are Starlings and Robins, in Europe the Robin's place is taken by the Redstart, in India it is mynahs and Black Kites; but wherever you go it is difficult to get away from House Sparrows. Seen in our inner cities the Sparrow is dull and dingy, but out in the country the beautiful chestnut colours of the male make it one of the most handsome birds. Indeed a great many birds only lack attraction because we see them so regularly and so easily. The male Chaffinch? The Bullfinch? The Nuthatch? All surely would be high on the list of 'wanted' birds were they not so common or widespread. A widely travelled friend of mine, an American with all the brashness and apt turn of phrase for which Americans are well known, refers to these species as 'trash birds'. Now that may seem a little unkind, but the point he is making is valid – that in any area there are dirt-common birds that will excite the visitor the day he arrives, but soon become part of the general background. What these birds are varies from place to place and amazingly can make bird-watchers terribly blasé about what would be highly valued species in other areas.

Among the families included in this volume there are birds as colourful, exotic and unusual as anyone could desire. Who could fail to be enthralled by the titmice as they crowd and squabble round the bird table? Their aerial mastery as they manoeuvre for position has to be seen in slow motion to be properly appreciated. Great Tit and Blue Tit may be the most common, but the regular peanut provider will be disappointed not to see Coal Tit, then Marsh and even Willow Tit. Watching the peanut dispenser and bird table and making a list of one's avian guests can be remarkably rewarding. I have recorded species as unlikely as Great Spotted Woodpecker and Siskin, and a fortunate enthusiast once spotted a Myrtle Warbler from America that proved to be a new bird for Britain.

Food may be the most obvious and effective ingredient in the bird gardener's armoury, but there are others besides. Providing nesting materials in spring and early summer can be exciting as birds

(Below) Male and female Blackcaps *Sylvia atricapilla*

fly to and fro with beakfuls of soft wool specially put out for them. If the weather is dry a tray or pool of mud will have Blackbirds, Song Thrushes and even House Martins paddling around gathering building materials for their nesting structures. The idea of a bird mud-centre evolved in response to complaints from my wife that our local Blackbirds were attacking the soft damp earth in her flower pots. It worked a treat. The same tactic (that is, free provision to prevent vandalism) might have saved the day for the nurseryman who discovered a nest decorated with all his neatly printed shrub labels that the birds had carefully removed one by one from his stock.

While providing nesting materials it is easy enough to go the whole hog and provide the nests themselves. Nest boxes are too well established in the repertoire to need any further comment, but it is terribly important to put them up correctly. Firstly, you must spread them out to the far corners of your estate, be it a back yard or an acre or more. Birds are territorial and a battery of homes nicely positioned around the house will fall in one or perhaps two territories. Set up in the far corners they may each fall in a different bird's domain. Secondly, ensure that the boxes are of different types. The small hole type will suit tits; the open-fronted is ideal for Robins and Spotted Flycatchers. I persuaded my local Spotted Flycatchers to nest in an old kettle strung up to a wall with the hole facing outwards. Thirdly, and most important, make sure that the nest box faces north-east and that the entrance hole is tilted slightly downwards to prevent any rain from blowing in. There are also specialist items such as the provision of artificial House Martins' nests fixed under the eaves to encourage a new colony, or shelves in garden sheds for Swallows to adopt, but far more successful is the provision of the right sort of cover. Making up an autumn bonfire of garden trimmings and prunings and forgetting to set fire to it will encourage Wrens and Dunnocks to nest. Leaving patches of brambles and nettles does the same for Whitethroats. A pile of sticks resting against a tree will provide a site for Song Thrushes, and ivy along a wall is marvellous for early nesters.

All these things help build up the population of ordinary common-or-garden(!) birds. Between them they have helped to make gardens one of the richest of all habitats. As the concern for birds grows our farming landscape is changing for the worse. Hedgerows are being ripped out to create larger fields for a more mechanised style of farming. Dells and ponds are filled in for the same reason. Along with the disappearing hedgerow goes the disappearing hedgerow bird just at the same time as the bird gardener is doing his best to encourage birds. Perhaps all we are doing is transferring the birds from one area to another, though what impact the lack of small insectivorous birds will have on the ecology of the farm I am not qualified to say. I do know that the Dutch have found it beneficial to erect Kestrel nest boxes on posts on their new tree-less polders to keep control of small mammals. Will we have to do the same on the new prairies of East Anglia?

Of all the birds of Europe none have had to learn to adapt to a man-made environment so totally as the birds of garden and hedgerow. Indeed, gardens and hedgerows did not exist without man. Living in such surroundings each and every species has had to make some adjustment. Those that were incapable of making such adjustments declined; those that were most adaptable flourished. Indeed some made the transition so well that it is difficult to see how they existed before man came along and changed the countryside. The House Sparrow and Starling we have already seen depend on us for food and shelter, but where did the Rook live before we created arable fields and copses of tall trees? Perhaps it is not totally accidental that the most recently evolved species are among the most adaptable.

Many of the birds in this volume are birds of hedgerow and garden more or less by accident. In fact they are birds of woodland edge that have found, in the corners of hedges and in those ill-considered little copses, an ideal habitat. Among my own favourites are the so-called Old World warblers, a family that includes marsh, leaf and scrub warblers, only some of which can be considered hedgerow birds. Part of their appeal is perhaps that their continual furtive activity affords the watcher only the most fleeting of glimpses, yet just occasionally a warbler will be confiding and show itself in full view. Then their grace and elegance can be seen. I remember finding a Willow Warbler's nest in a wooded garden a few years ago. The female was feeding young in the domed nest situated on the ground against a small mound. Back and forth she flew, and between each coming and going I shifted forward a pace until she was no more than three metres away and binoculars become irrelevant. Such tameness is not unusual among garden nesting birds. There is a story of a bird photographer who was erecting his hide near a Blue Tit's nest while the bird ignored his efforts and continued feeding its young. As a result he re-packed the hide and obtained the photographs he wanted standing in the open without concealment.

While they lack the charisma of eagles, storks, cranes or even godwits and sandpipers, garden and hedgerow birds do not lack interest. Because they live alongside us, and are generally plentiful, we can observe the details of their lives in a much more satisfying way than we can the more elusive, albeit spectacular, birds. We can see them every day, watch them in flocks and then as they establish and defend their territories. We can observe their migrations and their seasonal comings and goings. We can find their nests and watch the progress of the chicks to independence – being careful not to interfere or draw danger to their hiding places. There is so much that we can do with the common birds that surround us that the surprise is that no one is doing it! Even the most commonplace birds remain unstudied. What a wonderful opportunity there is for anyone who enjoys watching the birds on the bird table to add significantly to our knowledge.

Birds of Hedgerow
and Garden

ORDER **Passeriformes**
FAMILY # SYLVIIDAE: Old World Warblers

F. Blackburn/Bruce Coleman

R. Longo

R. Richter/Ardea

In some classifications the Old World warblers have been considered a sub-family and placed—together with thrushes, blackbirds, nightingales, robins and flycatchers—in the huge family Muscicapidae. Here, however, they are treated as a distinct family. They are small or medium-sized passerines, mainly distributed throughout the Old World and distinguished by having ten primaries. In English the generic term 'warblers' is the same as that given to their ecological counterparts in the New World: these, however, belong to a quite different family, the Parulidae or wood warblers.

Old World warblers are generally uniform greenish, brownish or grey in colour (although some tropical species are vividly coloured), and only a few species display sexual dimorphism. Even distinct species sometimes have similar coloration, which adds considerable complication to observation and study: even experts have to rely on slight structural differences such as the wing in order to distinguish the various species.

Besides insects, spiders and larvae, some species feed on berries and small fruits. Old World warblers are rather solitary shy birds, preferring to remain hidden in thick vegetation, among trees, bushes, reeds and tall grasses. The song of the male has a predominantly territorial function; each pair builds a nest in its territory, on the

(Above) Savi's Warbler *Locustella luscinioides* and (right) Reed Warbler *Acrocephalus scirpaceus.* (Facing page) Whitethroat *Sylvia communis.* (Page one) Blue Tit *Parus caeruleus*

F. Blackburn/Bruce Coleman

D. Sudia/Photo Researchers

(Right) Ruby-crowned Kinglet *Regulus calendula* and (above) Grasshopper Warbler *Locustella naevia*

ground or, more frequently, among bushes, in trees or among reeds.

About three hundred species of Old World warblers are recognised, with a distribution limited to the Old World. Many of these occur in Africa, where at least one hundred and fifty nesting species are found: about forty are European, twenty-five are native to southeast Asia and twenty-one are found in Australia. The remaining species are distributed unequally throughout Asia, from Asia Minor to India, China and Japan. Two genera are also found in America: the genus *Regulus* with two endemic species and *Phylloscopus* with one — the Arctic Warbler *P. borealis*—whose distribution is predominantly Palearctic. The invasion of the American continent (mainly Alaska) by the Arctic Warbler is recent, in all probability postglacial, and this is demonstrated by the fact that the American individuals of this species still winter, after performing a spectacular migration, in the tropics of the Old World. This is not unique: the Greenland race of the common Wheatear *Oenanthe oenanthe leucorrhoa* winters in Africa after migrating through Iceland, the British Isles and western Europe. Apart from the goldcrests and firecrests of the genus *Regulus* which are in any case 'aberrant' and considered by some authorities a separate family, all members of this family which are from temperate regions are strongly migratory. Their winter quarters are often great distances from the breeding range, a fact which appears extraordinary as these small birds are not strong fliers. However, the Willow Warbler *Phylloscopus trochilus* of eastern Siberia winters in East Africa, while the Arctic Warbler migrates in winter from Scandinavia, the USSR and western Siberia to Indonesia, the Philippines and New Guinea, thus travelling a distance of at least 12,000 kilometres twice a year.

The many species of the family are, however, grouped in only a few genera: in Europe the most common are *Sylvia* with fifteen species, *Acrocephalus* (nine species), *Phylloscopus* (twelve species), *Hippolais* and *Locustella* (six species each). All of these genera contain at least one pair of the so-called 'sibling species', very much alike and found over the same area, which confuse both experts and amateurs alike.

The genus *Sylvia* contains some of the best known European songsters, such as the Garden Warbler *S. borin* and the Blackcap *S. atricapilla*. The Lesser Whitethroat *S. curruca* is one of the most widespread and has many sub-species. Some species are typical of the Mediterranean, for example, the Dartford Warbler *S. undata* and Marmora's Warbler *S. sarda*. They are similar to one another and are often found in the same

M. D. England/Ardea

habitat, that is, semi-degraded maquis. The Sardinian Warbler *S. melanocephala*, Ménétries's Warbler *S. mystacea* and the Cyprus Warbler *S. melanothorax* are all more or less resident, while the Subalpine Warbler *S. cantillans* and the Spectacled Warbler *S. conspicillata* migrate in winter to tropical Africa. Some Mediterranean species also nest much further north: the Dartford Warbler, for example, is resident in southern England.

The genus *Hippolais* includes species which are all remarkably similar, with upper parts ranging in colour from light green to grey and underparts from white to more or less vivid sulphur-yellow.

Another group of warblers is found in thick damp vegetation: these are the species of the genus *Locustella*, most of which have a monotonous, drawn-out song reminiscent of grasshoppers (hence both the Latin name *Locustella* and the common name Grasshopper Warbler of one species). Only two species commonly nest in Britain: these are Savi's Warbler *L. luscinioides* and the Grasshopper Warbler *L. naevia*. They are both extremely shy birds and therefore appear to be much less widespread than they really are.

It is a short step from *Locustella* species to the reed warblers of the genus *Acrocephalus*. Many of the common names given to these species—Reed Warbler, Sedge Warbler, Marsh Warbler and so forth—are a good indication of the habitat of the majority of individuals: thick marsh vegetation

(Left) Melodious Warbler *Hippolais polyglotta* and (below) Chiffchaff *Phylloscopus collybita*

R. Messent/Ardea

H. Barnfather/Bruce Coleman

(Above) The Sedge Warbler *Acrocephalus schoeno-baenus* is one of the so-called reed warblers, most of which belong to the genus *Acrocephalus*. They are difficult to identify in the field as their plumage is very similar, being brown above and paler below with a whitish throat. They are also skulking species so are best identified by their song. (Below) World distribution of the family Sylviidae

and especially reed beds. In summer the monotonous and insistent call 'carek-carek' of the Great Reed Warbler *A. arundinaceus* may often be heard together with the similar but more subdued song of the Reed Warbler *A. scirpaceus*. The Marsh Warbler *A. palustris*, which closely resembles the Reed Warbler, prefers bramble-bushes and copses but also always near water. From amongst the vegetation the Marsh Warbler not only emits its own song, but also an astounding selection of imitations of the songs of other birds. This group of reed-dwelling warblers also includes another species, Cetti's Warbler *Cettia cetti*, which is easily recognisable by its loud, melodious song.

The leaf warblers constitute the genus *Phylloscopus* which is one of the most important genera. There are about thirty species, at least twelve of which regularly form part of the European avifauna. Leaf warblers are small yellowish or greenish warblers which are most easily distinguished by their songs. The tail sometimes appears slightly forked, and leaf warblers are often seen flicking their tails and wings. The Chiffchaff *P. collybita* and the Willow Warbler *P. trochilus* were at one time considered to be the same species: however, it now seems impossible not to give separate specific status to birds whose song is so different: a monotonous 'chiff-chaff-chiff-chiff-chaff' in the former and a cascade of liquid, descending musical notes in the latter.

The Greenish Warbler *P. trochiloides* has in recent years made spectacular advances westwards from its original Siberian range and is now found as far west as Finland and northeastern Germany. Many leaf warblers must migrate in winter to the tropics in order to find an adequate supply of the insects on which they feed, and there is even one genuinely tropical species: the Mountain Leaf Warbler *P. trivirgatus*, which nests in tropical mountain forests in Indonesia, New Guinea and the Solomon Islands. Whereas reed warblers often build nests attached to reed-stems which can slide up and down the stems depending on the water-level, leaf warblers prefer to conceal their carefully-built nests among grass or at the base of bushes. An even more beautifully-made spherical nest, lined with the softest of materials, from cotton to spiders' webs, is characteristic of most species of grass warblers of the genus *Cisticola*. Only one of this genus, the Fan-tailed Warbler or Zitting Cisticola *C. juncidis*, is found in Europe.

The family Sylviidae also includes many other species, found mainly in Africa, but also in Asia and the Australian region. Among the marsh-dwellers (or rather reed-dwellers) are the genera *Calamocichla* and *Bradypterus* whose species are also found in dry regions. In the tropics, leaf warblers are replaced by species of the genera *Seicercus*, *Abroscopus* and *Prinia*. The genera *Apalis* and *Eremomela* (consisting of the apalis and eremomelas respectively) occur in Africa alone and the tailor birds of the genus *Orthotomus* are present in Asia.

Besides the typical genera there are several other

more or less aberrant genera, which continue to be included in the family Sylviidae even if their exact relationship is not very clear. Some of them indeed constitute the links between the Sylviidae, Turdidae, Muscicapidae families and other groups. The genus *Regulus*, which includes the Goldcrest and Firecrest, deserves special mention: it is sometimes placed in a family of its own or sometimes grouped with the tits of the family Paridae. However, here it is classified with the family Sylviidae although some of its features are markedly different from the 'normal' warbler. These include the crest, sparse plumage and more vivid coloration, often with clear sexual dimorphism. The crest is red, orange or bright yellow, depending on the species; in the female this colour is more subdued or absent. There are five species, all dwellers in coniferous forests but which may also be found in other wooded regions. Three of these belong to the Old World avifauna: the Goldcrest *R. regulus*, with a wide distribution; the Firecrest *R. ignicapillus*, almost exclusively European; and *R. goodfellowi*, found only in the mountains of Formosa (some authorities consider it merely a sub-species of the Firecrest). The two other species, the Golden-crowned Kinglet *R. satrapa* and the Ruby-crowned Kinglet *R. calendula*, are North American.

Of the 'aberrant' species found outside Europe,

the so-called ground-warblers of the genus *Tesia* are worth noting. They have long legs and are only marginally arboreal in habit, factors that have sometimes led to their classification with the wrens of the family Troglodytidae or the babblers of the family Timaliidae. In central Asia two species of the genus *Leptopoecile* (or *Lophobasileus*) known as 'tit-warblers' are present. They resemble tits in their striking coloration.

(Left) Female Blackcap *Sylvia atricapilla.* (Below) Cetti's Warbler *Cettia cetti*

Cetti's Warbler
Cettia cetti

French: BOUSCARLE DE CETTI
Italian: USIGNOLO DI
FIUME
Spanish: RUISEÑOR BASTARDO
German: SEIDENSÄNGER

HABITAT Copses, thick, bushy vegetation, bogs, swamps and dense reed-beds.

IDENTIFICATION Length: 14 cm. Upper parts dark rufous-brown, narrow white eyestripe; underparts greyish, with flanks and under-tail coverts tending to brown; tail graduated and very rounded. Closely resembles the Nightingale, another rufous bird, but differs in smaller size and tail being shorter and less rufous than the upper parts. As this is a skulking species it is best identified by its distinctive call. See also page 58.

CALL A strident 'cheek-eek-eek-eek', a quavering 'tueek' or 'chueek', a soft 'weet' and a 'crr' of alarm.

REPRODUCTION Late April and early May onwards. Nest is a bulky cup of plant material and is constructed by the female. Eggs: generally three to five, deep brick-red in colour, smooth and glossy. The female alone incubates although both tend the young.

FOOD Insects; also worms and small molluscs.

DISTRIBUTION AND MOVEMENTS Breeds in southern Europe, North Africa, Mediterranean islands and around the Persian Gulf. Mainly sedentary. In Britain and Ireland is an increasingly frequent visitor and has colonised southern England in recent years.

SUB-SPECIES Sub-species are present in Asia.

French: LOCUSTELLE FASCIÉE
Italian: LOCUSTELLA DI GRAY
Spanish: BUSCARLA DE GRAY
German: RIESENSCHWIRL

Gray's Grasshopper Warbler
Locustella fasciolata

HABITAT Bushes and areas with tall, dense grasses; often in damp marshy ground. Sometimes also present in taiga.

IDENTIFICATION Length: 18 cm. Upper parts somewhat like those of Savi's Warbler, brownish above and whitish below. Tail coverts and tail more rufous, the eye-stripe is greyish and the margins of the wing coverts and flight feathers are more buff. From below, the front of the neck and the upper breast are greyish and appear 'scaly' due to the structure of the feathers which reflect the light at different angles. Juveniles darker but much like adults. See also page 58.

CALL The song is a short 'tutee-rutee . . . rutee-rutee'.

REPRODUCTION Little is known of this species which apparently nests on the ground near water, concealing the nest among thick vegetation. Four eggs are laid, dingy white in colour, glossy and thickly speckled.

FOOD Insects.

DISTRIBUTION AND MOVEMENTS An exclusively Asiatic species, nesting in a zone stretching from the Ob basin in the USSR to Japan. Migratory, wintering in the Philippines, the Moluccas, the Sunda islands and western New Guinea. Accidental in Europe in France and Denmark.

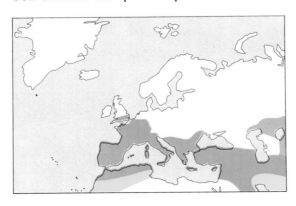

(Above) Cetti's Warbler (left) and Gray's Grasshopper Warbler (right). (Right) Breeding areas (yellow), wintering areas (magenta) and areas where Cetti's Warbler may be seen all year round (orange)

French: LOCUSTELLE
LUSCINIOÏDE
Italian: SALCIAIOLA
Spanish: BUSCARLA UNICOLOR
German: ROHRSCHWIRL

Savi's Warbler
Locustella luscinioides

HABITAT Breeds in marshes and swamps: also fens.

IDENTIFICATION Length: 14 cm. Adult male and female: upper parts uniform dark rufous-brown, short inconspicuous rufous eyestripe, brown cheeks; underparts and abdomen white or tinged light brown, remaining parts rufous-brown. Wide, strongly graduated tail. Less skulking and somewhat larger than the Grasshopper Warbler. See also page 58.

CALL An insistent, scolding 'tzuik' or 'tzuee'. A reeling very similar to Grasshopper Warbler, but lower in pitch and less prolonged.

REPRODUCTION From mid-April. Nest is built by the female alone, and consists of a cup of dead leaves and grass stems, which is situated at the base of reeds or tall grasses. Eggs: four to six, greyish-white. The female alone incubates for a period of twelve days: she also feeds the young, although the male may assist.

FOOD Chiefly insects.

DISTRIBUTION AND MOVEMENTS Europe, North Africa, western and southern USSR, steppes of western Siberia. Has colonised southeastern England in recent years and is now well established at several localities. A summer visitor and a vagrant away from the breeding grounds.

SUB-SPECIES A sub-species is present in Asia.

River Warbler
Locustella fluviatilis

HABITAT Damp, marshy ground, also woodland, and sometimes open steppes and town parks. Usually breeds by water.

IDENTIFICATION Length: 13 cm. Olive-brown in colour with no spotting or streaking on upper parts: this distinguishes it from the Grasshopper Warbler. Underparts pale with faint streaking on upper breast. Tail rounded, sometimes slightly rufous. Juveniles have more rufous-brown upper parts. See also page 58.

CALL Song similar to that of Grasshopper Warbler, but is slower and more rhythmical: it consists of a reeling 'derr-derr' which is uttered from the top of a bush. The call note is harsh.

REPRODUCTION From June onwards. Nest is usually built at the base of a shrub or sheltered by grasses. It is well hidden and constructed of grasses and leaves and is lined with finer grasses and sometimes with hair. Lays five or six eggs which are whitish with fine reddish or grey spotting, and are incubated for approximately thirteen days.

FOOD Insects.

DISTRIBUTION AND MOVEMENTS Nests from Scandinavia east to western Siberia and southwards to the Black Sea and the Caspian. Winters in southeastern Africa. An exceedingly rare vagrant to western Europe and Britain.

French: LOCUSTELLE FLUVIATILE
Italian: LOCUSTELLA FLUVIATILE
Spanish: BUSCARLA FLUVIAL
German: SCHLAGSCHWIRL

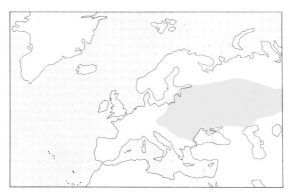

(Above) Savi's Warbler (left) and River Warbler (right). (Far left) Breeding areas (yellow) of Savi's Warbler and (left) breeding areas (yellow) of the River Warbler

Pallas's Grasshopper Warbler
Locustella certhiola

French: LOCUSTELLE DE PALLAS
Italian: LOCUSTELLA DEL PALLAS
Spanish: BUSCARLA DE PALLAS
German: STREIFENSCHWIRL

HABITAT Nests in water-meadows with thick bush and grass, or in copses with water courses and lush vegetation. Winters in rice-fields, reed-beds and marshes.

IDENTIFICATION Length: 13 cm. Very similar to Sedge Warbler. Adult male and female: upper parts, back and upper-tail coverts rufous, sometimes with some streaking which ends in the grey brown of the tail. Inconspicuous barring on tail; the centre of the blackish feathers widens to form a dark terminal band. All the tail feathers (except the central ones) have a narrow greyish tip. Under-tail coverts pale buff. Mantle streaked, usually darker than that of Sedge Warbler. Underparts generally greyish-white. Juveniles often have yellowish breast and flanks, with a sort of pectoral band formed by indistinct spotting. Habits similar to those of Grasshopper Warbler. See also page 58.

CALL Emits a 'chirr-chirr'. Sings in flight or when perched on bushes or plants.

REPRODUCTION From May onwards. Nest is like that of Grasshopper Warbler, built in grass tussocks or among tangled vegetation in mossy water-meadows: it is made of grasses and moss. Eggs: four to six, thickly speckled pinkish-brown, sometimes with dark threadmarks.

FOOD Small insects and larvae.

DISTRIBUTION AND MOVEMENTS Breeds in western Siberia, central Asia and east to Japan. Winters from India, Indochina and southeastern China to Ceylon, the Andaman Islands and the Philippines. Accidental in western Europe including Britain, where it is noted at Fair Isle from time to time.

SUB-SPECIES Many sub-species, including the nominate race, are present in Asia.

(Above) Pallas's Grasshopper Warbler

Grasshopper Warbler
Locustella naevia

HABITAT Swamps, water-meadows, marshes: also young conifer plantations, heathland and other areas with dry vegetation.

IDENTIFICATION Length: 13 cm. Most widespread species in Europe of the genus *Locustella*. Distinguishable by heavily streaked olive-brown upper parts, whitish or rufous underparts, light streaking on breast and the lightly barred and graduated tail. Rump is slightly rufous; dark eyestripe. See also page 58.

CALL A sharp, hard 'tcheek' which is repeated very rapidly when excited. Song is a rhythmic reeling sound which has been likened to a fisherman's reel being wound in. The song may be prolonged for several minutes.

REPRODUCTION May and June, exceptionally in July and August. The nest is built by both male and female from grasses and dry leaves and is lined with hair. It is generally regarded as one of the most difficult of all birds' nests to find. Eggs: generally six, sometimes four to seven, which are smooth and glossy. The basic colour is white although sometimes the purple or purple-brown speckling is so dense that the entire shell may appear tinted. Both sexes incubate the eggs for thirteen to fifteen days: both also tend the young.

FOOD Insects and their larvae.

DISTRIBUTION AND MOVEMENTS Breeds in central and northern Europe from Scandinavia, Britain and Ireland east across Eurasia to northwest Mongolia. Winters in Africa and southwestern Asia. In Britain and Ireland it is a widespread migrant breeder which is gradually extending its range northwards and westwards. Also occurs on passage.

SUB-SPECIES *L.n. naevia*: western Europe and east to the central USSR. *L.n. obscurior* (more olive): northern Caucasus. Other sub-species are present in Asia.

(Facing page top) Grasshopper Warbler. (Below) Breeding areas (yellow) and areas where the Grasshopper Warbler may be seen on passage (pink)

French: LOCUSTELLE TACHETÉE
Italian: FORAPAGLIE
MACCHIETTATO
Spanish: BUSCARLA PINTOJA
German: FELDSCHWIRL

French: LOCUSTELLE LANCÉOLÉE
Italian: LOCUSTELLA LANCEOLATA
Spanish: BUSCARLA LANCEOLADA
German: STRICHELSCHWIRL

Lanceolated Warbler
Locustella lanceolata

HABITAT Nests in thick vegetation by water or among reedbeds. Also found on taiga and in open forests.

IDENTIFICATION Length: 11 cm. Resembles the Grasshopper Warbler, but is smaller and has heavy brown-black streaking on the yellow-brown upper parts. Upper-tail coverts and tail dark brown, sometimes lacking the characteristic streaking. Distinctive dark streaking on the breast and flanks. Inconspicuous eye-stripe, creamy white in colour. Very skulking in habits and prefers to crawl through vegetation rather than fly. See also page 58.

CALL Emits a 'chir-chirr' like that of Pallas's Grasshopper Warbler: also a stifled, rolling note. Also reels in summer like a Grasshopper Warbler.

REPRODUCTION Mid-June onwards. The nest is a well-built cup of grasses, dead leaves and moss, which is constructed by the female in tall grass and herbage. Usually five white or very pale pink eggs are laid, which are heavily speckled with red or purple. Further information is lacking.

FOOD Probably insects.

DISTRIBUTION AND MOVEMENTS Breeds in the eastern USSR across Siberia and southwards to Korea and Japan. Winters in southern Asia. Accidental in western Europe, including Britain, where it is more or less confined to Fair Isle.

French: PHRAGMITE AQUATIQUE
Italian: PAGLIAROLO
Spanish: CARRICERÍN CEJUDO
German: SEGGENROHRSÄNGER

French: LUSCINIOLE À
MOUSTACHES
Italian: FORAPAGLIE
CASTAGNOLO
Spanish: CARRICERÍN REAL
German: TAMARISKENSÄNGER

Moustached Warbler
Lusciniola melanopogon

HABITAT Fresh water margins, especially reed-beds.

IDENTIFICATION Length: 13 cm. Very similar to the Sedge Warbler in size and coloration, but differs in having darker, more chestnut upper parts and a darker, almost black, crown. Also the eye-stripe and throat are whiter. Cheeks black, freckled white; underparts very white with flanks and undertail coverts rufous. Habitually cocks up and spreads the graduated tail. See also page 58.

CALL A scolding 'churr' like that of Sedge Warbler. Song resembles Nightingale's in some of the phrasing.

REPRODUCTION From April onwards. The nest is a deep cup made of grasses and bits of sedge, lined with reed-flowers, grasses and sometimes feathers. It is built over water in reeds or shrubs. Eggs: normally three or four, white or grey-white, spotted profusely with olive-brown. Both sexes care for the young.

FOOD Insects.

DISTRIBUTION AND MOVEMENTS Breeds in Spain and northern Africa, and north to Austria and east to northwest India. Winters in the southern part of the breeding range: some individuals also migrate to eastern Arabia and Africa south to the Sahara. Exceptionally a pair bred in Cambridgeshire in 1946, otherwise it is an extremely rare vagrant to Britain.

SUB-SPECIES A sub-species is present in Asia.

Aquatic Warbler
Acrocephalus paludicola

HABITAT Prefers low vegetation along water courses or open swamps with sedge.

IDENTIFICATION Length: 13 cm. Similar to the Sedge Warbler, but distinguished by conspicuous wide yellowish stripe on centre of crown, eyestripe buff rather than creamy, and more marked streaking on mantle extending to the rump. In general, appears distinctly yellowish. Breast and flanks have dark stripes which are very conspicuous and often visible even in winter. See also page 58.

CALL A scolding 'tak'. Song like Sedge Warbler, but with more regular patterned structure.

REPRODUCTION Mid-May onwards. Nest is made of grasses, plant down and spiders' webs, usually lined with feathers. Eggs: five or six, white, pale buff or olive closely speckled yellow-brown, sometimes with a few very fine, dark hair-streaks. The female alone generally incubates although both parents tend the young.

FOOD Chiefly insects.

DISTRIBUTION AND MOVEMENTS Breeds in northern Europe, in Finland, the Netherlands and through central Europe to Italy and east to the Caspian. Probably winters in tropical Africa. Is a regular, if rare, passage migrant in Britain and may occur on the southeast coast of England in some numbers. Rare visitor to Ireland.

(Above) Moustached Warbler (left) and Aquatic Warbler (right). (Right) Breeding areas (yellow), wintering areas (magenta), and areas where the Moustached Warbler may be seen all year round (orange). (Far right) Breeding areas (yellow) of the Aquatic Warbler

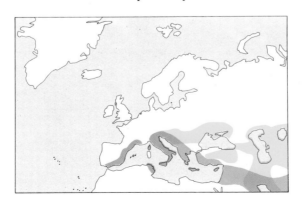

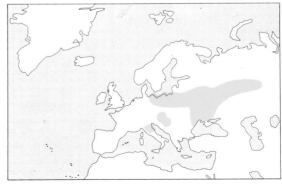

Sedge Warbler
Acrocephalus schoenobaenus

French: PHRAGMITE DES JONCS
Italian: FORAPAGLIE
Spanish: CARRICERÍN COMÚN
German: SCHILFROHRSÄNGER

HABITAT Frequents vegetation such as bushes and hedgerows fairly near water: may also be found among crops.

IDENTIFICATION Length: 13 cm. Distinguished from Reed Warbler by conspicuous creamy eyestripe and heavily streaked crown and upper parts. Sides of head brownish. Underparts creamy-white, tinged yellowish-rufous at sides, darker on flanks. Juveniles more yellowish with sparse spotting on throat and upper breast. The dark colour of the crown may cause confusion with Moustached Warbler. Sometimes has faint creamy stripe on crown which may lead to confusion with Aquatic, but rump unstreaked.

Often descends to ground level and creeps through dense vegetation. Perches on bushes or reed tops. Flight generally low, for short distances only, with tail spread and drooping. See also page 58.

CALL A scolding 'tuk', often repeated rapidly and a croaking 'chirr'. Song is a mixture of loud harsh notes and soft, musical notes. Sings both in the open and from cover as well as in flight.

REPRODUCTION Mid May through June. The nest is suspended in thick vegetation often near or over water but also among crops. It is a deep, bulky cup of dry grasses and moss and is lined with finer plant materials and hair. Eggs: five or six, pale green or pale olive-buff and thickly speckled with olive. Incubation is carried out mainly by the female for about thirteen days. The young are tended by both parents.

FOOD Insects and their larvae, also small spiders and worms.

DISTRIBUTION AND MOVEMENTS Breeds in Britain, Ireland and throughout continental Europe with the exception of Iberia and some Mediterranean coastal areas and east across Siberia and south to Iran. Migrates south of the breeding range, wintering in tropical and southern Africa. In Britain and Ireland it is a widespread migrant breeder to all counties, although sparse in some areas of northern Scotland and absent from Shetland. Also a passage visitor to both countries.

(Left) Breeding areas (yellow) and areas where the Sedge Warbler may be seen on passage (pink)

13

(Above) Sardinian Warbler *Sylvia melanocephala* and a young Cuckoo *Cuculus canorus* in the nest. (Right) Orphean Warbler *S. hortensis*. (Facing page) Male Blackcap *S. atricapilla* feeding its young which will remain in the nest for ten to fourteen days

14

L. Gaggero

French: ROUSSEROLLE DES
                BUISSONS
Italian: CANNAIOLA DI BLYTH
Spanish: CARRICERO DE BLYTH
German: BUSCHROHRSÄNGER

Blyth's Reed Warbler
Acrocephalus dumetorum

HABITAT Wide range of habitats with bushes and thick vegetation; frequently breeds by water although not necessarily.

IDENTIFICATION Length: 12 cm. Very difficult to distinguish in the field from the Marsh Warbler which it closely resembles in coloration. However, its upper parts are browner than the Marsh Warbler's. Also very similar to Reed Warbler but with darker, less rusty-brown upper parts. Bill is longer and thinner and forehead is steeper than that of other reed warblers. Wings are also shorter and more rounded: flight is whirring and more Wren-like. See also page 62.

CALL A distinct sharp 'tchk-tchk'; also a 'tap-tap' of alarm. Song very rich and varied, like that of the Marsh Warbler, with much mimicry. Generally sings from cover.

REPRODUCTION Nests in June. Nest resembles that of the Reed Warbler and is usually built close to a metre from the ground, supported by and partly hanging from stems. Eggs: four or five, highly variable, sometimes very like those of Marsh Warbler, sometimes suffused grey-brown with brown and grey markings. Further information is not available.

FOOD Probably insects.

DISTRIBUTION AND MOVEMENTS Breeds from Finland east across the USSR and western Siberia and south to the Caspian, Iran and Afghanistan. Winters in India and Ceylon. Accidental in Britain where a minor invasion (of less than ten individuals) occurred in the autumn of 1912. Otherwise exceptionally rare.

Paddyfield Warbler
Acrocephalus agricola

HABITAT Reed-beds, hedges, thick grass and swamp vegetation. Also frequents sparser low vegetation near water.

IDENTIFICATION Length: 12 cm. Very similar to the Reed Warbler. Plain rufous above, but lighter and more buffish than Reed Warbler. Also has a more pronounced whitish eyestripe than the Reed Warbler. Most noticeable features are the rufous margins to the secondary wing feathers. Underparts creamy white. Behaviour similar to that of the Reed Warbler. See also page 62.

CALL The call has been described as a 'chik-chik'. The song is like that of the Reed Warbler but without any harsh notes.

REPRODUCTION May and June. The nest, cylindrical in shape, resembles that of the Reed Warbler and Great Reed Warbler. It is built among reeds, sedge or among other waterside plants and shrubs. Eggs: four to six, similar to those of the Reed Warbler, but more heavily marked. The markings tend to be concentrated at the larger end. The female alone incubates but further details are lacking.

FOOD Probably mainly insects.

DISTRIBUTION AND MOVEMENTS Breeds in the southern USSR, Mongolia, Iran and Afghanistan: probably also in India. Winters in southern Iran and in India. The Paddyfield Warbler is a very rare vagrant to Britain.

SUB-SPECIES Sub-species are present in Asia.

(Above) Blyth's Reed Warbler. (Right) Breeding areas (yellow) and areas where Blyth's Reed Warbler may be seen on passage (pink)

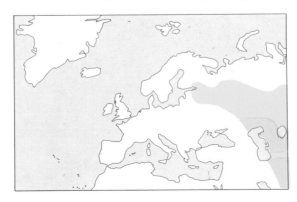

Marsh Warbler
Acrocephalus palustris

HABITAT Frequents areas with dense vegetation, often near fresh water; also marshy habitats. May also be found in crops and gardens.

IDENTIFICATION Length: 12 cm. Upper parts more olive than the Reed Warbler's and without the rufous tinge: underparts slightly whiter. Legs pale flesh colour. However, it is very difficult to distinguish the Marsh Warbler from Reed and Blyth's Reed Warbler by plumage alone: the song of the various species is the most reliable distinguishing feature. See also page 62.

CALL A very loud 'tik' or 'tchik' with variations. Song is varied and lively with a characteristic nasal note: 'azz-wee': its song is more musical and less uniform than the Reed Warbler's. An excellent mimic.

REPRODUCTION May onwards. Nest is built by the female among hedgerows, shrubs or other tall herbage. It consists of a cup of dry plant material which is suspended and supported by 'handles' that are fixed to the surrounding vegetation. The nest may be situated from half a metre to nearly three metres off the ground. It is often cylindrical, like the Reed Warbler's, but may taper towards the bottom (especially in higher nests). Eggs: four or five very pale bluish-green or grey eggs are laid. They are spotted and blotched olive-brown and grey. Both sexes incubate the eggs for about twelve days and both tend the young.

FOOD Insects and their larvae: also spiders and berries.

DISTRIBUTION AND MOVEMENTS Breeds in Europe from southern England and Scandinavia east to Iran. Winters in east Africa. In Britain is a very scarce migrant breeder in a few parts of southern England: accidental elsewhere. Has not been reliably identified in Ireland.

French: ROUSSEROLLE VERDEROLLE
Italian: CANNAIOLA VERDOGNOLA
Spanish: CARRICERO POLIGLOTA
German: SUMPFROHRSÄNGER

(Above) Marsh Warbler. (Left) Breeding areas (yellow) and areas where the Marsh Warbler may be seen on passage (pink)

French: ROUSSEROLLE ISABELLE
Italian: CANNAIOLA DI JERDON
Spanish: CARRICERO AGRÍCOLA
German: FELDROHRSÄNGER

(Right) Paddyfield Warbler

17

French: ROUSSEROLLE
EFFARVATTE
Italian: CANNAIOLA
Spanish: CARRICERO COMÚN
German: TEICHROHRSÄNGER

Great Reed Warbler
Acrocephalus arundinaceus

French: ROUSSEROLLE TURDOÏDE
Italian: CANNARECCIONE
Spanish: CARRICERO TORDAL
German: DROSSELROHRSÄNGER

HABITAT Freshwater margins—rivers, ponds and lakes—and especially reed-beds.

IDENTIFICATION Length: 19 cm. Largest warbler present in Europe. Adult male and female: upper parts warm olive-brown, crown darker, back, rump and upper-tail coverts more tawny. Underparts: chin, throat and centre of abdomen white, sometimes with narrow brown streaking under the throat. Remaining underparts and undertail coverts varying from creamy to tawny-brown, darker on flanks. Similar in colour and shape to Reed Warbler, but much larger, with stouter and more reddish bill, prominent pale eye-stripe and more strident voice.

Behaviour like that of Reed Warbler but is less shy. Perches on bushes, trees and even telegraph wires. Flight short and low, with tail spread; very rapid wing movements. See also page 62.

CALL A strident 'tak' or 'chack' and a low, vibrant croak; also a chatter of alarm like that of a shrike. Song like that of Reed Warbler, but variable; much louder, more guttural and croaking than that of Sedge Warbler, with a remarkable variety of grating sounds.

REPRODUCTION From May onwards. Nest is almost cylindrical in shape and is suspended from reeds, like that of the Reed Warbler, at about half a metre above the water. The nest is mainly built by the female of plant fibres, roots and leaves. It is lined with reed flowers, down, hair, and rarely with feathers. Eggs: four

to six, bluish or grey blotched with greenish or black. Both male and female incubate the eggs for fourteen or fifteen days: both also care for the young.

FOOD Insects and their larvae: also spiders and small fish.

DISTRIBUTION AND MOVEMENTS Breeds in Europe from Iberia, France, the Netherlands and Scandinavia east to the USSR. Also breeds in North Africa, and Asia Minor east to India, China and Japan. Migrates to tropical Africa and southern Asia. In Britain it is a more or less annual vagrant to southern England. Elsewhere it is a scarce vagrant.

SUB-SPECIES Sub-species are present in Asia.

(Above left) Great Reed Warbler. (Right) Breeding areas (yellow) and areas where the Great Reed Warbler may be seen on passage (pink)

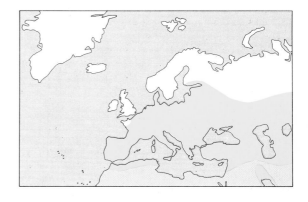

Reed Warbler
Acrocephalus scirpaceus

HABITAT Nests in reed-beds or among dense vegetation near water. Sometimes frequents parks, gardens and cultivated land.

IDENTIFICATION Length: 12 cm. Upper parts warm brown tending to rufous, especially on the back. Underparts buffish, shading into white of throat. The rufous tinge to the upper parts is one of the few differences between it and the Marsh and Blyth's Reed Warblers. However, the most reliable distinction between these species is the song. Lacks dark streaking on back and head unlike the Sedge Warbler, and has only a faint light eyestripe whereas the Sedge Warbler's is more conspicuous. Tail dark brown with narrow cream tips. Wings dark with narrow light brown tips. Moves with agility, although is generally shy and seldom emerges from cover. See also page 62.

CALL Song is a rather monotonous 'churr' which is repeated several times: has been likened to the sound of two pebbles being rubbed together. Is also a good mimic, but lacks the sweet notes of the Sedge Warbler.

REPRODUCTION May and June. Nest is built almost entirely by the female: it is a deep cylindrical cup which is constructed in reeds over water or in vegetation near water. Eggs: four, green-white, blotched and speckled with green or dull grey markings which may be concentrated to form a cap at the larger end of the shell. The eggs are incubated by both parents for about eleven or twelve days: both also tend the young.

FOOD Insects and their larvae: also small spiders, worms, small molluscs and berries.

DISTRIBUTION AND MOVEMENTS Breeds in Europe from Britain, France, Iberia and Scandinavia east across Eurasia and south to the Mediterranean, Caspian and Iran. Also breeds in northwest Africa. Migrates to tropical Africa. In Britain is a common breeding bird wherever large reed-beds occur, but does not extend as far north as Scotland: has bred on occasion in Ireland. Occurs on passage to Britain and Ireland.

SUB-SPECIES A sub-species is present in Asia.

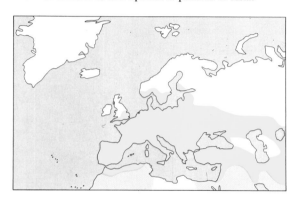

(Facing page, near left) Reed Warbler. (Left) Breeding areas (yellow) and areas where the Reed Warbler may be seen on passage (pink)

French: ROUSSEROLLE À GROS BEC
Italian: CANNARECCIONE BECCOGROSSO
Spanish: CARRICERO PICOGORDO
German: DICKSCHNABELSÄNGER

Thick-billed Warbler
Acrocephalus aedon

HABITAT Thick bushes and hedges, especially in damp or marshy areas and along freshwater margins.

IDENTIFICATION Length: 19 cm. Resembles the Great Reed Warbler in size, shape and coloration: the two are difficult to distinguish. However, the Thick billed's rump is even more rufous and its general coloration is more olive-brown. The bill is heavier and shorter; wings also shorter. Lacks the pale eye-stripe. In the hand may be immediately identified, not only by the above characteristics, but also by the rather long and broad first primary. More shy than the Great Reed Warbler, although it ascends to the top of bushes or trees to sing. See also page 62.

CALL Song is reminiscent of Icterine Warbler's and the Nightingale's. Call note consists of a 'chock-chock'.

REPRODUCTION The nest is built a short distance from the ground among reeds or other vegetation. Five to six eggs are laid which vary in colour, but which are usually spotted or even unmarked pink.

FOOD Probably chiefly insects.

DISTRIBUTION AND MOVEMENTS Breeds from southern Siberia east to China and Korea. Migratory, wintering in India, Burma, and southeast China. Accidental in Europe where it has been identified at Fair Isle.

French: HYPOLAÏS POLYGLOTTE
Italian: CANAPINO
Spanish: ZARCERO COMÚN
German: ORPHEUSSPÖTTER

Melodious Warbler
Hippolais polyglotta

(Below right) Breeding areas (yellow) and areas where the Melodious Warbler may be seen on passage (pink)

HABITAT Nests in thick vegetation, gardens or copses, usually close to water. Also frequents more open areas including parks.

IDENTIFICATION Length: 13 cm. Very similar to Icterine Warbler, but song distinguishes it in the field. Also appears more compact, with shorter, more rounded wings, not extending beyond base of tail. Characteristic contrast between yellowish underparts and browner, duller upper parts. Legs vary from blue-grey to brownish in colour. Yellowish wing-patch, present in many adults, less marked than in Icterine Warbler; absent in juveniles which are browner in coloration. Bill broad: dark upper mandible, pinkish lower mandible. Underparts more yellow than in Icterine Warbler. See also page 64.

CALL Emits a chirping and twittering call note. Song is musical, rich and varied, fairly low-pitched and more liquid and hurried than that of the Icterine Warbler.

REPRODUCTION Late May onwards. Nest is a deep cup built in the fork of a shrub or tree, one to two metres above the ground. The female builds the nest of plant stems, grasses and spiders' webs and lines it with finer materials. Eggs: usually four, ground colour pinkish tinged violet, with dark spotting and streaking.

The female alone incubates for twelve to thirteen days. Both parents care for the young.

FOOD Chiefly insects and their larvae.

DISTRIBUTION AND MOVEMENTS Breeds in southwest Europe in France, Switzerland, Italy, Sicily and Iberia. Also breeds in northwest Africa. Migrates to tropical western Africa. In Britain and Ireland is a vagrant which occurs more or less annually in autumn, mostly to coastal areas.

R. Longo

(Above left) Melodious Warbler *Hippolais polyglotta:* this western counterpart of the Icterine Warbler is best distinguished from the latter by its song. (Left) Grasshopper Warbler *Locustella naevia.* Like other species of the genus *Locustella* it is extremely shy and frequents dense cover

S. Roberts/Ardea

French: HYPOLAÏS DES OLIVIERS
Italian: CANAPINO LEVANTINO
Spanish: ZARCERO GRANDE
German: OLIVENSPÖTTER

Olive-tree Warbler
Hippolais olivetorum

HABITAT Areas with scattered trees, open woodland, olive groves and scrub.

IDENTIFICATION Length: 15 cm. One of the larger warblers, with grey-brown plumage, contrasting with the pale, almost white borders of the secondaries. The bill is conspicuously long and the pale eyestripe is also noticeable. Underparts are dingy white. Skulking habits. See also page 64.

CALL Loud, melodious song, with a rapid succession of notes: its song is louder and deeper than that of other *Hippolais* warblers. Call consists of 'tic' or 'tr-truc'.

REPRODUCTION Probably from May onwards. Nests in a tree or bush, sometimes near the ground, but also up to three metres off the ground. Usually lays four pale pinkish eggs with sparse black markings. Further information unavailable.

DISTRIBUTION AND MOVEMENTS Breeds in the Balkan peninsula, Turkey, Syria and Israel. Migratory, wintering chiefly in eastern Africa. Accidental elsewhere in Europe.

Icterine Warbler
Hippolais icterina

HABITAT Gardens, crops, forest edges and riversides.

IDENTIFICATION Length: 13 cm. Very similar to Melodious Warbler, with yellow underparts and bluish-grey legs. High forehead, unstreaked plumage, squarer tail and broader bill distinguish the Icterine and other warblers of the genus *Hippolais* from reed and leaf warblers.

Song distinguishes the Icterine from Melodious Warbler. Both have olive-green upper parts, brownish wings and tail, and a yellow eyestripe. Underparts yellow. Active and lively in behaviour. See also page 64.

CALL Principal call is a distinctive, liquid 'dideroid': also a harsh 'tek-tek'. Song is loud and vehement, with a variety of harsh, musical notes. Somewhat reminiscent of the Marsh Warbler's song.

REPRODUCTION Late May onwards. Nest is built by male and female from grasses, wool, roots and other plant material. It is situated in a large shrub or small tree between one and four metres from the ground. Eggs: four or five, dull pink-purple lightly spotted and streaked with black. Both male and female incubate the eggs for thirteen days. Both also care for the young.

FOOD Chiefly insects and their larvae; sometimes small spiders, snails and berries.

DISTRIBUTION AND MOVEMENTS Breeds from northernmost Europe south to France and northern Italy and eastwards to the USSR and Iran. Winters in tropical and southern Africa. In Britain and Ireland is an annual, if scarce, visitor in autumn, the majority recorded at Fair Isle. Is also said to have bred once, in 1907, in Wiltshire.

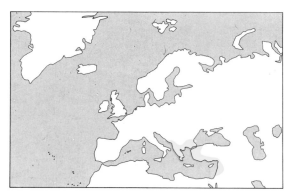

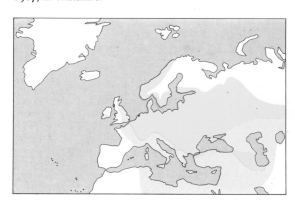

(Above) Olive-Tree Warbler. (Near right) Breeding areas (yellow) of the Olive-tree Warbler

French: HYPOLAÏS ICTÉRINE
Italian: CANAPINO MAGGIORE
Spanish: ZARCERO ICTERINO
German: GELBSPÖTTER

(Above) Icterine Warbler.
(Facing page, near left)
Breeding areas (yellow) and
areas where the Icterine
Warbler may be seen on
passage (pink)

French: HYPOLAÏS PÂLE
Italian: CANAPINO PALLIDO
Spanish: ZARCERO PÁLIDO
German: BLASSPÖTTER

Olivaceous Warbler

Hippolais pallida

HABITAT Nests in bushy areas including gardens, orchards, crops and olive-groves.

IDENTIFICATION Length: 13 cm. Resembles Icterine and Melodious Warblers in silhouette and behaviour. Differs in having uniform light brown upper parts, darker wings and tail, buffish-white underparts and whitish eye rings. Also has buff eyestripe and generally lacks any greenish or yellowish tinge. More flattened crown. In spring, possibly some yellowish tinge on underparts. See also page 64.

CALL A clear 'tak', 'trakk' or 'tchak-tchak' like Icterine Warbler's. Song resembles the Garden Warbler's but is more varied.

REPRODUCTION From late April. Nest is a strongly constructed neat cup of twigs and grasses which is built from one third of a metre to a metre off the ground. Usually lays three glossy pale grey-white eggs with sparse black markings. The female alone incubates for twelve or thirteen days.

FOOD Probably only insects.

DISTRIBUTION AND MOVEMENTS Breeds from Spain through southeast Europe to Asia Minor, Near East, Iraq and Iran to northern Afghanistan. Also breeds in northwest Africa. Winters mainly in tropical Africa. A rare vagrant to Britain and Ireland.

SUB-SPECIES *H. p. opaca*: Spain, Morocco, Algeria and Tunisia. *H. p. elaeica*: southeast Europe, Asia Minor and Asia. Other sub-species are present in Africa.

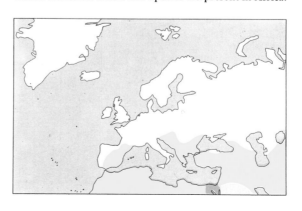

(Above) Olivaceous Warbler.
(Left) Breeding areas (yellow),
areas where the Olivaceous
Warbler may be seen all year
round (orange) and on
passage (pink)

23

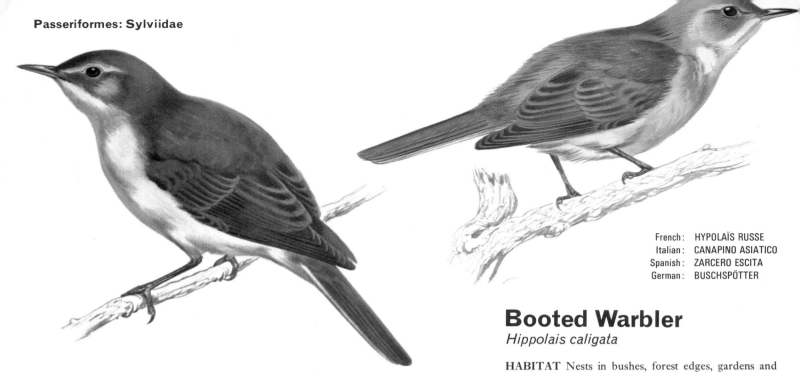

French: HYPOLAÏS RUSSE
Italian: CANAPINO ASIATICO
Spanish: ZARCERO ESCITA
German: BUSCHSPÖTTER

French: HYPOLAÏS D'UPCHER
Italian: CANAPINO LANGUIDO
German: DORNBUSCHSPÖTTER

Upcher's Warbler
Hippolais languida

HABITAT Open, arid areas, scrub, gardens and vineyards.

IDENTIFICATION Length: 14 cm. Much the same size as the Melodious Warbler, but differs in paler, more greyish coloration and has a conspicuous eyestripe. Wings a little darker with pale margins. Legs light brown (not grey). Underparts whitish, darker on breast and yellowish on under-tail coverts. Very difficult to distinguish from the Olivaceous Warbler. See also page 64.

CALL A sharp 'chick-chick'.

REPRODUCTION From late May. The nest is built among bushes and stunted desert trees at a height of up to two metres from the ground. It is a thin-walled but strong cup. Three to five pale lilac eggs with sparse black and grey speckling are laid. Further details are lacking.

FOOD Insects.

DISTRIBUTION AND MOVEMENTS Breeds from the Mediterranean coasts of Asia Minor eastwards to Afghanistan. Winters in India, Saudi Arabia and eastern Africa. Accidental in Europe.

Booted Warbler
Hippolais caligata

HABITAT Nests in bushes, forest edges, gardens and cultivated areas: also semi-desert regions.

IDENTIFICATION Length: 12 cm. Upper parts grey-brown tending to rufous; underparts white, tinged with buff on flanks. Outer-tail feathers white. Legs dark brown. Similar to Olivaceous Warbler, but the Olivaceous has a larger bill and less buff on the underparts. See also page 64.

CALL Usual note is a sharp 'click'. The song is loud and babbling and consists of variations on a 'chrek-chrek'.

REPRODUCTION Late May onwards. Nest is usually built on the ground among shrubs, although it may sometimes be slightly raised off the ground. Eggs: five to six, dull purplish-pink with sparse black speckling and sometimes streaking. The female mainly incubates, although she is assisted by the male. No further information is available.

FOOD Mainly insects.

DISTRIBUTION AND MOVEMENTS Breeds in northern and central USSR and south to Iran. Migrates to India and southern Arabia. In Britain is a very rare vagrant, mostly to Fair Isle.

SUB-SPECIES As well as the nominate race *H. c. caligata*, found in the USSR, there is another sub-species in Asia.

(Above left) Upcher's Warbler and (right) Booted Warbler. (Right) Breeding areas (yellow) and areas where Upcher's Warbler may be seen on passage (pink). (Far right) Breeding areas (yellow) of the Booted Warbler

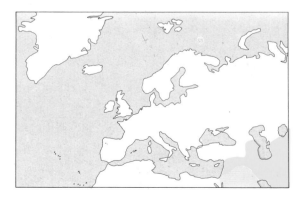

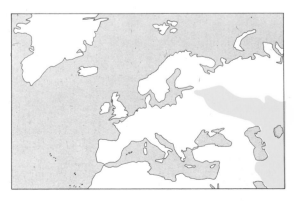

D. Green/Bruce Coleman

Eric Hosking

(Above) Female Whitethroat *Sylvia communis:* like the male she has rufous wings. (Left) Icterine Warbler *Hippolais icterina* at the nest

French : FAUVETTE NAINE
Italian : STERPAZZOLA NANA
Spanish : CURRUCA SAHARIANA
German : WÜSTENGRASMÜCKE

Desert Warbler
Sylvia nana

HABITAT Steppes, desert and semi-desert areas.

IDENTIFICATION Length: 11 cm. Smallest and palest of the scrub warblers. Upper parts are a pinkish-sandy colour with some reddish coloration on the white-edged tail. Underparts very pale. Male and female are alike. See also page 68.

CALL Emits a weak grating call. Its brief, simple and bell-like song is often uttered in display flight.

REPRODUCTION From April onwards. It builds its nest in very dense, often thorny bushes up to a metre off the ground. The nest is a deep strong cup of plant fibres and grasses. Four to six eggs are laid which are white or pale blue, finely marked with brown or grey-brown. Both sexes incubate the eggs.

FOOD Mainly insects and larvae.

DISTRIBUTION AND MOVEMENTS Breeds in arid regions of northern Africa and in Saharan Africa and steppes and deserts in much of Asia, including the Middle East and Caspian region. It is a migrant, particularly in the eastern part of its distribution area, and winters in India, Egypt, Saudi Arabia and northern Africa.

SUB-SPECIES *S. n. nana*: southern USSR and central Asia. *S. n. deserti* (paler) northwest Africa. The nesting area of a third sub-species—*S. n. theresae*—is not known, but it occurs in Pakistan during the winter.

Orphean Warbler
Sylvia hortensis

HABITAT Wooded or cultivated land: also parks.

IDENTIFICATION Length: 15 cm. Larger and stouter than the similar Blackcap. Dark hood extends below the eye and shades into the grey coloration of the mantle; white throat and outer tail feathers. Squarish tail. Female's crown is paler and its upper parts are browner: the juvenile's crown is darker than its mantle. Prominent white eyes and jet-black cheeks help to identify this species. See also page 66.

CALL Harsh grating alarm note: 'trrr'. Song is a repetitive thrush-like warble.

REPRODUCTION From late April. Nest is a loosely built cup which is situated one or two metres up in a bush or small tree. Eggs: four or five, whitish, spotted with brown. Both sexes incubate the eggs.

FOOD Insects and fruit.

DISTRIBUTION AND MOVEMENTS Breeds across southern Europe from Spain east to Asia Minor and India. Winters in tropical and northern Africa and Asia. Is a very rare vagrant to Britain.

SUB-SPECIES *S. h. hortensis*: western Europe and northern Africa. *S. h. crassirostris*: eastern Europe and Asia Minor. Other sub-species are present in Asia.

(Above) The sub-species *S.n. deserti* of the Desert Warbler (foreground) and adult Desert Warbler. (Near right) Breeding areas (yellow), wintering areas (magenta) and areas where the Desert Warbler may be seen all year round (orange)

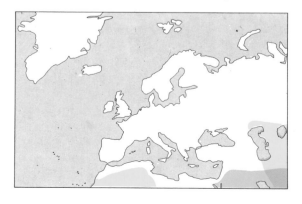

French: FAUVETTE ORPHÉE
Italian: BIGIA GROSSA
Spanish: CURRUCA MIRLONA
German: ORPHEUSGRASMÜCKE

(Above) Orphean Warbler.
(Facing page, near left)
Breeding areas (yellow) and
areas where the Orphean
Warbler may be seen on
passage (pink)

Barred Warbler
Sylvia nisoria

HABITAT Woodland edges, bushy areas, hedgerows and scrub.

IDENTIFICATION Length: 15 cm. One of the larger warblers of the genus *Sylvia* which occurs in Europe. Adults: grey upper parts; grey-white underparts heavily barred dark grey. Dark brown wings with two white wing-bars which may be clearly defined or indistinct. White outer tail feathers: yellow eyes. Juveniles have only faint barring or no barring at all. The large size and predominantly grey coloration are then the best field marks. See also page 66.

CALL A vibrant 'raar' and a dry 'ts-chak'. Song similar to the Garden Warbler's but is harsher and emitted in shorter bursts.

REPRODUCTION Late May onwards. Nest is a loosely built deep cup of plant material which is frequently situated in thorn thickets or in the fork or branches of a tree. It may be built a metre to two-and-a-half metres off the ground. Eggs: five or six, pale grey speckled with buffish-grey. Both sexes incubate the eggs for twelve to fifteen days. The young are tended in the nest by both parents.

FOOD Insects and larvae.

DISTRIBUTION AND MOVEMENTS Breeds from southern Scandinavia, Germany, northern France and Italy east through Europe to Asia Minor and Afghanistan: also northwards to the central USSR. Winters in southern Arabia south to tropical Africa. It is a regular passage visitor to Britain and Ireland in small numbers.

SUB-SPECIES A sub-species is present in Asia.

French: FAUVETTE ÉPERVIÈRE
Italian: BIGIA PADOVANA
Spanish: CURRUCA GAVILANA
German: SPERBERGRASMÜCKE

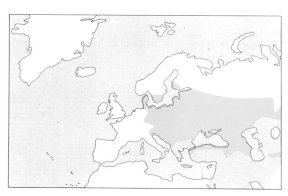

(Above right) Barred Warbler
(foreground) and juvenile.
(Left) Breeding areas (yellow)
and areas where the Barred
Warbler may be seen on
passage (pink)

French: FAUVETTE DES JARDINS
Italian: BECCAFICO
Spanish: CURRUCA MOSQUITERA
German: GARTENGRASMÜCKE

Garden Warbler
Sylvia borin

HABITAT Mixed woods with abundant undergrowth, scrub, parks and gardens.

IDENTIFICATION Length: 13 cm. Pale buff under-parts; uniform dull grey-brown upper parts. Grey legs. The lack of a supercilium and slight eye-ring are the best distinguishing features in this otherwise rather featureless bird, which resembles the warblers of the genus *Hippolais*. See also page 66.

CALL A harsh 'tek-tek'. Song resembles the Blackcap's: it is a quiet warbling but without the higher louder notes of the Blackcap.

REPRODUCTION From late May. The nest is a substantial cup, usually situated among plant stems or in a fork of small branches. May nest about a third of a metre off the ground but also up to two-and-a-half metres high. Lays four or five, sometimes three to seven, smooth and glossy eggs which vary in colour but are often white, buff or pinkish and blotched with light olive, brown, purplish and grey. Markings are usually rather sparse. Both parents incubate the eggs for eleven or twelve days and both tend the young.

FOOD Insects and larvae: also worms, fruit and berries.

DISTRIBUTION AND MOVEMENTS Europe (except for the southernmost regions), western Siberia and Transcaucasia. It migrates to tropical and southern Africa. Breeds in Eurasia from Scandinavia, Britain, Ireland and Iberia eastwards across the USSR. Also breeds southwards, perhaps to Iran. Winters in tropical Africa. In Britain it is a numerous breeder in England and Wales (resident from April to September), but very rare in Scotland: also a scarce breeder in Ireland. It is also a passage visitor to both Britain and Ireland, particularly to the south and east coasts of England in early autumn.

SUB-SPECIES *S. b. borin*: present in most parts of Europe. *S. b. woodwardi* (paler and greyer): from the Lower Volga eastwards.

(Right) Breeding areas (yellow) and areas where the Garden Warbler may be seen on passage (pink)

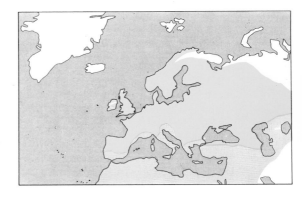

Blackcap
Sylvia atricapilla

French: FAUVETTE À TÊTE NOIRE
Italian: CAPINERA
Spanish: CURRUCA CAPIROTADA
German: MÖNCHSGRASMÜCKE

HABITAT Forests, scrub with scattered trees, gardens, orchards and parks.

IDENTIFICATION Length: 14 cm. Male can be identified by its very clearly defined black crown (hence its English name) which extends to its eyes. Also may be distinguished by its greyish upper parts and its light grey underparts, neck and sides of the head. Female: clearly defined but less conspicuous brown crown; grey upper parts, sides of the head, neck and underparts. Juveniles: more rufous upper parts and more yellowish underparts. It differs from the Orphean Warbler and the Sardinian Warbler in having the clearly defined cap and in the absence of white in its tail feathers.

It is very active and lively, and spends much time among trees and bushes. It is less retiring than the Garden Warbler. See also page 66.

CALL A hard, grumbling 'tak-tak', repeated rapidly if it is alarmed; also a harsh 'char-rr'. Its warbling song contains many more phrases than the Garden Warbler's, but is less sustained and higher-pitched. Also more mimetic.

REPRODUCTION From May onwards. The nest is located in low bushes or on the low branch of a tree. It consists of a cup of dry grasses and roots which is smaller and neater than the Garden Warbler's nest. Five white eggs, tinted buffish, olive or pink are laid. They are blotched and speckled with brown, olive, grey or reddish. Both sexes incubate the eggs for twelve or thirteen days and both tend the young.

FOOD Insects, fruit and berries: occasionally worms.

DISTRIBUTION AND MOVEMENTS Breeds throughout Europe (except for the northernmost regions) east to Siberia and south to northwest Africa. Winters from the Mediterranean basin south to central Africa: some also winter in western Europe as far north as Britain and Ireland. In Britain it is a widespread and numerous breeding bird in England and Wales but is decidedly rare in Scotland: also rare in Ireland. Also occurs as a passage visitor and a few winter in southwest England and Ireland.

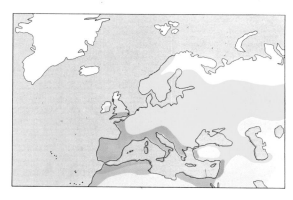

(Above) Male Blackcap (foreground) and female. (Left) Breeding areas (yellow), wintering areas (magenta), areas where the Blackcap may be seen all year round (orange) and on passage (pink)

(Right) Lesser Whitethroat *Sylvia curruca*, (below) Sardinian Warbler *S. melanocephala* and (below right) Barred Warbler *S. nisoria*. Like most warblers of the genus *Sylvia* they inhabit scrub and bushes

W. Murray/Bruce Coleman

M. D. England/Ardea

V. Ollson

M. D. England/Ardea

(Above) Subalpine Warbler
Sylvia cantillans, (below)
Sedge Warbler *Acrocephalus
schoenobaenus*

S. Roberts/Ardea

French: FAUVETTE BABILLARDE
Italian: BIGIARELLA
Spanish: CURRUCA ZARCERILLA
German: KLAPPERGRASMÜCKE

French: FAUVETTE GRISETTE
Italian: STERPAZZOLA
Spanish: CURRUCA ZARCERA
German: DORNGRASMÜCKE

Whitethroat

Sylvia communis

HABITAT Frequents areas with dense vegetation, scrub, hedgerows and sometimes gardens.

IDENTIFICATION Length: 14 cm. Male: dull brown upper parts contrast with the rufous coverts and the borders of the secondaries. Grey hood extends below the eye (pale grey in spring and summer and dark grey in winter) in contrast with the pure white of its throat. Very light rufous underparts tinged with pink. Female: darker and duller coloration with a brownish head and pinkish breast. These characteristics, together with its more slender build and its long tail, distinguish it from the more sturdily built Garden Warbler.

The Whitethroat is very lively and restless. It spends much of its time in hedges or dense, low vegetation from which it suddenly emerges only to quickly disappear again with its crest raised, its white throat puffed out and its tail spread. It is rarely seen on the ground. See also page 66.

CALL A loud, raucous, grumbling 'charr'. Song is a brief staccato burst.

REPRODUCTION From early May onwards. The nest is situated in low bushes, hedges or thorn-bushes, or in long grass, close to the ground. May occasionally build its nest on the ground or up to five metres above it. The male builds the nest before the arrival of a female: the female may use it or build her own. Four or five eggs are laid which may vary considerably in appearance; they are generally greenish or pale blue with light green, olive or buff markings. Incubation is carried out by both

sexes and takes eleven to thirteen days. The offspring are fed by both parents.

FOOD Insects and larvae; also spiders and berries.

DISTRIBUTION AND MOVEMENTS Breeds in northern Africa, Europe (apart from the northernmost regions) east across the USSR and south to Iran and Afghanistan. Winters in tropical and southern Africa. In Britain and Ireland is an abundant migrant breeder in most counties as well as a passage visitor in good numbers.

SUB-SPECIES *S. c. communis*: western Europe and North Africa (from Morocco to Tunisia). *S. c. volgensis* (paler): the USSR. *S. c. icterops* (greyer): the eastern Mediterranean and the Caucasus.

(Above left) Whitethroat. (Right) Breeding areas (yellow) and areas where the Whitethroat may be seen on passage (pink)

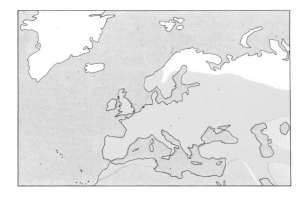

Lesser Whitethroat
Sylvia curruca

HABITAT Scrub and hedgerow like the Whitethroat, but also more open woodland and parks.

IDENTIFICATION Length: 13 cm. Dark patch on the ear coverts is more pronounced than that of any other white-throated warbler present in Europe. It is similar to the Whitethroat, but smaller and more compact. Also lacks the rufous on the wings. Its upper parts are greyer and its underparts whiter than the Whitethroat's. White underparts washed with buff-pink on the flanks. Juveniles in the autumn: darker, more chestnut overall coloration than that of adults. More retiring in its behaviour than the Whitethroat. See also page 66.

CALL Its principal note resembles the Blackcap's: a hard and persistent 'tekk-tekk'. Also a 'shar-rr' like the Whitethroat's, but emitted less frequently. Its song consists of the rapid repetition of a single note— 'cheeka-cheeka-cheeka' often preceded by a series of soft, low notes. It sings from within dense vegetation.

REPRODUCTION From early May onwards. Both male and female build the nest which is situated in thick hedges, bushes or scrub and is smaller and thinner than the Whitethroat's. It is usually built less than a metre off the ground. Eggs: four to six eggs are laid which have grey (or occasionally pink) marks and speckles. Incubation is carried out by both sexes and takes ten or eleven days. The offspring are cared for by both parents.

FOOD Insects, larvae, fruit and berries. Also occasionally spiders and small worms.

DISTRIBUTION AND MOVEMENTS Breeds in Europe from Scandinavia, Britain and France east to Siberia and northern China. It winters in tropical Africa. In Britain it is a fairly numerous migrant breeder which is confined to southern England, being more or less a rarity in Scotland and scarce even in Wales. Occurs on passage in Britain, but is still most often seen in the south and west. Is also a passage visitor to Ireland.

SUB-SPECIES Sub-species are present in Asia.

Spectacled Warbler
Sylvia conspicillata

HABITAT Arid regions with low bushes.

IDENTIFICATION Length: 12 cm. Resembles a dark Whitethroat or a pale Subalpine Warbler. Male's head dark grey, back and tail brown: the tail is edged with white. Wings have reddish-brown borders. Chin and throat white. Underparts pink-brown, becoming paler on the abdomen. Female's coloration is more subdued, especially the underparts which are paler. Reddish margins of the secondaries make this species easy to distinguish from all other warblers with the exception of the Whitethroat. Pale eyering not conspicuous.

CALL Emits a rattling 'kirr'. Song is a brief 'whieet' like the Whitethroat's.

REPRODUCTION From late February. Nests in a low dense bush, often close to the ground. Lays four or five, sometimes three to six pale greenish or buff-white eggs which are finely marked with light olive or grey-green. Both sexes incubate the eggs for twelve to fourteen days and both tend the young.

FOOD Small insects and small invertebrates.

DISTRIBUTION AND MOVEMENTS Breeds from Iberia east to Italy and also in northwest Africa. It is also present in the Middle East, Canary Islands and Cape Verde Island. The Spectacled Warbler is a partial migrant and winters mainly just south of its breeding range. Elsewhere in Europe, including Britain, it is a rare vagrant.

French: FAUVETTE MASQUÉE
Italian: STERPAZZOLA DI SARDEGNA
Spanish: CURRUCA TOMILLERA
German: BRILLENGRASMÜCKE

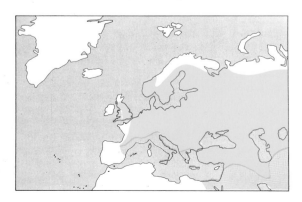

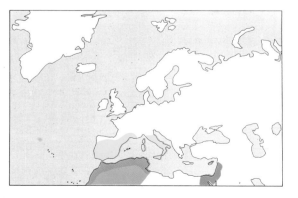

(Facing page, near left) Lesser Whitethroat. (Above) Spectacled Warbler. (Far left) Breeding areas (yellow) and areas where the Lesser Whitethroat may be seen on passage (pink). (Left) Breeding areas (yellow), wintering areas (magenta) and areas where the Spectacled Warbler may be seen all year round (orange)

French: FAUVETTE
MÉLANOCÉPHALE
Italian: OCCHIOCOTTO
Spanish: CURRUCA CABECINEGRA
German: SAMTKOPFGRASMÜCKE

French: FAUVETTE
MÉLANOCÉPHALE DE
CHYPRE
Italian: BIGIA DI CIPRO
German: ZYPERN-
SAMTKOPFGRASMÜCKE

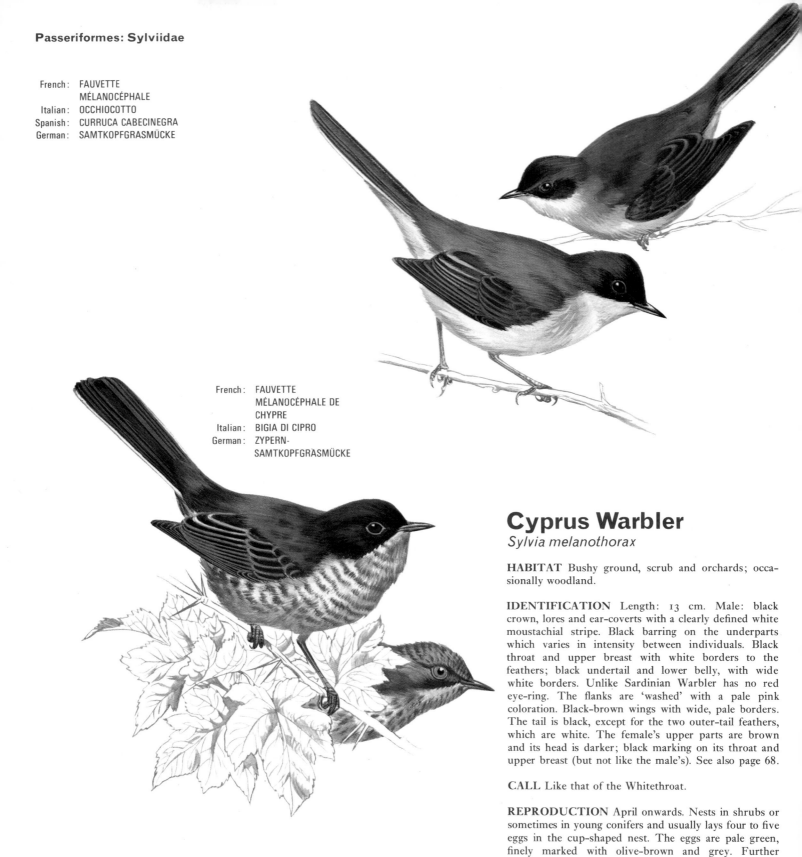

Cyprus Warbler
Sylvia melanothorax

HABITAT Bushy ground, scrub and orchards; occasionally woodland.

IDENTIFICATION Length: 13 cm. Male: black crown, lores and ear-coverts with a clearly defined white moustachial stripe. Black barring on the underparts which varies in intensity between individuals. Black throat and upper breast with white borders to the feathers; black undertail and lower belly, with wide white borders. Unlike Sardinian Warbler has no red eye-ring. The flanks are 'washed' with a pale pink coloration. Black-brown wings with wide, pale borders. The tail is black, except for the two outer-tail feathers, which are white. The female's upper parts are brown and its head is darker; black marking on its throat and upper breast (but not like the male's). See also page 68.

CALL Like that of the Whitethroat.

REPRODUCTION April onwards. Nests in shrubs or sometimes in young conifers and usually lays four to five eggs in the cup-shaped nest. The eggs are pale green, finely marked with olive-brown and grey. Further information is not available.

FOOD Insects.

DISTRIBUTION AND MOVEMENTS It is confined to Cyprus, although it sometimes travels in winter and has been seen on rare occasions in Asia Minor, the Lebanon and Israel. Some authorities classify this species as a race of the Sardinian Warbler.

(Above) Male Cyprus Warbler
(foreground) and female

Sardinian Warbler
Sylvia melanocephala

HABITAT Open woodland, scrub, parks and gardens: very occasionally in urban areas.

IDENTIFICATION Length: 13 cm. Male resembles a Blackcap but the glossy black crown extends below the eye. Grey rump and upper parts, white chin and throat, off-white underparts with greyish flanks and a graduated blackish tail which is often spread. Outer tail feathers white and very conspicuous in flight. Conspicuous red eye and red eye-ring. Female Sardinian Warbler is much browner, and the crown is only slightly darker grey than its upper parts so there is little contrast. Resembles the Lesser Whitethroat but its coloration is a warmer deep brown. Female's eye-ring is still prominent but paler than the male's. See also page 66.

CALL Emits strident, scolding notes: a 'tee-tee' which is repeated several times. The song resembles the Whitethroat's but it is more musical and sustained.

REPRODUCTION From mid March onwards. The cup-shaped nest may be built close to the ground or over two metres off the ground in shrubs, climbing plants and other vegetation. Usually lays three or four glossy eggs which vary greatly in colour from white to greenish to pink or buff. The eggs are speckled and mottled with a variety of colours. Incubation is carried out by both sexes for thirteen or fourteen days.

FOOD Mainly small insects, larvae and small spiders. Also fruit in season.

DISTRIBUTION AND MOVEMENTS Breeds around the Mediterranean basin and in the Canary Islands. Mainly sedentary although some individuals winter in the Sahara, northern Iraq and Saudi Arabia. In Britain it has been recorded as a vagrant on only a few occasions.

Rüppell's Warbler
Sylvia rüppelli

HABITAT Scrub, low bushes, gardens, rocky areas and sometimes on coasts.

IDENTIFICATION Length: 14 cm. The adult male is easily identified by its completely black head and throat. Has a thin white moustachial stripe: eyes red. Female's upper parts grey-brown with only a few traces of black coloration on the head: both sexes have distinctive reddish legs. Both female and juvenile are hard to distinguish from those of the Sardinian Warbler which shares some of its range. See also page 66.

CALL Like that of the Sardinian Warbler but interspersed with a harsher rattle.

REPRODUCTION From mid-April. The nest is a cup of plant stems and grasses which is lined with plant fibres: it is often situated in a bush. Lays three to five eggs which are white, sometimes tinged buff or greenish, and finely, but profusely, marked with olive, light brown or grey. Both sexes incubate the eggs for about thirteen days.

FOOD Mainly small insects and spiders.

DISTRIBUTION AND MOVEMENTS Breeds in Crete and the Aegean Islands as well as in Asia Minor. It migrates from the eastern Mediterranean to winter in East Africa. Further north in Europe it is an extremely rare vagrant.

French: FAUVETTE MASQUÉE
Italian: BIGIA DI RÜPPELL
Spanish: CURRUCA DE RÜPPELL
German: MASKENGRASMÜCKE

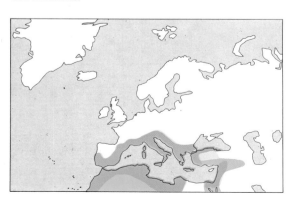

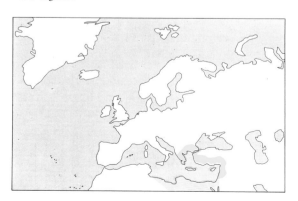

(Facing page top) Female Sardinian Warbler (above) and male (below). (Far left) Wintering areas (magenta), areas where the Sardinian Warbler may be seen all year round (orange) and on passage (pink). (Above) Male Rüppell's Warbler (foreground) and female. (Left) Breeding areas (yellow) and areas where Rüppell's Warbler may be seen on passage (pink)

French: FAUVETTE DE
MÉNÉTRIES
Italian: BIGIA DI MÉNÉTRIES
Spanish: CURRUCA DE MÉNÉTRIES
German: ÖSTLICHE-
SAMTKOPFGRASMÜCKE

Ménétries' Warbler
Sylvia mystacea

HABITAT It frequents plains and the lower slopes of mountains, particularly in areas where tamarisk bushes are plentiful. Also found along rivers and in plains and orchards.

IDENTIFICATION Length: 13 cm. Very similar to the Sardinian Warbler. The adult male has a black forehead and crown which merge into the nape. Remaining upper parts are ash grey, except for its wings, which are edged with brown, without any white coloration. Blackish tail. Pinkish underparts are a distinguishing feature. White moustachial stripe between the black of the cheeks and the pink of the throat. The female is like the male but its upper parts are brown rather than black or grey, although they sometimes have a little grey coloration. Generally a restless and skulking species. See also page 68.

CALL Alarm note: 'tak-tak'. Song consists of rattling and hissing notes.

REPRODUCTION From May onwards. It nests in low bushes—especially tamarisks—building its nest on the ground or up to a metre above it. Eggs: three to five white or faintly greenish with olive-brown or grey

markings are laid. Incubation takes fourteen days, but further details are not available.

FOOD Mainly insects.

DISTRIBUTION AND MOVEMENTS Breeds in Asia Minor, southern USSR, the shores of the Caspian Sea and east across Iran and Afghanistan as far as Lake Aral. It winters in Africa and is rare further north and west.

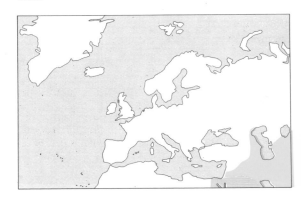

(Right) Breeding areas (yellow) and areas where Ménétries' Warbler may be seen on passage (pink)

Subalpine Warbler
Sylvia cantillans

French: FAUVETTE PASSERINETTE
Italian: STERPAZZOLINA
Spanish: CURRUCA CARRASQUEÑA
German: BARTGRASMÜCKE

HABITAT Scrub, bushes and thickets or rocky, broken ground.

IDENTIFICATION Length: 12 cm. Resembles a small Dartford Warbler. The male's upper parts are bluish-grey except for its wings and tail which are tinged with brown. Chin, throat and breast are reddish: this coloration is separated from the grey of its head by a conspicuous white moustachial stripe which is a key feature to the identification of this species. The female is browner. See also page 68.

CALL Emits a distinctive soft 'tec-tec'. Song is like the Sardinian Warbler's, but more musical with no harsh notes.

REPRODUCTION From mid-April. Nests in low shrubs or creepers, and lays three or four eggs in the cup-shaped nest. Eggs are glossy white or pale greenish, buff or pinkish. They are finely speckled with olive, brown, grey or purple-red. The female alone usually incubates for about twelve days although the male sometimes assists. Both tend the young.

FOOD Small insects and other invertebrates.

DISTRIBUTION AND MOVEMENTS Breeds in southern Europe from Iberia east to Asia Minor and Syria: also in northwest Africa. Mainly migratory and most frequently winters in Africa south of the Sahara. Vagrant to Britain and Ireland.

SUB-SPECIES The nominate sub-species *S. c. cantillans* is found in Iberia, southern France, Italy, Sardinia, Corsica and Sicily. *S. c. albistriata*: Yugoslavia east to Asia Minor and Syria. *S. c. inornata*: northwest Africa.

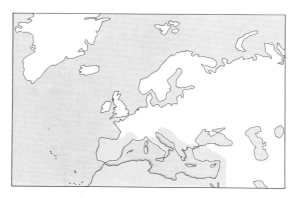

(Above) Male Subalpine Warbler (left) and female. (Left) Breeding areas (yellow) and areas where the Subalpine Warbler may be seen on passage (pink)

French: FAUVETTE SARDE
Italian: MAGNANINA SARDA
Spanish: CURRUCA SARDA
German: SARDENGRASMÜCKE

Marmora's Warbler
Sylvia sarda

HABITAT Scrub of Mediterranean islands.

IDENTIFICATION Length: 12 cm. This species is easy to identify on account of its dark coloration: it appears almost black from a distance. The male is the same shape and size as the Dartford Warbler, but has slate-grey underparts with slightly browner coloration on its wings and tail, and paler coloration from the centre of its breast to its undertail. The female is paler— a pinkish grey-brown. Red eye and eye-ring. See also page 68.

CALL Call is distinctive 'tsiig'. Its song is like the Dartford Warbler's but less harsh.

REPRODUCTION From April onwards. The cup-shaped nest is situated in a low shrub, either very near to the ground or sometimes a metre above. Lays three or four white, pale grey or greenish eggs which are mottled with grey or brownish. Both parents tend the young.

FOOD Probably mainly insects.

DISTRIBUTION AND MOVEMENTS It is a sedentary species although some individuals are found south of their nesting sites during the winter. Breeds on the Spanish mainland, Corsica, Sardinia, Sicily and small Mediterranean islands and on the coast of Tunisia.

SUB-SPECIES *S. s. balearica*: (slightly smaller with pink-tinged breast): the Balearic Islands.

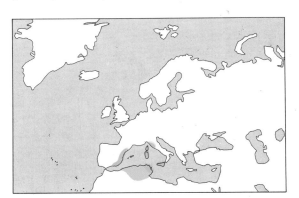

(Right) Male Marmora's Warbler (foreground) and female. (Top right) Wintering areas (magenta) and areas where Marmora's Warbler may be seen all year round (orange)

Dartford Warbler
Sylvia undata

French: FAUVETTE PITCHOU
Italian: MAGNANINA
Spanish: CURRUCA RABILARGA
German: PROVENCEGRASMÜCKE

HABITAT Heaths, open woodland and scrub.

IDENTIFICATION Length: 12 cm. Although it is often only seen fleetingly as it dives from one bush to another, its small size, very dark coloration and its white-edged dark tail (which is often raised or fanned out) are distinguishing features. Male: dark brown upper parts merging into the slate-grey coloration of its head; dark purple-brown underparts. Females and juveniles are paler and browner. The throat and chin have white markings in the autumn. Orange-red eye and eye-ring. See also page 68.

CALL Similar notes to those of the Whitethroat, but more grating, metallic and incisive: 'tcheer-rr'. Also more melodious and liquid variations. The short song is more metallic than the Whitethroat's.

REPRODUCTION Usually from mid-April. The nest is situated very near the ground or up to a metre off the ground in low shrubs. Three or four pale green or whitish eggs are laid with olive-green and lead grey markings, and occasionally reddish-chestnut markings. Incubation is mainly carried out by the female for twelve or thirteen days. The young are cared for by both parents.

FOOD Mainly insects; also spiders and berries.

DISTRIBUTION AND MOVEMENTS Breeds from southern England, western France and Iberia east to Italy. Also breeds in northwest Africa. Mainly sedentary. In Britain it is a resident in small numbers in the extreme south of England where it is badly hit by hard winters.

SUB-SPECIES *S. u. dartfordiensis*: southern England, Channel Islands and northwest France. *S. u. undata*: southern France, northern and central Spain, Italy, Corsica, Sardinia and Sicily. *S. u. naevalbens*: southeast Italy. *S. u. toni*: Portugal, southern Spain and northern Africa.

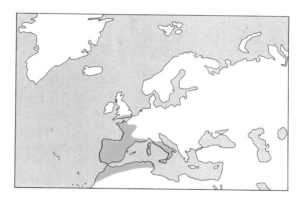

(Above) Areas where the Dartford Warbler may be seen all year round (orange)

(Right) Blackcap *Sylvia atricapilla:* the male's black crown makes him easily identifiable. (Below) Male and female Blackcaps at the nest

French: POUILLOT FITIS
Italian: LUÌ GROSSO
Spanish: MOSQUITERO MUSICAL
German: FITISLAUBSÄNGER

Willow Warbler
Phylloscopus trochilus

HABITAT Open woodland, bushy and sparsely wooded areas: also gardens.

IDENTIFICATION Length: 11 cm. Very similar to the Chiffchaff from which it may be distinguished by its song and its yellow-brown rather than blackish legs. Colours of its plumage are also more clearly defined: upper parts are greener and underparts yellower. The supercilium is also more conspicuous.

CALL A mournful 'wee-eet' which is similar to the Chiffchaff's call. Its distinctive melodious and trilling song starts gently and slowly and then grows louder and more emphatic.

REPRODUCTION From late April onwards. Usually six or seven eggs, white speckled with brown, are laid in the spherical nest which is usually situated on the ground in herbage. The nest is made by the female of grass, plant stems, moss, roots and bits of rotten wood. It is entered from the side. The female alone incubates for about thirteen days although both parents tend the young which remain in the nest for thirteen to sixteen days.

FOOD Insects, larvae, spiders and occasionally small worms. Also feeds on soft berries in autumn.

DISTRIBUTION AND MOVEMENTS Breeds from Britain, Ireland and Scandinavia east across northern Eurasia. Migrant, wintering in tropical and southern Africa. In Britain and Ireland it is an abundant migrant breeder in all areas except Shetland and only locally in the Outer Hebrides and Orkney. It is also a passage visitor to Britain and Ireland.

SUB-SPECIES *P.t. acredula:* Scandinavia, eastern Europe and western Siberia. Another sub-species is present in central and eastern Siberia.

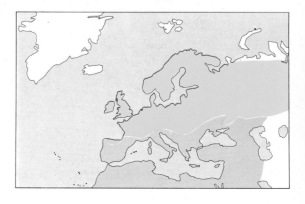

(Right) Breeding areas (yellow) and areas where the Willow Warbler may be seen on passage (pink). (Preceding page) Willow Warbler *P. trochilus* at the nest

Chiffchaff
Phylloscopus collybita

HABITAT Similar to that of the Willow Warbler, but generally in areas with taller trees.

IDENTIFICATION Length: 11 cm. Brown upper parts shading into olive-green: slightly greener tail. Underparts tinged with white; pale brown and yellowish coloration. Very similar to the Willow Warbler but coloration is generally somewhat duller and has darker legs. However, the two species are best distinguished by their songs.

CALL Emits a monosyllabic 'hweet'. Song is a repeated 'chiff-chaff' (hence its English name) sometimes interspersed with a guttural 'chirr'.

REPRODUCTION From late April onwards. The nest is a domed structure of plant material which is thickly lined with feathers. It is built by the female on the ground or slightly above in herbage. Usually lays four to nine shiny white eggs with dark markings. However second broods usually contain only four or five eggs. Incubation, which is carried out by the female alone, lasts thirteen or fourteen days. The chicks are tended mainly by the female.

FOOD Insects, larvae and spiders.

DISTRIBUTION AND MOVEMENTS Breeds in western and central Europe, northwest Africa, the Canary Islands and Asia. Most populations are migratory and winter in Africa, the eastern Mediterranean, Arabia and southeast Asia. In Britain and Ireland it is a numerous migrant breeder but is rather scarce in northern England and in Scotland. The Chiffchaff is resident from mid-March to October although a few may overwinter, mainly in south west England. Also occurs as a passage visitor and some individuals winter on coasts, mostly of southern England and the Irish Sea.

SUB-SPECIES *P.c. abietinus*: Scandinavia and the western USSR southwards to Iran. Other sub-species are present in Asia.

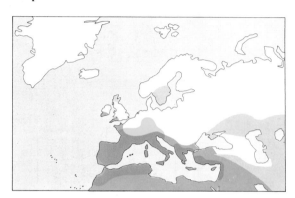

French: POUILLOT VÉLOCE
Italian: LUÌ PICCOLO
Spanish: MOSQUITERO COMÚN
German: ZILPZALP

(Above left) Breeding areas (yellow), wintering areas (magenta), areas where the Chiffchaff may be seen all year round (orange) and on passage (pink)

Bonelli's Warbler
Phylloscopus bonelli

HABITAT Woods and forests in hilly areas.

IDENTIFICATION Length: 11 cm. Distinguishable from other leaf warblers of the genus *Phylloscopus* by the pale grey front half of the body. There is a touch of yellow on the rump and a yellow marking on the wing. Underparts are paler than the Willow Warbler's.

CALL A soft 'ho-eet'. Its song, which is based on the same note, is like the Wood Warbler's trill but slower, more musical and more distinctly disyllabic.

REPRODUCTION From early May. Nest is a domed structure with a side entrance: it consists mainly of grass and is lined with finer grasses. The nest is built by the female and is situated on the ground, often in a hollow or in a bank. Eggs: four to six smooth and glossy white eggs, profusely marked with red-brown or purple brown, are laid. The dark markings are usually concentrated at the larger end. The female alone incubates, but further information is unavailable.

FOOD Mainly insects.

DISTRIBUTION AND MOVEMENTS Breeds from Iberia and France east through southern Europe to Asia Minor and the Near East. Also breeds in northwest Africa. Migratory, wintering in tropical Africa. In Britain it is a rare vagrant which has occurred mainly in the early autumn.

SUB-SPECIES *P.b. orientalis:* the Balkan peninsula and Asia Minor.

Wood Warbler
Phylloscopus sibilatrix

HABITAT Deciduous woods (especially beech) and coniferous woods.

IDENTIFICATION Length: 12 cm. One of the largest leaf warblers of the genus *Phylloscopus* present in Europe. May be distinguished from other species of the genus by its larger size, long wings and the brighter and more contrasting coloration. Yellow-green upper parts, conspicuous yellow eyestripe, yellow throat and breast and white underparts. Coloration of juveniles is less vivid.

CALL Has two distinct songs: a tremulous drawn-out trill and a soft 'dee-urr'.

REPRODUCTION From late May. The female builds the nest on the ground in undergrowth or in a hollow. The nest is a domed structure of leaves, grasses and stems. Usually lays six or seven smooth and glossy white eggs which are profusely marked with reddish-brown. The female alone incubates for about thirteen days. Both sexes tend the young.

FOOD Insects and larvae: occasionally berries.

DISTRIBUTION AND MOVEMENTS Breeds from Scandinavia, Britain and France east across Eurasia to the Caucasus. Migrant, and winters in tropical Africa. European birds migrate southeast in autumn. Breeds in Britain and Ireland and is most numerous in the wetter western hill districts. However, it is sparse or absent from the Scottish islands and Ireland. Also occurs as a passage visitor to Britain.

(Above) Bonelli's Warbler. (Near right) Breeding areas (yellow) and areas where Bonelli's Warbler may be seen on passage (pink)

Dusky Warbler
Phylloscopus fuscatus

French: POUILLOT BRUN
Italian: LUÌ SCURO
Spanish: MOSQUITERO SOMBRÍO
German: DUNKLER LAUBSÄNGER

HABITAT Low bushes or woods; often found near marshes, but also inhabits arid ground.

IDENTIFICATION Length: 11 cm. Smaller than the similar Radde's Warbler and has a thinner bill. It has the darkest plumage of the European species of the genus *Phylloscopus*. Lacks green or yellow coloration: has a buff not yellow eyestripe. Brown upper parts, pale underparts and brown speckles on its ear-coverts. Often feeds on the ground.

CALL Its usual call note is a harsh 'tchake-tchake'. Its song is a brief and repetitive 't-ya'.

REPRODUCTION From mid-June onwards. It normally nests near water, but sometimes on barren hillsides. The nest is situated on the ground, at the foot of a bush; it is made of dry grasses and moss, lined with feathers. There are five or six plain white eggs per clutch.

FOOD Mainly small insects.

DISTRIBUTION AND MOVEMENTS Breeds in Siberia, eastern Asia, the eastern Himalayas and China. Winters in India and southern China. Accidental in Britain.

SUB-SPECIES Sub-species are present in Asia.

French: POUILLOT SIFFLEUR
Italian: LUÌ VERDE
Spanish: MOSQUITERO SILBADOR
German: WALDLAUBSÄNGER

(Above) Dusky Warbler and (left) Wood Warbler. (Facing page, near left) Breeding areas (yellow) and areas where the Wood Warbler may be seen on passage (pink)

French: POUILLOT DE PALLAS
Italian: LUÌ DEL PALLAS
Spanish: MOSQUITERO DE PALLAS
German: GOLDHÄHNCHEN-
LAUBSÄNGER

Pallas's Warbler
Phylloscopus proregulus

French: POUILLOT À GRANDS
SOURCILS
Italian: LUÌ FORESTIERO
Spanish: MOSQUITERO BILISTADO
German: GELBBRAUEN-
LAUBSÄNGER

HABITAT Mixed or coniferous forests.

IDENTIFICATION Length: 9 cm. Smallest leaf warbler which occurs in Europe. Yellow rump makes this species easily recognisable—this feature is most visible when the bird is hovering. Looks more like a Goldcrest than a member of the genus *Phylloscopus* because of its habit of hovering in the foliage of trees in search of insects. Its double yellow wing-bar, the wide pale yellow streak down the centre of its crown and its brighter yellow eyestripe are other distinctive features.

CALL A thin 'weesp', shriller than that of the Yellow-browed Warbler.

REPRODUCTION Its well-built, domed nest is usually situated close to the ground. There are five or six white eggs with purple-grey or red-brown speckles. Further information is lacking.

FOOD Mainly insects.

DISTRIBUTION AND MOVEMENTS It nests in Siberia and China south to the Himalayas. Winters in southeast Asia. Vagrant to Europe, but is identified with increasing frequency in Britain and Ireland.

SUB-SPECIES In addition to the nominate sub-species, which is accidental in various parts of western Europe, sub-species are present in Asia.

(Above left) Pallas's Warbler and (right) Yellow-browed Warbler

Yellow-browed Warbler
Phylloscopus inornatus

HABITAT Coniferous forests and mixed woodland.

IDENTIFICATION Length: 10 cm. Pale green upper parts tinged with yellow. Its smaller size and more marked pale yellow eyestripe distinguishes it from the Willow Warbler. Off-white underparts and off-white double wing bar, greenish rump. May have a pale streak along its crown and a lighter rump which cause it to resemble Pallas's Warbler although the latter has a clearly defined dark and yellowish head pattern.

CALL Call resembles the Chiffchaff's but is louder. Its tremulous and monotonous song consists of the rapid repetitions of the note 'fee-tee'.

REPRODUCTION Late June onwards. Nests on the ground, often against a tussock, mound or tree root. Nest is a domed structure with a side entrance. Eggs: five or six, white finely speckled with red-brown. No further information is available.

FOOD Mainly small insects.

DISTRIBUTION AND MOVEMENTS Breeds across northern Asia and south to Afghanistan: winters in southern Asia. Occurs in western Europe as an accidental, but is recorded regularly in autumn in Britain and Ireland.

SUB-SPECIES Sub-species are present in Asia.

Radde's Warbler
Phylloscopus schwarzi

French: POUILLOT DE SCHWARZ
Italian: LUÌ DI RADDE
Spanish: MOSQUITERO DE SCHWARZ
German: BARTLAUBSÄNGER

HABITAT Deciduous woods and areas with scattered trees, often close to rivers.

IDENTIFICATION Length: 13 cm. Similar to the Dusky Warbler but larger and has paler upper parts. Also generally more olive and less reddish in coloration. The eyestripe is more conspicuous as is the large bill. Skulking in habits. Assumes an erect posture which is reminiscent of the Reed Warbler.

CALL Emits a soft whistling 'tweet'.

REPRODUCTION The almost spherical nest is constructed of plant material and is entered from the top. It is usually situated near the ground. Four or five white eggs with rust-coloured markings are laid. Further information is lacking.

FOOD Mainly insects.

DISTRIBUTION AND MOVEMENTS Breeds in southern Siberia and southwards to Korea. Winters mainly in Vietnam, Laos, Cambodia and southern China. Accidental in Europe, and it has occurred in Britain as a vagrant on a number of occasions in widely scattered localities.

French: POUILLOT BORÉAL
Italian: LUÌ BOREALE
Spanish: MOSQUITERO BOREAL
German: NORDISCHER
LAUBSÄNGER

Arctic Warbler
Phylloscopus borealis

HABITAT Arctic and sub-arctic forests and scrub.

IDENTIFICATION Length: 12 cm. Greenish upper parts tinged with grey-brown; whitish underparts, parts tinged with grey-brown; whitish underparts, with traces of yellow on the flanks. Narrow off-white wing bar. Sometimes the trace of a second wing bar is visible, but equally both may be worn away. Very prominent yellow supercilium which extends to the nape, and a dark stripe through the eye which distinguishes it from the Willow and Wood Warblers. Yellow-brown legs.

CALL Song is a repeated 'tzeek' followed by a brief chattering sequence.

REPRODUCTION From late June. The nest is a domed structure with a side entrance. It is usually built into dead vegetation so that only the entrance shows. May sometimes be built in herbage up to a metre off the ground. Five to six (sometimes three to seven) eggs are laid which are finely spotted with red brown. The female alone incubates. Further information about reproduction is lacking.

FOOD Insects.

DISTRIBUTION AND MOVEMENTS Breeds across northern Eurasia from Scandinavia to the Bering Strait and across into Alaska. It migrates eastwards and is very rare in Europe away from its Scandinavian breeding grounds. In Britain and Ireland it is a rare vagrant.

SUB-SPECIES *P.b. talovka* is present in the western part of the range east to Siberia and northwest Mongolia. Others, including the nominate sub-species, are present in Asia and Alaska.

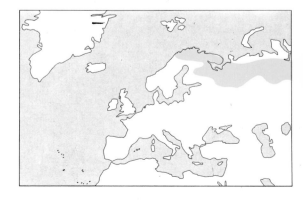

(Above) Adult Arctic Warbler (top) and juvenile. (Right) Breeding areas (yellow) of the Arctic Warbler

Green Warbler
Phylloscopus nitidus

HABITAT Breeds in woods in mountainous areas.

IDENTIFICATION Length: 11 cm. Very similar to the Wood Warbler but its plumage is brighter green and less yellowish on the upper parts. Sometimes this species is regarded as a race of the Greenish Warbler. Underparts yellow, not white like the Wood Warbler's. Bright yellow cheeks and supercilium: pale yellow wing-bar. When the plumage is new a second narrow wing-bar may also be visible. Legs range in colour from deep olive to grey.

CALL Emits a 'chee-wee'. Song is a repetitive 'tss-tri-tss'.

REPRODUCTION From mid May. The nest is a domed structure of grass stems, roots and moss with a side entrance. It is usually situated on the ground. Four to six white eggs are laid, but further information is lacking.

FOOD Insects and larvae.

DISTRIBUTION AND MOVEMENTS Breeds in the Caucasus from the Black Sea to the Caspian and also in northern Iran and Afghanistan. Migrates south to India and Ceylon.

French: POUILLOT VERT
Italian: LUÌ NITIDO
Spanish: MOSQUITERO VERDE
German: KAUKASUS GRÜNLAUBSÄNGER

(Left) Breeding areas (yellow) of the Green Warbler

Greenish Warbler
Phylloscopus trochiloides

HABITAT Breeds in forest edges and open woodland.

IDENTIFICATION Length: 11 cm. May be distinguished from the Willow Warbler by its pale yellow wing-bar and more conspicuous eyestripe: also by the white underparts. Smaller and greyer than the Arctic Warbler. The olive-green upper parts shade into brown; flanks and sides of the breast yellow-white. Legs are dark.

CALL A double note: 'tess-ay'. The song consists of a high-pitched and warbling wren-like trill.

REPRODUCTION From mid-June. The female builds a domed nest on the ground under a bush. Eggs: four to six smooth but non-glossy white eggs are laid. Incubation is carried out by the female alone although both parents tend the young.

FOOD Probably insects.

DISTRIBUTION AND MOVEMENTS Breeds from southern Finland, Germany and the Baltic countries east across the USSR to China and south to Afghanistan. Winters in Indo-China. Outside its Scandinavian breeding grounds it is a rare vagrant over most of Europe, including Britain and Ireland, where it does, however, occur with slightly more frequency than the Arctic Warbler.

SUB-SPECIES The sub-species *P.t. viridanus* is present in Europe. Other sub-species, including the nominate one, are present in Asia.

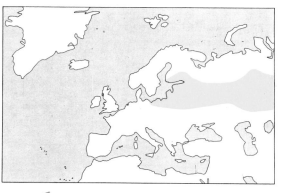

French: POUILLOT VERDÂTRE
Italian: LUÌ VERDASTRO
Spanish: MOSQUITERO TROQUILOIDE
German: GRÜNER LAUBSÄNGER

(Left) Breeding areas (yellow) of the Greenish Warbler

49

F. V. Blackburn/Bruce Coleman

(Left) Wood Warbler *Phylloscopus sibilatrix*, (below) Willow Warbler *P. trochilus* and (facing page) Chiffchaff *P. collybita*. These small greenish and yellowish leaf warblers are most easily distinguished from one another by their songs

H. Mickelsson

French: ROITELET HUPPÉ
Italian: REGOLO
Spanish: REYEZUELO SENCILLO
German: WINTERGOLDHÄHNCHEN

Goldcrest
Regulus regulus

HABITAT Mixed and coniferous woodland: also undergrowth, hedgerows, parks and gardens.

IDENTIFICATION Length: 9 cm. One of the smallest warblers breeding in Europe. Distinguishable from all other warblers by its black bordered crest. Crest is orange in the male, yellow in the female. Brown forehead, rest of the head (except for the crest) olive-grey. Upper parts grey-green, underparts pale olive. Bill brown-black; legs pale grey-brown; iris brown. Double wing-bar with a dark mark alongside. Juveniles: top of the head uniform green-brown: lacks the crest.

During nuptial display the male erects and undulates his crest, and performs excited jerky movements.

CALL A thin and high pitched 'sisisi'. The song consists of a repeated soft and very high pitched double note 'ceder-ceder' which ends in a short trill.

REPRODUCTION From late April. Nests in tall trees, building a suspended nest at a fork of twigs at the end of a branch. Alternatively the nest may be built in the sheltered fork of a tree. Both sexes build the nest, but the male's participation varies. The nest is a deep thick cup of mosses and lichen. It may be built so tightly against the foliage or twigs above that entrance to the small egg cavity is restricted. Eggs: seven to ten, sometimes only five or six, varying in colour from white to yellowish with some brown or pink speckling. The female alone incubates for fourteen to seventeen days.

The young are tended by both parents and leave the nest after sixteen to twenty-one days. Double brooded.

FOOD Insects and larvae.

DISTRIBUTION AND MOVEMENTS Breeds throughout Europe except for the extreme north and south, and discontinuously east across Asia to Japan. Winters in the south of the breeding range and beyond to the Mediterranean, Iran and southern China. In Britain and Ireland it is a widespread breeder as well as a winter and passage visitor.

SUB-SPECIES *R.r. buturlini* (more grey-green): Crimea. Other sub-species are present in Asia.

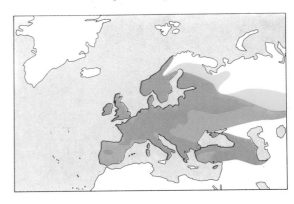

(Above) Male Goldcrest (foreground) and female. (Right) Breeding areas (yellow), wintering areas (magenta) and areas where the Goldcrest may be seen all year round (orange)

Firecrest
Regulus ignicapillus

French: ROITELET À TRIPLE BANDEAU
Italian: FIORRANCINO
Spanish: REYEZUELO LISTADO
German: SOMMERGOLDHÄHNCHEN

HABITAT Like that of Goldcrest, including deciduous and coniferous woodland.

IDENTIFICATION Length: 9 cm. Along with the Goldcrest is one of Europe's smallest breeding birds. Bright orange-red crest, bordered by two black stripes meeting in front. White stripe above eye with black streak through eye and white patch under eye distinguish it from the Goldcrest. Upper parts yellow-green; underparts pale grey-brown except for white belly. Bill black; legs brown. Remaining parts as Goldcrest. Female has yellow crest. Juveniles: faintly marked black and white streaks on head, but no crest.

CALL The usual call is a 'tseet' which is less high pitched than the Goldcrest's. The song consists of the repetition of a single high-pitched note 'siss'.

REPRODUCTION From early May. The female builds the nest at the end of branches of conifers, deciduous trees and bushes. It is very similar to the Goldcrest's nest. Eggs: seven to eleven, sometimes twelve, white with a pinkish tint and a cap at the larger end of fine reddish speckling. Only the female incubates for fourteen or fifteen days. The young are able to leave the nest after nineteen or twenty days. Double brooded.

FOOD Insects and larvae: also spiders.

DISTRIBUTION AND MOVEMENTS Breeds in central and western Europe from Denmark and the southwest USSR south to the Mediterranean, the Balkans and Asia Minor. Also breeds in northern Africa, Madeira and the Canaries. Partially migratory, wintering in the south of the breeding range. The Firecrest colonised southern England in recent years and has spread gradually northwards: however, it remains a very rare breeder in this country. It is not known whether these individuals are resident or migratory. Also occurs as a winter visitor in small numbers in southwest England and occasionally elsewhere. Occurs as a passage visitor to southern England, Wales and southwest Ireland. Rare vagrant elsewhere.

SUB-SPECIES *R.i. balearicus* (greyer): Balearic Islands and northern Africa. *R.i. madeirensis:* Madeira. *R.i. teneriffae:* Canaries.

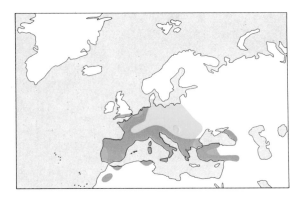

(Above) Male Firecrest (top) and female. (Left) Breeding areas (yellow), wintering areas (magenta), areas where the Firecrest may be seen all year round (orange) and on passage (pink)

French: PRINIA GRACILE
Italian: PRINIA GRACILE
German: STREIFEN-PRINIA

Graceful Warbler
Prinia gracilis

(Below right) Areas where the Graceful Warbler may be seen all year round (orange)

HABITAT Desert scrub and dry grassy areas: also cultivated land and gardens. Sometimes found along river banks.

IDENTIFICATION Length: 10 cm. The long graduated tail comprises over half the length of this small species. Upper parts grey-brown, strongly streaked dark on the crown and back. Underparts white tinged greyish on the flanks. Outer tail feathers edged with white and have a distinct black subterminal patch. Flight feathers are a warm brown. The long tail is often carried cocked up and fanned out, and is sometimes twitched from side to side. The sexes are similar.

CALL A triple 'brrip' and variations. The song is a high pitched and repeated 'zer-wit'.

REPRODUCTION From late March: the breeding period is prolonged. The nest is a fairly loose domed structure with a side entrance. The nest is built up to a metre off the ground in long grass or bushes. The clutch consists of three glossy pinkish eggs which are faintly speckled with red-brown although the coloration varies in different localities. Both sexes incubate for

twelve to fourteen days. The male alone may tend the fledglings while the female builds a new nest as this species has two or three broods per year.

FOOD Insects, spiders and perhaps seeds.

DISTRIBUTION AND MOVEMENTS Breeds in eastern Egypt, southern Turkey and Asia Minor. Also breeds in east Africa.

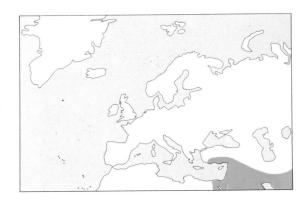

Fan-tailed Warbler
Cisticola juncidis

HABITAT Freshwater margins and marshes. Also cultivated areas, grassland and road verges.

IDENTIFICATION Length: 10 cm. In Africa known as the Zitting Cisticola. A small rufous-brown bird with pale underparts tinged rufous. Head and back streaked. Tail short and graduated, often spread like a fan; tail feathers are tipped white and have a black sub-terminal patch. Bill slender.
  Fairly restless but skulking in behaviour, and most easily observed during its undulating courtship flight when it utters its characteristic song. Sometimes runs on the ground when hunting insects.

CALL A short 'tew'. Song consists of an insistent 'chip, chip'.

REPRODUCTION From late March: the breeding season is prolonged. The species is double, possibly treble, brooded. The nest is an intricate, elongated pear-shaped structure woven of grasses and spiders' web, between grass and rush stems often only a few centimetres from the ground. The entrance is situated slightly to the side at the top part. Eggs: four to six, rather elongated and glossy, varying in colour from white to pinkish-white and pale blue, sometimes speckled red-brown. Both sexes incubate for about ten days.

FOOD Mainly insects and their larvae.

DISTRIBUTION AND MOVEMENTS Breeds in southern Europe and Mediterranean region, Africa, southern Arabia, southern Asia and its islands east to China and Japan. Also breeds in the Indo-Malayan region and northern Australia. In the Mediterranean region it is sedentary although it undertakes irregular winter movements. Has recently spread up the west coast of France to the Channel coast. Accidental in Britain and Ireland, but may colonise in the future.

SUB-SPECIES *C.j. cisticola* (slightly darker): North Africa, Iberia, southern France and the western shores of the Mediterranean. Many other sub-species are present in the rest of the range.

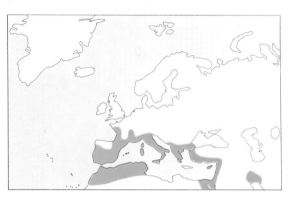

French: CISTICOLE DES JONCS
Italian: BECCAMOSCHINO
Spanish: BUITRÓN
German: CISTENSÄNGER

(Left) Areas where the Fan-tailed Warbler may be seen all year round (orange)

F. V. Blackburn

F. V. Blackburn/Bruce Coleman

Eric Hosking

(Above) Female Goldcrest *Regulus regulus*. (Left) Wood Warbler *Phylloscopus sibilatrix* and (facing page) Chiffchaff *P. collybita* at the side entrances to their nests

Identification of warblers

The following illustrations—showing members of the family Sylviidae—have been selected to highlight features which distinguish these otherwise very similar birds. In many cases the physical differences between species are minute and virtually undetectable in the field: for this reason it has not been felt relevant to illustrate these species in flight. Warblers are most reliably distinguished by their songs or, in the hand, by wing formulae.

1: LANCEOLATED WARBLER *(Locustella lanceolata)* The grey-green upper parts (a) are heavily streaked. The tail is short and seen from underneath (b) has a dark tip. Distinctive dark streaks on breast and flanks.

2: PALLAS'S GRASSHOPPER WARBLER *(Locustella certhiola)* The upper parts (a) are streaked as in Lanceolated Warbler. Diagnostic features are rufous rump and pale tips to tail feathers (b).

3: GRASSHOPPER WARBLER *(Locustella naevia)* Upper parts (a) are less heavily streaked than in the two preceding species. Undertail coverts (b) are streaked and the tail feathers are dark.

4: SEDGE WARBLER *(Acrocephalus schoenobaenus)* Distinguishing features are the light eye-stripe, dark crown, uniform rufous rump and square tail.

5: AQUATIC WARBLER *(Acrocephalus paludicola)* Distinguishable by the pale streak on crown, yellowish coloration, streaked mantle and rump.

6: MOUSTACHED WARBLER *(Lusciniola melanopogon)* The white eye-stripe, very dark crown, dark rufous upper parts, dark, rounded tail enable this species to be identified.

7: GRAY'S GRASSHOPPER WARBLER *(Locustella fasciolata)* Strong bill, light eye-stripe, tail long, pointed and graduated. Adults differ from juveniles (a) in having the throat white. From below, undertail coverts (b) are yellow.

8: SAVI'S WARBLER *(Locustella luscinioides)* Primaries are fairly short (a). The tail is rounded and from below (b) the tail-feathers have a narrow black band. May also be distinguished by its white chin. In general is less skulking in behaviour than the similar Grasshopper Warbler.

9: RIVER WARBLER *(Locustella fluviatilis)* Upper parts are greenish-grey: has rounded tail and long primaries. In some individuals the breast is conspicuously streaked (a) while in others streaking is much lighter (b). The tail, seen from below (c), has pale tips to the coverts.

(Below) Sedge Warbler
Acrocephalus schoenobaenus

A. Fatras/Ardea

M.D. England/Ardea

D. Sudia/Photo Researchers

(Above) Fan-tailed Warbler
Cisticola juncidis. (Right)
Ruby-crowned Kinglet
Regulus calendula from North
America. (Below left)
Firecrest *R. ignicapillus* and
(right) Golden-crowned
Kinglet *R. satrapa,* another
North American kinglet

K. Maslowski/Photo Researchers

Bruce Coleman

Reed warblers

1: GREAT REED WARBLER (*Acrocephalus arundinaceus*) A large bird with a robust bill. The legs are dark and the primaries fairly long (a). The tail (b) is of medium length and rounded like that of many other reed warblers.

2: THICK-BILLED REED WARBLER (*Acrocephalus aëdon*) Very similar to the Great Reed Warbler, but may be distinguished by shorter primaries (a) and graduated tail (b).

3: CETTI'S WARBLER (*Cettia cetti*) Different in form from other warblers, being 'chubbier'. Also perches in a more upright position (a). Distinguishing features are the dark rufous-brown upper parts and tail. Seen from below (b) the dark tail feathers contrast with the pale undertail coverts.

4: REED WARBLER (*Acrocephalus scirpaceus*) Has a pale eystripe and fairly long primaries. Slight rufous tinge to the upper parts but best distinguished from Marsh and Blyth's Reed Warblers by its song. Only rarely breeds away from reed beds.

5: PADDYFIELD WARBLER (*Acrocephalus agricola*) Distinguished from Reed Warbler and Marsh Warbler by shorter primaries, more rufous coloration and pale eyestripe. However the Reed, Marsh and Blyth's Reed Warblers are all confusingly alike.

6: MARSH WARBLER (*Acrocephalus palustris*) Distinguished from Reed Warbler by more olive-brown colour of upper parts and by its lighter throat. However, it is very difficult to distinguish from Reed and Blyth's Reed Warblers in the field except by its song.

7: BLYTH'S REED WARBLER (*Acrocephalus dumetorum*) Very similar to Marsh and Reed Warblers but may be distinguished by longer tail and longer thin bill.

(Below) Great Reed Warbler *Acrocephalus arundinaceus* at the nest: it is the largest warbler present in Europe. (Preceding page) Dartford Warbler *Sylvia undata*

A. Fatras/Ardea

Hippolais warblers

1: **ICTERINE WARBLER** *(Hippolais icterina)* Has a heavy bill, pale eyestripe, greenish or greyish upper parts and yellow underparts. Yellowish bar on wings. Very difficult to distinguish from the Melodious Warbler although the Icterine has longer and more pointed wings: different songs also distinguish the two species.

2: **MELODIOUS WARBLER** *(Hippolais polyglotta)* Distinguished from Icterine Warbler mainly by song, but also by its shorter and more rounded wings, slightly duller coloration and less peaked crown.

3: **OLIVACEOUS WARBLER** *(Hippolais pallida)* Has pale eyestripe, long bill, greyish-brown upper parts, pale wing-bar and pale borders to the flight-feathers (a). The outer tail-feathers are edged white (b).

4: **BOOTED WARBLER** *(Hippolais caligata)* Smallest species of the genus *Hippolais* present in Europe. More slender than other members of the genus *Hippolais* and more like the Reed Warbler. Distinguished from Olivaceous Warbler by the smaller bill and whitish outer tail feathers.

5: **OLIVE-TREE WARBLER** *(Hippolais olivetorum)* Largest species of the genus *Hippolais* present in

Europe. Has very long wings and tail, heavy bill, pale eyestripe and wing bar, pale borders to flight feathers and wing coverts, greyish legs (a). Borders of outer tail-feathers are white (b). A skulking species which frequents areas with scattered trees.

6: **UPCHER'S WARBLER** *(Hippolais languida)* Distinguished by light eyestripe, light greyish upper parts: almost indistinguishable in the field from the Olivaceous Warbler except by its call. The primaries are long and the upper-tail coverts a rather warm colour (a). The tail feathers are bordered white like the Booted Warbler's (b).

7: **GRACEFUL WARBLER** *(Prinia gracilis)* A very small warbler. Back and flanks barred, very long, graduated tail (a). In flight (b) the long tail is characteristic. The tail is often held cocked up and fanned outwards.

8: **FAN-TAILED WARBLER** *(Cisticola juncidis)* Another very small warbler. Conspicuous streaking on upper parts; short wings and tail (a). The underside of all the tail-feathers (b) is bordered white. In flight (c) the wings are broad and the short, graduated tail spread in a fan-shape. This species is most easily detected in its jerky, high song flight.

(Below) Melodious Warbler
Hippolais polyglotta

A. Fatras/Ardea

Sylvia warblers

1: ORPHEAN WARBLER *(Sylvia hortensis)* While adults have well-defined characteristics such as the staring white eye, jet-black crown and cheeks, juveniles (illustrated here) may be confused with juvenile Barred Warblers. They may be distinguished, however, by their shorter tail which has no pale spots at the base.

2: BARRED WARBLER *(Sylvia nisoria)* Juveniles (a) are unbarred, have a heavy bill, dark eye, pale borders to wing coverts and flight feathers, long, square tail. Outer tail feathers are edged white (b).

3: GARDEN WARBLER *(Sylvia borin)* This species is best distinguished by its uniform plumage and lack of any conspicuous feature; it has no eyering and also, unlike most other warblers, does not have a white throat. Rounded head and short bill are also useful characteristics to note.

4: BLACKCAP *(Sylvia atricapilla)* The adult male is unmistakable by virtue of his black cap which does not extend onto the cheeks. The female (illustrated here) may be identified by its rufous crown.

(Below) Sardinian Warbler *Sylvia melanocephala*: the jet-black head and red eye are conspicuous features

5: SARDINIAN WARBLER *(Sylvia melanocephala)* Juveniles (a) are fairly similar to females, and have a greyish head, brown back and rump. The male resembles a male Blackcap except the whole head is jet black and the red eye is conspicuous. The wings are short and the tail graduated. The outer tail-feathers (b) are distinctively white in this species. In flight (c) the long, slender tail is characteristic.

6: WHITETHROAT *(Sylvia communis)* The female, illustrated here, is more uniform in coloration than the male, with rufous rump and borders to wing coverts and flight-feathers. The male has a grey head, white throat and rufous wings.

7: RÜPPELL'S WARBLER *(Sylvia rüppelli)* Juveniles (a) have grey head, red eye-ring, grey-brown back, grey rump, dark tail, pale borders to wing coverts and flight-feathers in spring plumage. The outer tail-feathers (b) have white patches. In flight (c) the silhouette is heavier than that of Sardinian Warbler.

The adult male is the only warbler of Europe with a black head and throat. White moustache and red eye are also distinguishing features.

8: LESSER WHITETHROAT *(Sylvia curruca)* Has greyish head, dark ear coverts, grey rump, outer tail-feathers bordered white (a). In flight (b) has broader, shorter wings than any of the preceding species: no rufous on wings.

A. Fatras/Ardea

9: HUME'S LESSER WHITETHROAT *(Sylvia althaea)* Features distinguishing this species from the Lesser Whitethroat are the more uniformly dark head and larger stouter bill.

10: DESERT WARBLER *(Sylvia nana)* Very small and pale warbler: sand-coloured plumage with centre of tail-feathers dark, outer tail-feathers bordered white.

11: DARTFORD WARBLER *(Sylvia undata)* Adults are readily recognised by dark greyish upper parts and purple-brown underparts: cocked-up tail also distinctive. However, juveniles (a) are easily confused with juvenile Marmora's Warbler but may be distinguished by buffish throat and breast. In flight (b) both species have an identical silhouette.

12: MARMORA'S WARBLER *(Sylvia sarda)* Grey underparts distinguish Marmora's Warbler from the Dartford Warbler. Juveniles (illustrated here) are distinguished by grey throat and breast.

13: MÉNÉTRIES'S WARBLER *(Sylvia mystacea)* Very similar to the Sardinian Warbler but the pinkish

underparts are distinctive. Female (a) has brown upper parts. Tail is dark and graduated, outer tail-feathers (b) white.

14: CYPRUS WARBLER *(Sylvia melanothorax)* Very similar to Sardinian Warbler but easily distinguished by the black markings on the throat and breast. Short wings, tail dark and graduated (a). Outer tail-feathers (b) white.

15: SPECTACLED WARBLER *(Sylvia conspicillata)* Female (a) has paler coloration than male and has a striking chestnut wing patch. Outer tail-feathers (b) are whitish. In general resembles a pale Subalpine Warbler or a dark Whitethroat.

16: SUBALPINE WARBLER *(Sylvia cantillans)* Resembles a small pale Dartford Warbler, but white moustachial stripe of the male is conspicuous. Female (a) is paler and more uniform in coloration than male. Upper parts greyish, the wings are rufous, underparts rufous, with white undertail coverts. In flight the tail appears square and the outer tail-feathers (b) have white patches.

(Right) Spectacled Warbler *Sylvia conspicillata.* (Overleaf, pages 70–71) Male Blackcap *Sylvia atricapilla* feeding its young

M. D. England/Ardea

Leaf warblers

1: ARCTIC WARBLER *(Phylloscopus borealis)* The long yellow supercilium is characteristic; back is grey-green, underparts whitish (a). Arctic and Greenish Warblers are very similar but may be distinguished from one another by the wing formulae: the Arctic Warbler (b) has a shorter first primary and longer second primary than Greenish Warbler.

2: GREENISH WARBLER *(Phylloscopus trochiloides)* Has small bill, very conspicuous supercilium which distinguishes it from the Willow Warbler, pale wing bar, dark legs (a). The wing is illustrated in figure (b).

3: WILLOW WARBLER *(Phylloscopus trochilus)* Adult (a) has pale eyestripe and white underparts washed yellow; no wing bar. Juveniles (b) have much more yellow on underparts. Specimens have been found in Scotland and Siberia which display a brown phase (c),

lacking any yellow coloration. This is the most common warbler in much of northern Europe.

4: BONELLI'S WARBLER *(Phylloscopus bonelli)* Pale head, greyish-green back, yellow rump. Underparts whitish; yellow bar on wing.

5: WOOD WARBLER *(Phylloscopus sibilatrix)* The largest leaf-warbler present in Europe. Has yellow supercilium, throat and upper parts, white belly. Flight-feathers dark with light borders; wings long.

6: CHIFFCHAFF *(Phylloscopus collybita)* The Siberian sub-species *P.c. tristis,* possibly accidental in Europe, has brownish upper parts and whitish underparts (a). The European form, in summer plumage, is shown in (b). Distinguished from Willow Warbler by darker legs, but most reliably distinguished by its song:

(Right) Willow Warbler *Phylloscopus trochilus*: it is the most common warbler in much of northern Europe. In the field it is very difficult to distinguish from the Chiffchaff, and the two species are most reliably identified by their songs

B. Bevan/Ardea

7: YELLOW-BROWED WARBLER *(Phylloscopus inornatus)* Adult (a) has pale supercilium, back and rump of the same colour, two light wing bars, whitish throat, breast and belly. Juveniles (b) have more buff on head and underparts.

8: PALLAS'S WARBLER *(Phylloscopus proregulus)* Smallest leaf-warbler present in Europe. Adult (a) and juvenile (b) have striped crown and two yellow wing bars. Seen from behind (c) the striped crown and yellow rump are particularly conspicuous.

9: GOLDCREST *(Regulus regulus)* Distinguishable from all other leaf warblers by its tiny bill and black-bordered crest. The female (illustrated here) has a yellow centre to crest, not orange as in male. The wings have a dark mark along the double wing bars.

10: FIRECREST *(Regulus ignicapillus)* Juvenile (illustrated here) and adults have black and white eyestripes which distinguish this species from the Goldcrest. Flight-feathers have no pale borders and underparts are whitish. Crest orange, but juveniles have no crest.

11: RADDE'S WARBLER *(Phylloscopus schwarzi)* Adult (a) has light supercilium, white throat and buffiish underparts. Juvenile (b) has distinctly yellow underparts. Bill thicker than that of Dusky Warbler, and tail quite long.

12: DUSKY WARBLER *(Phylloscopus fuscatus)* Juvenile (a) and adult (b) have pale supercilium and dark streak through eye. Underparts buff in juvenile, whitish in adult. Smaller and thinner-billed than Radde's Warbler.

(Below) Goldcrest *Regulus regulus*

F. V. Blackburn

H. Mickelsson

The family Muscicapidae or flycatchers is a group of about three hundred and thirty species which have well-defined characteristics. The fairly flat and broad bills are edged with fine hairs and the legs have short tarsi, slightly reminiscent of those of swallows of the family Hirundinidae. The dimensions of flycatchers vary, the smallest being the size of a Goldcrest and the largest as big as a large thrush. The plumage is frequently brightly coloured and sexual dimorphism is often present. Some species have squarish tails, others have graduated tails and paradise flycatchers of the genus *Terpsiphone* often have exceptionally long tails (especially the males), whose almost thread-like central feathers which may be twice as long as their bodies. Some species have vividly coloured wattles, particularly around the eyes. As their English name indicates, members of this family feed on flying insects: they make frequent sallies from their perch, catch an insect and then return to the perch. They are rarely seen on the ground.

About one hundred and forty species are allocated to the sub-family Muscicapinae or Old World flycatchers. They all bear some resemblance to the

(Left) African Paradise Flycatcher *Terpsiphone viridis*. (Below left) Collared Flycatcher *Ficedula albicollis* and (below) Pied Flycatcher *F. hypoleuca*. (Facing page) Spotted Flycatcher *Muscicapa striata*. The Collared, Pied and Spotted Flycatchers all breed in Europe. Like other flycatchers they have a broad, flattened bill for feeding on flying insects

European species such as those of the genera *Ficedula* and *Muscicapa*. However, the limits of this group are not clearly defined. For example, birds of the genus *Muscicapella* from tropical Asia have rather thin bills surrounded by rictal bristles. However, a characteristic that they have in common is the habit of catching insects in flight, swooping on their prey from branches or other perches, but the

B. J. Coates

(Above) Spot-wing Monarch Flycatcher *Monarcha guttula* from Australasia: it is one of the so-called monarch flycatchers. (Below) World distribution of the family Muscicapidae

larger species, such as those of the African genus *Bradornis*, take off from the ground in pursuit of insects in the manner of certain shrikes of the family Lanidae. Although they are basically solitary in their behaviour, some species, particularly those of the genus *Newtonia* from Madagascar such as the Common Newtonia *N. brunneicauda*, live in small groups deep in the foliage of trees. The other sub-families are the Rhipidurinae or fantail flycatchers and the Monarchinae or monarch flycatchers.

The carefully built nests of flycatchers are usually cup-shaped and are situated in bushes, on the ends of horizontal branches, in holes in trees, in cracks in rocks or in banks of earth and sand. Some species, like those of the Australian genus *Microeca* which includes the Australian Brown Flycatcher *M. leucophaea*, build nests which are only big enough to hold one egg. Other species, such as those of the genera *Dendrobiastes* and *Ochromela*, build almost spherical nests with side entrances between exposed tree roots or on the ground itself. Certain African species usually lay their eggs in the abandoned nests of weavers of the family Ploceidae. Another African species, Cassin's Grey Flycather *Alseonax cassini*, sometimes lays its eggs in swallows' nests.

Of the European species, the Pied Flycatcher *Ficedula hypoleuca* and the Collared Flycatcher *F. albicollis* also breed in nest-boxes. The males are polygamous and may defend several territories at the same time. The Spotted Flycatcher *Muscicapa striata*, which is distributed throughout Europe and most of Asia, does not appear to have territorial habits. As a rule, the Palearctic species have fairly large clutches (the Pied Flycatcher may lay as many as eleven eggs), while the tropical species produce very few young.

The family is distributed throughout almost the entire Old World (except for the northernmost regions of Asia) and extends to the Pacific to Hawaii and the Marquesas Islands. Species from northern and temperate zones are migrant: Palearctic species winter in the tropics.

Certain birds belonging to the typically American family Tyrannidae are often referred to as flycatchers, both because they have similar habits and because of evolutionary convergence which has made them resemble flycatchers of the Old World. However, they are quite distinct from the family Muscicapidae.

W. R. Taylor/Ardea

B. J. Coates/Ardea

Eric Hosking

(Top) Australian Brown Flycatcher *Microeca leucophaea*.
(Above) Black-and-Yellow Monarch Flycatcher
Monarcha chrysomela. (Right and overleaf, page 80)
Spotted Flycatcher *Muscicapa striata*: this grey-brown
species breeds throughout Europe and is a common bird
in parks and gardens

Eric Hosking

Pied Flycatcher
Ficedula hypoleuca

French : GOBEMOUCHE NOIR
Italian : BALIA NERA
Spanish : PAPAMOSCAS
CERROJILLO
German : TRAUERSCHNAPPER

HABITAT Forests, wooded areas, parks and gardens.

IDENTIFICATION Length: 13 cm. Males in summer plumage strikingly black and white. Black upper parts with a white marking on the forehead. Conspicuous white wing-bar. Black tail feathers, some edged with white. Black legs and bill. In winter plumage the male is like the female except for a white mark on the forehead and the flight feathers and tail feathers are darker. Female: grey-brown upper parts (no patch on the forehead); greyish-white underparts; extensive white on the wings. Juveniles: deep brown upper parts with reddish patches; yellowish underparts with brown patches on the throat and breast. On occasions it is polygamous and consequently the male takes less interest in its offspring, leaving this duty to the female. See also page 86.

CALL A Swallow-like 'whit'. Song consists of variations and repetitions of the note 'tree'.

REPRODUCTION From early May. It nests in holes in trees or walls or in nest boxes. The female builds a large, loose cup of leaves, grass, roots and moss which is lined with hair, feathers and plant material. Usually four to seven (rarely one to eleven) eggs of a uniform, pale blue colour are laid. Occasionally the eggs are marked with a few dark reddish-brown speckles. Incubation takes twelve or thirteen days and is carried out by the female alone. The young are tended by both parents and leave the nest after thirteen to sixteen days. Normally one clutch.

FOOD Mainly insects: also molluscs and berries.

DISTRIBUTION AND MOVEMENTS Breeds in northern Eurasia from Scandinavia, Britain and Germany east to Siberia. Also breeds locally in France, Iberia, Italy, the Balkans and Crimea: also northwest Africa. Winters in tropical Africa. In Britain it is confined as a breeding bird to the hilly, wooded districts of the north and west, although it is only sparsely distributed in Scotland. It has only bred occasionally in other areas. Absent from Ireland. It is a common passage visitor to coastal areas of Britain and Ireland.

SUB-SPECIES Sub-species are present in Asia and Africa.

(Above) Female Pied Flycatcher (bottom) and male. (Below) Breeding areas (yellow) and areas where the Pied Flycatcher may be seen on passage (pink)

French: GOBEMOUCHE A COLLIER
Italian: BALIA DAL COLLARE
Spanish: PAPAMOSCAS COLLARINO
German: HALSBANDSCHNAPPER

Collared Flycatcher
Ficedula albicollis

(Above) Female Collared Flycatcher (left) and male. (Right) Breeding areas (yellow) and areas where the Collared Flycatcher may be seen on passage (pink)

HABITAT Like that of the Pied Flycatcher.

IDENTIFICATION Length: 13 cm. White marking on forehead; black crown and sides of the head. Conspicuous broad white collar distinguishes it from the Pied Flycatcher, and white on the forehead and wings is more extensive. Black upper parts, apart from its whitish rump; white underparts; black tail feathers. Black bill and legs. Female: like the female Pied Flycatcher but with greyer upper parts, more extensive white on the wing and a very pale, inconspicuous semi-collar. Juveniles: like young Pied Flycatchers, with indistinct collars. See also page 86.

CALL Call is like that of the Pied Flycatcher: a 'whit'. Song softer and more uniform than the Pied Flycatcher's.

REPRODUCTION From early May. The nest is a small cup made mostly of moss and plant fibres. It is built mainly by the female and situated in a tree hole, a hole in a building or wall or in a nest box. Usually lays six or seven smooth, pale blue eggs. The female alone incubates although both male and female tend the young.

FOOD Mainly insects.

DISTRIBUTION AND MOVEMENTS Breeds mainly in central and southeast Europe from the Baltic region east to the USSR. Also breeds locally in eastern France, northern Italy, Greece and Asia Minor east to Iran. Winters in tropical Africa. Is a very rare vagrant to Britain: all except one have occured in the spring.

SUB-SPECIES Sub-species of the Collared Flycatcher are present in Asia.

Red-breasted Flycatcher
Ficedula parva

French: GOBEMOUCHE NAIN
Italian: PIGLIAMOSCHE
PETTIROSSO
Spanish: PAPAMOSCAS PAPIRROJO
German: ZWERGSCHNAPPER

HABITAT Breeds in forests, particularly those with large deciduous trees.

IDENTIFICATION Length: 11 cm. Smallest flycatcher present in Europe. Grey-brown upper parts; brownish upper-tail coverts; white eye-ring; grey sides of the head and neck. Throat and breast of male red—a feature which makes him easily identifiable. Underparts variable in colour from grey-white to pure white with yellowish tinges on the flanks. Tail is frequently flicked up showing bold white marks at base of tail of both male and female. Lacks white wing-bar. Female: upper parts like the male's but no red on throat and breast; white underparts with yellowish tinge on throat and flanks. Juveniles: brown and reddish markings on the upper parts; reddish throat and breast with brown borders; the remaining underparts white. See also page 86.

CALL Emits a short sharp 'chiik': also chattering notes. Song is variable, sometimes reminiscent of the Wood Warbler, and also emits bell-like notes.

REPRODUCTION From early May. The nest is built mainly by the female and is a small cup of moss and plant fibres. It is situated in a tree hole, on twigs or in a hole in a wall. Five or six whitish eggs are laid which are finely covered with reddish markings. On rare occasions there may be four or seven eggs. Incubation is carried out by the female alone but the incubation period is not known. The young are tended by both parents.

FOOD Insects and larvae: also fruit and berries.

DISTRIBUTION AND MOVEMENTS Breeds in Eurasia from Finland and Germany east to Siberia and south to Austria, the Balkans, Caucasus and Iran. Winters in southeast Asia. In Britain and Ireland it is a scarce passage visitor mainly in autumn. It has been identified with increasing regularity in recent years.

SUB-SPECIES Sub-species are present in Asia.

(Above) Female Red-breasted Flycatcher (bottom) and male. (Left) Breeding areas of the Red-breasted Flycatcher (yellow)

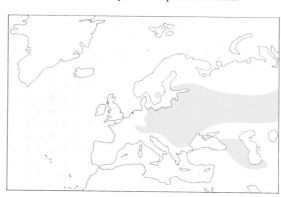

Brown Flycatcher
Muscicapa latirostris

HABITAT Prefers deciduous woods and thickets.

IDENTIFICATION Length: 12 cm. Male and female alike; uniform brown or grey-brown upper parts; narrow, dirty white eye-ring. White throat. Dark brown tail feathers and flight feathers. Resembles the Spotted Flycatcher but is smaller and has no streaks on the head and breast. Its brownish coloration makes it similar to female flycatchers of the European species, but unlike the female Red-breasted it has no white at the base of the tail and unlike the female Pied or Collared it lacks a white mark on the wing. Juveniles: like adults, but most of the feathers on the upper parts have pale, tan-coloured speckles on the tips. See also page 86.

CALL Voice is similar to the Spotted Flycatcher's.

REPRODUCTION From May onwards. Nests on branches close to the trunk of a tree. The carefully constructed, cup-shaped nest is lined with lichens. Four or five pale grey-green eggs, sometimes marked with reddish streaks, are laid.

FOOD Insects.

DISTRIBUTION AND MOVEMENTS Eastern Asia. Migrant and winters in southeast Asia. Accidental in Europe in Norway and the Faeroes.

French: GOBEMOUCHE BRUN
Italian: PIGLIAMOSCHE BECCOLARGO
Spanish: PAPAMOSCAS PARDO
German: BRAUNNSCHNAPPER

Spotted Flycatcher
Muscicapa striata

HABITAT Forest edges, orchards, parks and gardens. Common in suburban areas.

IDENTIFICATION Length: 14 cm. Grey-brown upper parts with dark brown stripes on the sides of the throat, breast and flanks. Brownish coloration under the wings; brown flight feathers with pale borders visible on the secondaries; dark brown wing coverts with reddish margins; brown tail feathers. Blackish bill and black legs. The sexes are alike. Juveniles: spotted brown-grey plumage: white belly. See also page 86.

CALL A shrill 'tzee'. Song consists of sharp, grating notes.

REPRODUCTION From May. It nests about two to four metres off the ground (although sometimes less than a metre to nine metres off the ground) on twigs against tree trunks, in crevices or holes in trees, on ledges or in creepers. Mainly the female builds the cup-shaped nest of grass, roots, lichen and other plant material. It is lined with feathers, hair and plant fibres. Four or five eggs are laid—rarely two to seven—which are greenish-white or bluish and often heavily blotched with purple-grey and reddish-brown. Usually the female alone incubates the eggs for eleven to fifteen days. The female feeds the young with insects brought by the male, although later both bring food.

FOOD Insects, earthworms and berries.

DISTRIBUTION AND MOVEMENTS Breeds in Eurasia from Scandinavia, Britain, Ireland and Iberia east to Siberia and Mongolia and southwards to the Mediterranean region, northwest Africa, Persian Gulf and the Himalayas. Winters in tropical and southern Africa, Arabia and northern India. In Britain and Ireland it is a widespread and numerous breeding bird in all counties except Shetland. The Spotted Flycatcher is also an abundant passage visitor.

SUB-SPECIES *M. s. inexpectata*: the Crimea. *M. s. balearica*: Balearic Islands. *M. s. tyrrhenica*: Corsica and Sardinia. There are other sub-species in Asia.

French: GOBEMOUCHE GRIS
Italian: PIGLIAMOSCHE
Spanish: PAPAMOSCAS GRIS
German: GRAUSCHNAPPER

(Far left) Brown Flycatcher (left) Spotted Flycatcher. (Below) Breeding areas (yellow), wintering areas (magenta) and areas where the Spotted Flycatcher may be seen on passage (pink). (Right) Spotted Flycatcher *M. striata* at the nest

Identification of flycatchers

1: PIED FLYCATCHER *(Ficedula hypoleuca)* The female (a) has brownish upper parts, while the male (b) is black and white. Unlike the Collared Flycatcher, both sexes have white outer-tail feathers. In flight the female and juvenile (c) appear brown with short white wing-bars; the male (d) also has similar wing-bars, but plumage is black.

2: COLLARED FLYCATCHER *(Ficedula albicollis)* The female (a) has brownish upper parts with a faint collar; rump is whitish and has much more white on its wings than the Pied Flycatcher. In flight (b) the long wing-bars are fairly conspicuous. The male (c) has a well-defined collar, a greyish-white rump and black and white wings. In flight (d), its white collar, long wing-bars and pale rump are prominent. Like other flycatchers is rarely seen on the ground.

3: RED-BREASTED FLYCATCHER *(Ficedula parva)* The female and juveniles seen from below (a) have dirty white throats, breasts and bellies, while the male (b) has a red throat and upper breast and grey cheeks and crown. Both sexes have partly white outer-tail feathers. In flight (c) it is the only flycatcher with a white tail with a dark T-shaped pattern.

4: SPOTTED FLYCATCHER *(Muscicapa striata)* The head (a) is streaked. The juvenile (b) is also fairly heavily streaked on the underparts while the adult (c) has fewer streaks. In flight (d) it is a uniform brownish colour.

5: BROWN FLYCATCHER *(Muscicapa latirostris)* It has a white eye-ring (a) and differs from the Spotted Flycatcher in having off-white underparts without any streaks (b) and a shorter tail.

(Right) Female Pied Flycatcher
F hypoleuca

F. V. Blackburn

M. Wilkes/Aquila

The tits of the family Paridae are small and active insectivorous birds which are often seen in flocks. The typical coloration of the majority of species is a combination of brown, olive-green and greenish-grey on the upper parts, and white, pale yellow or buff on the underparts. Some species have sharply contrasting black and white coloration, particularly on the head, and some also have crests.

Tits generally range in size from ten or eleven centimetres to about twenty centimetres in length in species with long tails. Despite their fairly uniform characteristics, both structurally and in terms of behaviour, it is not certain if tits are monophyletic in origin, that is, derived from a single parent form. The close resemblance of the species may be due to evolutionary convergence.

Other characteristics of the family Paridae are the pointed, elongated wings, rather short tarsi (although those of the family Muscicapidae are still shorter) the fairly long toes with very sharp, curved, laterally compressed claws. Tits are nimble climbers, and it is quite frequent to observe them hanging upside down from the ends of small, thin branches.

The diet of these species consists mainly of small insects and larvae but in many temperate regions it is supplemented by seeds (including quite hard ones), especially during the winter. Other substances they feed upon include the resin of trees.

Most tits are resident, although some species undertake irregular journeys to lower altitudes when bad weather prevents them from finding food. Only a few species are truly migrant. Tits are common in areas with scattered trees, including deciduous and coniferous woodland, gardens, orchards, parks and hedgerows. They are well-known birds in the towns and cities of Europe, especially in Britain where they break the tinfoil on the top of milk bottles to obtain cream.

The nest is situated in a variety of habitats, but usually in association with trees. However, nest sites not only include holes in trees and on branches, but also in a wall or bank or among rocks. The nest is carefully built out of materials such as grass, moss, spiders' webs, roots and lichens. Tits are among the species which adapt most readily to nestboxes, and they also regularly visit bird tables. The female usually builds the nest in which she lays her white eggs. Broods are often large, and both adults feed the young with insects brought in the bill.

The family may be divided into three sub-families: these are the true tits of the sub-family Parinae, the long-tailed tits of the sub-family Aegithalinae and the penduline tits of the sub-family Remizinae.

(Right) The Coal Tit *P. ater* is the smallest tit which breeds in Britain. (Facing page) Willow Tit *P. montanus*

P. Hinchliffe/Bruce Coleman

There are about forty-five species of true or typical tits of the sub-family Parinae. Their distribution is very wide, and they inhabit areas with scattered trees. Some species are migratory while others are resident and remain through the winter in cold regions where they manage to survive by virtue of stockpiled food (such as nuts) which they collect in the summer and store in cracks of trees and in rock crevices.

The majority of species belong to the genus *Parus*. The Great Tit *P. major*, the Blue Tit *P. caeruleus*, the Coal Tit *P. ater*, the Marsh Tit *P. palustris*, the Willow Tit *P. montanus*, and the Crested Tit *P. cristatus* are among the well-known European species of this genus. The sexes are similar, and summer and winter plumage is generally alike.

There are seven species of long-tailed tit of the sub-family Aegithaline if the Common Bushtit *P. minimus* of the American genus *Psaltriparus* is included instead of being classified as a separate family. Five species belong to the genus *Aegithalos*: this includes the Long-tailed Tit *A. caudatus*. It is a widespread and typical member of the genus and is distributed throughout Eurasia. The other four species are less well known and are more localised, inhabiting southeast Asia. The Pygmy Titmouse *Psaltria exilis* is found exclusively in Java and is closer to the Common Bushtit, than the Eurasian Long-tailed Tit.

The typical representative of the sub-family

(Above) Marsh Tit *P. palustris.*
(Below left) World distribution of
the family Paridae and (below)
Long-tailed Tit *A. caudatus*:
more than half its length is
constituted by the tail

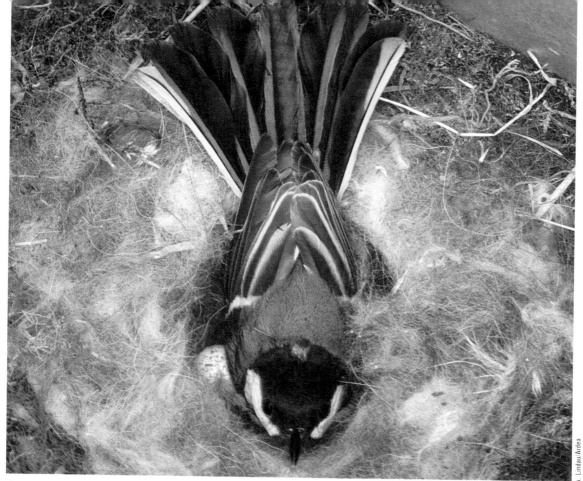

A. Lindau/Ardea

(Left) Great Tit *P. major*: the black and white head of this species is unmistakeable. (Below) Penduline Tit *R. pendulinus* at the nest: the nest is often suspended from thin twigs at the end of a branch, and the side entrance tube is distinctive

A. Blomgren

Remizinae, which consists of nine species, is the Penduline Tit *Remiz pendulinus*. It is well known for its unusual flask-shaped nest with a side entrance tube, and is suspended from thin twigs at the tip of a branch. This elaborate nest takes the male and female about two weeks to construct. The Penduline Tit is among the most brightly coloured members of the family, and may also be distinguished by its preference for living near water in marshes, fens and by freshwater margins.

The main difference between penduline tits and other tits is the shape of the bill which is narrower and more pointed. Many of the species of the sub-family Remizinae are found in Africa although the Verdin *Auriparus flaviceps* is North American. The Fire-capped Tit *Cephalopyrus flammiceps* of Asia belongs to the monotypic genus *Cephalopyrus* while the remaining seven species belong to the genus *Remiz*. This genus includes the already mentioned Penduline Tit *R. pendulinus*, the African Penduline Tit *R. caroli* and the Cappoc Tit *R. punctifrons*.

B. Bevan/Ardea

(Above) Blue Tit *P. caeruleus* and (below) Siberian Tit *P. cinctus*: this species is distinguished from the Marsh and Willow Tits by its browner crown and nape

E. Nilsson

Marsh Tit
Parus palustris

French: MESANGE NONNETTE
Italian: CINCIA BIGIA
Spanish: CARBONERO PALUSTRE
German: SUMPFMEISE

HABITAT Frequents deciduous woodland and scrub.

IDENTIFICATION Length: 11 cm. Adult (male and female alike): shiny, jet black forehead, crown, nape and chin. Brown mantle, scapulars, back, rump and upper-tail coverts. Cheeks and ear-coverts white; whitish-brown sides of the neck. Underparts: dirty white tinged with rufous-brown on the flanks; bill black; grey-blue legs. Very similar to Willow Tit and best distinguished from it by voice. However, Marsh Tit has no pale patch on the wing, although this is not easy to observe in the field. Juvenile: resembles adult but is tinged greyish and the underparts are white.

CALL Call is a 'pitchu', also a 'tchaay' which is less grating than the Willow Tit's. Song is a monotonous and rattling 'schep-schep'.

REPRODUCTION From mid-April. Nest is a cup of moss lined with hair and feathers to form a felted layer. It is built by the female alone, and is situated in a natural hole in a stump or tree or sometimes in a wall: she may occasionally excavate a hole. Eggs: usually six to nine white eggs with reddish-brown speckles, though some clutches may contain five to eleven eggs. Usually single brooded in the north of the range, often double brooded in the south. Incubation is carried out by the female alone for thirteen to seventeen days. Both parents tend the young who remain in the nest for sixteen to twenty-one days.

FOOD Mainly insects and larvae: also consumes seeds and berries.

DISTRIBUTION AND MOVEMENTS Breeds discontinuously in Eurasia from Scandinavia, Britain and northern Spain east to the Urals and southwards to southern Italy, Asia Minor and southeast Asia. Sedentary. Is a widespread, but not numerous, resident breeder in England and Wales. In Scotland is restricted to the southeast; absent altogether from Ireland.

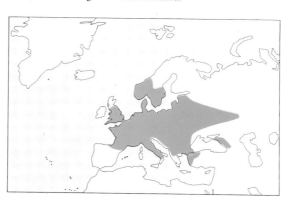

(Left) Areas where the Marsh Tit may be seen all year round (orange)

Willow Tit
Parus montanus

HABITAT Deciduous and coniferous woodland and scrub: also marshy areas with shrub vegetation.

IDENTIFICATION Length: 11 cm. Can be distinguished from the Marsh Tit by its duller and spotted black rather than glossy jet black crown, and the pale area on the wing formed by the light coloured margins of its secondaries. Its flanks are a deeper rufous colour than the Marsh Tit's and its black bib is larger. However the most reliable way to distinguish between the Willow Tit and the Marsh Tit is by voice.

CALL Typical call note is a grating and harsh 'tsshey' or 'aeg'. Has two distinct songs: a 'piu-piu' which resembles the Wood Warbler's and an intermittent liquid song like the Garden Warbler.

REPRODUCTION From mid-April. Nests in a dead tree or stump where the wood is soft enough to allow the bird to excavate its own cavity. However, it also occasionally nests in a natural cavity or woodpecker hole. The female digs the cavity and lines it with hair and a few feathers. Six to nine (rarely five to thirteen) eggs are laid. They are smooth and glossy white in colour with variable amounts of reddish markings which may be concentrated at the larger end. The female alone incubates the eggs for thirteen to fifteen days. Both parents tend the young.

FOOD Insects, larvae and seeds.

DISTRIBUTION AND MOVEMENTS Breeds from Scandinavia, Britain, France and the Balkans east across Eurasia to Japan. Essentially sedentary. In Britain it is a widespread although sparse resident breeder in England, Wales and southern Scotland. Does not occur in Ireland even as a vagrant. The sub-species *P. m. borealis* from northern Europe has occurred in Britain as a rare vagrant.

SUB-SPECIES *P. m. borealis:* Scandinavia east to Siberia. *P. m. kleinschmidti:* Britain.

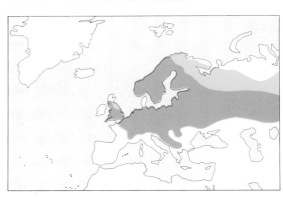

(Below) Willow Tit. (Right) Breeding areas (yellow) and areas where the Willow Tit may be seen all year round (orange)

French: MESANGE BOREALE
Italian: CINCIA BIGIA ALPESTRE
Spanish: CARBONERO SIBILINO
German: WEIDENMEISE

French: MESANGE LUGUBRE
Italian: CINCIA DALMATINA
Spanish: CARBONERO LUGUBRE
German: TRAUERMEISE

Siberian Tit
Parus cinctus

HABITAT Mainly coniferous forests.

IDENTIFICATION Length: 13 cm. Resembles the Marsh Tit, but its crown is chocolate-brown and it has a larger, dark marking on its chin and throat. White cheeks, white underparts with buff flanks. Grey-brown upper parts tinged with red-brown. In general may be distinguished by reddish-brown coloration of upper parts.

CALL Very similar to the Willow Tit's but its call is a longer and more drawn out 'eeez-eeez'.

REPRODUCTION From late May. Nests in a hole in a tree: nest is often situated less than a metre to four metres off the ground. The female excavates the hole (although a natural cavity or woodpecker hole may be used) and makes a cup-shaped nest of moss which is lined with hair. Six to ten smooth and glossy white eggs are laid which are lightly speckled with reddish-brown. The female alone incubates for about fifteen days but both parents tend the young.

FOOD Insects and seeds.

(Below right) Siberian Tit.
(Above right) Wintering areas (magenta) and areas where the Siberian Tit may be seen all year round (orange)

DISTRIBUTION AND MOVEMENTS Breeds in northern Europe from Scandinavia east across northern Eurasia to Siberia. Also breeds in northwest North America.

SUB-SPECIES *P. c. lapponicus:* eastern part of the range as far as the Pacific coast of Siberia. Also present in Alaska and northwest Canada.

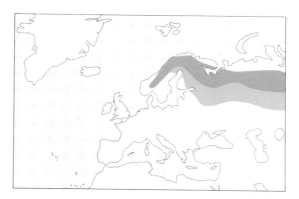

French: MESANGE LAPONE
Italian: CINCIA SIBERIANA
Spanish: CARBONERO LAPON
German: LAPPLANDSMEISE

Sombre Tit
Parus lugubris

HABITAT Woods and rocky country: also parks, gardens and scrub.

IDENTIFICATION Length: 14 cm. Resembles a large Willow or Marsh Tit, but with browner nape and a larger black throat patch. Grey-brown upper parts, off-white face and sides of the neck. Cheeks whiter than those of the Willow or Marsh Tit.

CALL Call and song like that of the Great Tit but also emits a 'churr'.

REPRODUCTION From March onwards. The nest is situated in a tree hole and consists of a cup of plant material lined with feathers. Five to seven, occasionally as many as ten eggs are laid which are white speckled with reddish-brown. Information on incubation is lacking.

FOOD Chiefly insects.

DISTRIBUTION AND MOVEMENTS Breeds in the Balkan peninsula including Yugoslavia and Greece east through Asia Minor to Iran.

SUB-SPECIES *P. l. lugens:* Greece. *P. l. anatoliae:* Asia Minor. There are other sub-species in Asia.

(Facing page, near left)
Sombre Tit. (Left)
Areas where the Sombre Tit may be seen all year round (orange)

95

French: MESANGE NOIRE
Italian: CINCIA MORA
Spanish: CARBONERO GARRAPINOS
German: · TANNENMEISE

Coal Tit
Parus ater

HABITAT Coniferous and deciduous woodlands; also town parks and gardens.

IDENTIFICATION Length: 11 cm. Together with the Blue Tit is one of the smallest tits of Europe. It is the only black-crowned tit with a large white patch on the nape. Silky white cheeks and black bib and upper breast; olive-grey upper parts with a narrow white double wingbar. Off-white underparts with buff flanks. Black bill. Blue-grey legs. Juveniles: nape, cheeks and the underparts are yellowish.

CALL Similar to the Great Tit's although the Coal Tit's wide range of calls are higher-pitched. Song resembles the so-called saw-sharpening song of the Great Tit: also emits a Goldcrest-like 'tsee'.

REPRODUCTION From late April. Nests in a hole in a tree, wall or bank: occasionally on the ground. Nest is a cup of moss lined with feathers and hair. Eggs: seven to nine smooth white and finely speckled reddish-brown. The female alone incubates for fourteen to eighteen days: both parents tend the young.

FOOD Insects, larvae and seeds.

DISTRIBUTION AND MOVEMENTS Breeds from Scandinavia, Britain, Ireland and Iberia east across Eurasia to Kamchatka. Also breeds south to northwest Africa, Greece, Iran and southern China. Northern populations are partially migratory, wintering just south of the breeding range and beyond. In Britain and Ireland it is a widely distributed resident breeder although absent from Shetland and Orkney. Also occurs as a winter and passage visitor.

SUB-SPECIES *P. a. hibernicus:* Ireland except for the northeast. *P. a. britannicus:* Britain and northeast Ireland. *P. a. sardus:* Corsica and Sardinia. *P. a. moltchanovi:* the southern Crimea. *P. a. michalowskii:* the Caucasus. *P. a. vieirae:* Iberian Peninsula. *P. a. cypriotes:* Cyprus. There are numerous other sub-species present in Asia and Africa.

(Right) Breeding areas (yellow), wintering areas (magenta) and areas where the Coal Tit may be seen all year round (orange)

Crested Tit

Parus cristatus

French: MESANGE HUPPEE
Italian: CINCIA DAL CIUFFO
Spanish: HERRERILLO CAPUCHINO
German: HAUBENMEISE

HABITAT Mainly coniferous woods, but also frequents mixed woods.

IDENTIFICATION Length: 12 cm. Easily identified by its prominent black and white crest: it is the only tit and only really small bird of Europe with a crest. Off-white face has a curved black marking running from the eye into the white cheek. Narrow collar and bib are black. Warm, grey-brown upper parts; off-white underparts with buff flanks. Bill black: bluish legs. Lacks a wing-bar. The female's crest is shorter and its collar is narrower. Juveniles: very short crest, darker back, indistinct collar and dirty white coloration. During the nesting season there are frequent battles over the possession of a female and on these occasions the male's crest is erected. Sometimes hunts for food on tree trunks like a treecreeper.

CALL More restricted than that of other tits. Emits soft trilling notes and a 'sii-sii-sii'.

REPRODUCTION From late April. It nests in holes in rotting trees or stumps. The hole is excavated and the nest built by the female. The nest is a cup of moss and lichen lined with hair or wool. It usually lays four to eight eggs which are white with dense, reddish-brown speckles which are often concentrated at the larger end where they form a cap. Incubation lasts about thirteen to eighteen days and is carried out by the female alone. Both parents care for the young.

FOOD Mainly insects: also larvae and seeds.

DISTRIBUTION AND MOVEMENTS Breeds from Scotland and Scandinavia east across the USSR and south across most of continental Europe to Iberia, northern Italy and Greece. Mainly sedentary. In Britain it is scarce resident breeder confined to the Scottish Highlands. Rare vagrant elsewhere.

SUB-SPECIES *P. c. cristatus:* Scandinavia, USSR, eastern Balkans. *P. c. scoticus:* Scotland. *P. c. mitratus:* continental Europe except for Brittany and parts of Iberia. *P. c. abadiei:* Brittany. *P. c. weigoldi:* Iberia. Other sub-species are present throughout Asia.

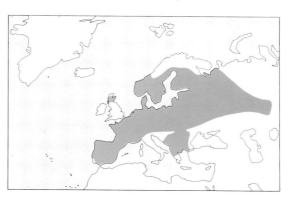

(Left) Areas where the Crested Tit may be seen all year round (orange)

French: MESANGE BLEUE
Italian: CINCIARELLA
Spanish: HERRERILLO COMUN
German: BLAUMEISE

Blue Tit
Parus caeruleus

(Right) Breeding areas (yellow) and areas where the Blue Tit may be seen all year round (orange)

HABITAT Areas with scattered trees including town parks and gardens. Also common in hedgerows.

IDENTIFICATION Length: 12 cm. Easily identified as it is the only tit with blue wings, tail and crown: the bright blue on the crown is especially noticeable. Yellow underparts. White cheeks; black line runs through the eye, round the nape and cheeks. White border to the blue crown; greenish back with yellowish coloration on the rump. Black bill with brownish tip. Deep, slate blue legs. Female: slightly less vivid coloration. Juveniles: greenish-brown upper parts and yellowish cheeks.

CALL Most typical of the many calls is a scolding 'tsee-tsee-tseet'. Song is a cheery 'tsu-tsuhu-hu'.

REPRODUCTION From mid-April. Nests in a hole or cavity usually in a tree or wall, but also in banks and nest boxes. Nest is a cup of moss, leaves, hair and grass which is lined with down, feathers and hair. It is built by the female. Eggs: seven to twelve (sometimes five to sixteen) which are smooth and glossy white with a variable amount of purple-red or reddish-brown speckles. The female alone incubates for twelve to sixteen days. Both tend the young who remain in the nest for fifteen to twenty-three days.

FOOD Mainly insects and larvae: also fruits.

DISTRIBUTION AND MOVEMENTS Breeds from Britain, Ireland and Scandinavia east across virtually all of Europe and southwards to northwest Africa, the Canaries, Asia Minor and Iran. Northern populations are partially migratory, moving south within the breeding range. In Britain and Ireland it is an abundant and widespread resident breeder in all counties except Orkney and Shetland, and only in Stornoway in the Outer Hebrides. The British and Irish populations are essentially sedentary but movements over one hundred kilometres have been recorded. Also occurs as a winter visitor from the continent in highly variable numbers.

SUB-SPECIES *P. c. balearicus:* the Balearic Islands. *P. c. ogliastrae:* Portugal, Spain, Corsica, Sardinia, Greece and Crete. *P. c. satunini:* the Crimea. *P. c. obscurus:* Britain, Ireland and the Channel Islands. There are numerous other sub-species in Asia and Africa.

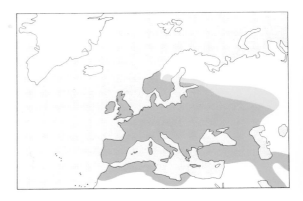

David Sewell

H. Kinloch/Aquila

(Above and left) The Blue Tit *P. caeruleus* is commonly seen in suburban gardens where it frequently pecks tinfoil on milk bottles to obtain the cream underneath, and happily consumes food, such as nuts, which is put out for it

French: MESANGE AZUREE
Italian: CINCIARELLA AZZURRA
Spanish: HERRERILLO CIANEO
German: LASURMEISE

Azure Tit
Parus cyanus

(Right) Areas where the Azure Tit may be seen all year round (orange)

HABITAT Scrub and birch woods, especially by freshwater margins.

IDENTIFICATION Length: 13 cm. The Asiatic counterpart of the Blue Tit (may hybridise with it) with the same overall pattern but larger, whiter with much less blue and with a conspicuously long tail. Its head is white with a narrow dark blue stripe running across its eye to its collar. Blue-grey upper parts and white underparts with a bluish-grey marking in the centre of the throat and upper breast. Its blue wings have a distinctive wide, white U-shaped marking.

CALL Its call note is similar to the Long-tailed Tit's: a 'tsirup'.

REPRODUCTION From mid-May. Usually nests in a cavity in a tree from a metre and a half up to five metres off the ground. The nest is a cup of dry grasses and hair. Eggs: usually nine to eleven smooth white with purple-red spots. The female alone incubates for thirteen or fourteen days. Both male and female tend the young.

FOOD Chiefly insects.

DISTRIBUTION AND MOVEMENTS Breeds from the western USSR east to Siberia. Basically sedentary. Accidental in the Netherlands and France.

SUB-SPECIES Sub-species are present in Asia.

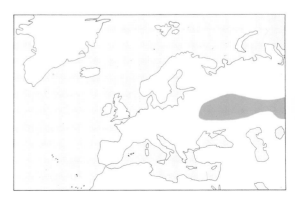

Great Tit
Parus major

French: MESANGE CHARBONNIERE
Italian: CINCIALLEGRA
Spanish: CARBONERO COMUN
German: KOHLMEISE

HABITAT Woodland, orchards, gardens and parks and other areas with scattered trees.

IDENTIFICATION Length: 14 cm. Black head and throat with bluish highlights; white cheeks. Yellow underparts with a broad black bib down the middle. Back: yellowish, olive-green on the nape and grey on the rump. Black flight feathers. Black bill and greyish-blue legs. The sexes are alike, as is summer and winter plumage. Juveniles have black parts of adult brownish and white parts are yellowish.

CALL Has a very extensive vocabulary. Calls include a 'piink' like the Chaffinch's and calls like those of other tits except louder. Song includes a 'tcheet' and also a rasping song which has been likened to a saw being sharpened.

REPRODUCTION From late March. The female builds a cup-shaped nest of roots, moss and grasses lined with hair, plant down and sometimes feathers. Nests in a hole in a tree, rocks or walls: will also use nest boxes. Eggs: eight to thirteen, white with purplish-red speckles and blotches. The female alone incubates for about thirteen days. Both tend the young. Usually double brooded, although not in Britain.

FOOD Insects, larvae, molluscs and earthworms: also berries and seeds.

DISTRIBUTION AND MOVEMENTS Breeds through much of Eurasia from Scandinavia, Britain and Ireland east to Japan. Also breeds south to northwest Africa, the Middle East, Iran and Indonesia. Partially migratory: northern populations move to southern parts of the breeding range. In Britain and Ireland the Great Tit is a numerous and abundant resident breeder except in Orkney and Shetland. British and Irish populations are sedentary although some individuals may move distances over a hundred kilometres in autumn and winter. Also occurs irregularly as a winter visitor from the continent.

SUB-SPECIES *P.m. newtoni*: Britain and Ireland. The nominate sub-species *P.m. major* is present in southeast England. *P.m. aphrodite*: Balearic Islands, Greece and Crete. There are other sub-species present in Africa and Asia.

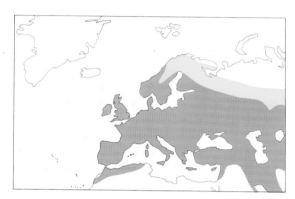

(Left) Breeding areas (yellow) and areas where the Great Tit may be seen all year round (orange)

French: MESANGE A LONGUE
QUEUE
Italian: CODIBUGNOLO O CINCIA
CODONA
Spanish: MITO
German: SCHWANZMEISE

Long-tailed Tit
Aegithalos caudatus

HABITAT Coniferous and deciduous woods and scrub. Less often seen in parks and gardens than other tits.

IDENTIFICATION Length: 14 cm. Extremely long tail comprises over half the length of this species, and is a distinguishing feature. White head, neck and underparts. Northern and eastern forms have pure white head while the western race has a black eyestripe and the southern race a greyish eyestripe. Pinkish rump. The back is usually black but may sometimes be grey; white underparts and pinkish flanks (which vary in intensity of coloration). Blackish-brown flight feathers, the inner ones edged with white. Juveniles: chocolate-brown sides of the head and nape, brown back and remaining plumage like that of adults.

Flight is slow, weak and undulating. In winter it forms flocks that fly in lines from one tree to the next.

CALL Emits a soft 'tupp' and a 'tsirup'. Song is a combination of the call notes but is rarely heard.

REPRODUCTION From March onwards. Nest is a large domed structure with a side entrance. It is built by both male and female of moss bound with spiders' webs and hair, and is coated on the outside with lichen: the nest takes up to three weeks to build. It is usually situated in brambles or thick bushes from a metre to five metres off the ground, but may also be built in a tree up to twenty metres off the ground. Eggs: usually eight to twelve (sometimes five to sixteen), white and finely speckled with purplish-red or unmarked. Mainly the female incu-

bates for twelve to fourteen days. Both tend the young who remain in the nest for fourteen days.

FOOD Mainly insects.

DISTRIBUTION AND MOVEMENTS Breeds from Scandinavia, Britain, Ireland and Iberia east across Eurasia to Japan and south to Sicily and Iran. Northern populations may sometimes winter in the south of the breeding range. In Britain and Ireland is a widely distributed species which breeds in most counties although not in Orkney, Shetland and the Outer Hebrides.

SUB-SPECIES Numerous sub-species have been described through its range: *A. c. rosaceus* is present in Britain and Ireland.

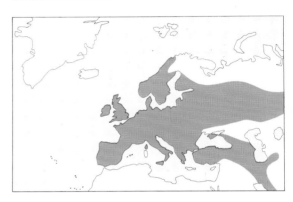

(Below) The British and Irish sub-species of the Long-tailed Tit *A.c. rosaceus* (foreground) and the northern and eastern form (behind). (Right) Areas where the Long-tailed Tit may be seen all year round (orange)

Penduline Tit
Remiz pendulinus

French: MESANGE REMIZ
Italian: PENDOLINO
Spanish: PAJARO MOSCON
German: BEUTELMEISE

HABITAT Marshes, fens and by freshwater margins.

IDENTIFICATION Length: 11 cm. Easily recognised by its contrasting brown and grey coloration. Head and throat are grey-white with a large black patch extending through the eye to the ear-coverts. Mantle chestnut, wings brown-grey with a light patch on the flight-feathers; underparts buffish-white. Juveniles lack the black patch on head and chestnut on back.

CALL Call is a soft, plaintive 'tsee' similar to the Robin's. Also utters a characteristic 'tsee-tsee'.

REPRODUCTION From late April. The nest is a distinctive flask-shaped construction with a tubular side entrance. It is suspended from twigs of bushes or trees, often over water. Both male and female build the nest which may take two weeks to complete. The nest is built of plant down, seed cases and fibres which form a thick felted material. The eggs, five to ten in number, are white, sometimes with a pink flush when first laid. The female alone incubates for about fourteen days. Both tend the young who remain in the nest for sixteen to eighteen days.

FOOD Mostly small insects and spiders: also seeds.

DISTRIBUTION AND MOVEMENTS Breeds from the southern Baltic east across Siberia and south to Iran and Afghanistan. Also breeds locally in eastern Spain, southern France and Italy. Sedentary and migratory: some populations winter south to Iraq and northern India. In Europe is extending its range to the northwest. Has occurred in Britain as a vagrant.

SUB-SPECIES *R. p. menzbieri:* Turkey and south-western Asia. Other sub-species are present in Asia.

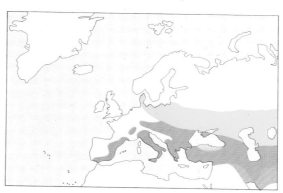

(Below) Penduline Tit (foreground) and juvenile. (Left) Breeding areas (yellow), wintering areas (magenta), areas where the Penduline Tit may be seen all year round (orange) and on passage (pink)

Eric Hosking

(Left) Great Tit *Parus major*, (below) Blue Tit *P. caeruleus* and (facing page) Marsh Tit *P. palustris*. These small insectivorous birds are common in woodland, and the Blue and Great Tits may often be seen in town parks and gardens

David Hosking

ORDER Passeriformes
FAMILY **SITTIDAE: Nuthatches**

J. S. Wightman/Ardea

The family Sittidae or nuthatches consists of twenty-four species of small, tree-climbing birds. The tails are short and often square, and they have large heads and strong, pointed bills. This powerful bill is used to open the nuts and seeds on which nuthatches feed, although the tougher shelled ones are often wedged into cracks in the bark of trees and hammered open. Nuthatches also feed on insects and spiders. The tarsi are of short to medium length and the toes have strong, hooked claws. Nuthatches are the only birds which habitually descend trees with their heads downwards.

Nuthatches vary in length from nine to nineteen centimetres. The plumage in most species is blue-grey above and pale greyish beneath. The underparts are generally unstreaked. The crown is often dark—brown or black. Most species have a conspicuous black or grey eyestripe and some have a dark crown. A few species differ from this general scheme of coloration and have black or velvety dark blue plumage. The sexes are alike.

Nuthatches are sedentary except some Red-breasted Nuthatches *Sitta canadensis* migrate in winter. The non-migratory species hoard food and carefully conceal it in natural cavities.

The nest is generally built in hollows in trees or rocks; some species may dig cavities in rotten trees. The Nuthatch *Sitta europaea* reduces the size of the entrance to the nest cavity by plastering it up with earth and mud, probably for protection from predators. Species such as the Rock Nuthatch *Sitta tephronota* build an entrance tube of mud which leads into the nest.

The family has a predominantly Holarctic distribution: the species of the genus *Sitta* are found mostly in Eurasia, but four occur in North America. The genus *Neositta* (six species) is limited to Australia and New Guinea, where an endemic form, the Pink-faced Nuthatch *Daphoenositta miranda*, is also found. The Wallcreeper *Tichodroma muraria* is found only in the high mountain ranges

J. A. Hancock/Photo Researchers

(Above and left) Nuthatch *Sitta europaea:* it is the most widespread and common nuthatch present in Europe. (Facing page) Rock Nuthatch *S. neumayer.* It is easily confused with the Nuthatch but its coloration is usually drabber

S. C. Porter/Bruce Coleman

W. Weisser/Ardea

(Right) White-breasted Nuthatch *Sitta carolinensis* with food. This species is found in North and Central America. (Below) World distribution of the family

of Europe and Asia. It flutters up vertical faces with half-open wings displaying the splendid crimson of the flight feathers.

Madagascar also possesses an endemic species, the Madagascar Nuthatch *Hypositta corallirostris*: according to some authorities it is an aberrant species of the family Vangidae or vanga shrikes of that island.

The genus *Sitta* includes the true nuthatches, the most common being the Nuthatch *S. europaea*. It is widely distributed in Europe and Asia and is also the only species to have established itself in Africa. A rare and endangered species is the Corsican Nuthatch *Sitta whiteheadi* which is confined to Corsica. It was once considered, on the basis of structural characteristics, conspecific with the American Red-breasted Nuthatch *Sitta canadensis*, but its quite distinct vocal and behavioural characteristics merit separate specific status.

The largest of all the nuthatches is the Giant Nuthatch *Sitta magna* which is found in the high mountain ranges of southeast Asia.

Some brilliantly-coloured nuthatches are found in southern Asia: these include the Velvet-fronted Nuthatch *Sitta frontalis*, the Azure Nuthatch *S. azurea* of Indonesia and the Beautiful Nuthatch *S. formosa*, which is found from Sikkim to eastern Assam. Asia is the home of the Eastern Rock Nuthatch *S. tephronota*. It is easily confused with the Rock Nuthatch *S. neumayer*.

Wallcreeper
Tichodroma muraria

French: TICHODROME ÉCHELETTE
Italian: PICCHIO MURAIOLO
Spanish: TREPARRISCOS
German: MAUERLAUFER

HABITAT Cliffs, rocky and mountainous areas: also stone buildings.

IDENTIFICATION Length: 16 cm. Long curved bill, like that of the Treecreeper, is a conspicuous feature. Upper parts ash-grey; black bib on throat and neck. Wing coverts crimson, white-spotted wings and tail. Often flicks its wings and exposes the distinctive crimson feathers. Bill and legs black. Juveniles have brownish-grey throat and more white on wings, with ochre patches on primaries and secondaries.

During courtship the male circles round the female with spread wings and vibrating tail, at the same time rapidly extending and withdrawing his head.

CALL Voice resembles the Treecreeper's but is louder, and is habitually emitted while climbing.

REPRODUCTION Mid-May onwards. Nests in rock crevices or holes often at considerable height. The female alone builds the bulky cup-shaped nest of moss, grass and roots: it is lined with hair and feathers. Eggs: usually four sometimes three or five, white in colour generally with fine sparse red-brown speckling. The female alone incubates for eighteen days. Both parents tend the young which remain in the nest for twenty-one to twenty-six days.

FOOD Insects and their larvae.

DISTRIBUTION AND MOVEMENTS Breeds in mountainous areas of southern Europe from Iberia east across Eurasia to the Himalayas and China. Sedentary, although may move to lower altitudes in winter. Has occurred in Britain as a vagrant on only a handful of occasions.

SUB-SPECIES Sub-species of the Wallcreeper are present in Asia.

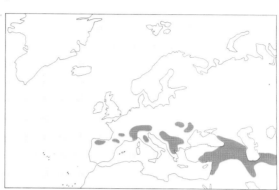

(Left) Areas where the Wallcreeper may be seen all year round (orange)

(Overleaf) Nuthatch *Sitta europaea*: the underparts vary in coloration from white to deep orange-buff

109

French: SITTELLE TORCHEPOT
Italian: PICCHIO MURATORE
Spanish: TREPADOR AZUL
German: KLEIBER

Nuthatch
Sitta europaea

HABITAT Wooded areas, parkland and gardens: may be seen at bird tables.

IDENTIFICATION Length: 14 cm. Most common and widespread nuthatch of Europe. Upper parts blue-grey; black streak from bill through eye to side of neck. Underparts vary from white belly in the north of its range to deep rufous-yellow in the south. Throat white; flanks chestnut. Bill slate-coloured: legs yellowish-brown. Juveniles lack chestnut coloration: some white on tail.

CALL Emits loud ringing calls including a 'chwet-chwet'. Song is a loud repetitive 'twee'.

REPRODUCTION From late April. Mainly the female builds the nest which is a loose cup of dead leaves and bits of bark. The nest is situated in a tree hole, hole in a wall or nest box with the entrance plastered to size with mud. Eggs: six to nine, rarely four to thirteen, white speckled with reddish-brown. Incubation period is normally fourteen or fifteen days, but may be up to eighteen days. Young are tended by both parents for twenty-two to twenty-five days.

FOOD Chiefly insects, but also seeds and nuts.

DISTRIBUTION AND MOVEMENTS Breeds from southern Scandinavia, Britain and Iberia east across Eurasia to Indochina. Also breeds in northwest Africa. Basically sedentary, but large scale irruptive movements to the west or the south sometimes occur among Siberian populations. In Britain is a widely distributed resident breeder in England and Wales, but only wanders occasionally to Scotland. The Nuthatch is absent, even as a vagrant, from Ireland.

SUB-SPECIES *S. e. caesia*: Central, southeastern and western Europe. *S. e. cisalpina*: Italy, Yugoslavia, southeastern France and southern Switzerland. *S. e. hispaniensis*: Spain and Portugal. Many other sub-species are present in Asia.

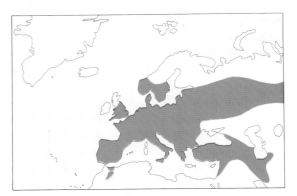

(Below) Nuthatch (top) and the northern race which may be distinguished by its white belly. (Right) Areas where the Nuthatch may be seen all year round (orange)

Kruper's Nuthatch
Sitta kruperi

HABITAT Coniferous forests in hilly and mountainous areas.

IDENTIFICATION Length: 12 cm. Similar in size to the Corsican Nuthatch, but easily recognised by the dark reddish-brown band on the breast. Small size and black crown also help to distinguish it. Upper parts grey, underparts whitish from cheeks to breast, except for the red-brown patch; flanks and under-tail coverts greyish. Very active species: often seen feeding on the outer branches of trees.

CALL A soft 'pwit': also a harsh 'swee'.

REPRODUCTION From late April. Nest is a cup of moss, hair, wool and feathers which is situated in a hole in a tree, in an old woodpecker hole or in a cavity behind dead bark. Unlike the Nuthatch's nest the entrance is not plastered. Lays five or six white eggs speckled with dark red or purple-red. Further information is not available.

FOOD Insects.

DISTRIBUTION AND MOVEMENTS Breeds in Asia Minor and the southern Caucasus. Sedentary.

(Below) Kruper's Nuthatch.
(Above) Areas where Kruper's Nuthatch may be seen all year round (orange)

French: SITTELLE DE KRUPER
Italian: PICCHIO MURATORE DI KRUPER
Spanish: TREPADOR DE KRUPER
German: KRUPER ZWERGKLEIBER

Rock Nuthatch
Sitta neumayer

HABITAT Mountainous regions; also cliffs and rocky outcrops.

IDENTIFICATION Length: 14 cm. Very like the Nuthatch, but has drabber coloration: underparts paler and browner, flanks and under-tail coverts buffish not chestnut. Tail lacks the white markings of the Nuthatch. Different habitats also distinguish the two species: the Rock Nuthatch frequents rocky not forested areas.

CALL Resembles the Nuthatch's but also has a rich fluty call. Song is a series of shrill piping notes.

REPRODUCTION From mid-April. Nests in a crevice among rocks or in a hollow. Builds a rounded structure of hardened mud with projecting tubular entrance. Lined inside with hair, wool and feathers. Nest may take ten days to build. Eggs: six to ten (sometimes as many as thirteen), white with light red or purple-red blotches and speckles. The female alone incubates but further details are not known.

FOOD Chiefly insects and spiders.

DISTRIBUTION AND MOVEMENTS Breeds in southeastern Europe including Yugoslavia and Greece. Also breeds in Asia Minor, the Middle East, northern Iraq and Iran.

SUB-SPECIES Sub-species are present in Asia.

French: SITTELLE DES ROCHERS
Italian: PICCHIO MURATORE DI ROCCIA
Spanish: TREPADOR RUPESTRE
German: FELSENKLEIBER

(Below) Rock Nuthatch.
(Below left) Areas where the Rock Nuthatch may be seen all year round (orange)

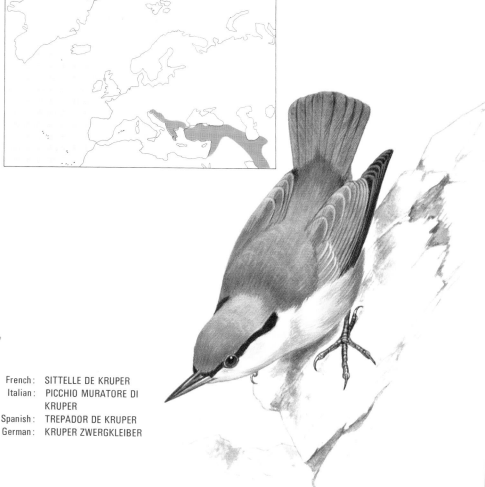

French: SITTELLE CORSE
Italian: PICCHIO MURATORE
       CORSO
Spanish: TREPADOR CORSO
German: KORSIKANISCHER
       KLEIBER

Corsican Nuthatch
Sitta whiteheadi

HABITAT Confined to mountainous pine forests of Corsica.

IDENTIFICATION Length: 12 cm. Noticeably smaller than the Nuthatch. Male easily recognised by black crown and wide black eyestripe. Conspicuous white stripe over black eyestripe. Upper parts grey; underparts white. Female darker, with slate-grey crown. Frequently associates with tits, especially in winter. Has been considered conspecific with Red-breasted Nuthatch, but now regarded as a species in its own right. Restricted range—Corsica only—distinguishes this species from the Nuthatch as it is not present in Corsica.

CALL Utters a weak 'piu-piu-piu-piu' and other notes which are quieter than the Nuthatch's.

REPRODUCTION From late April. Nests in a natural tree hole or old woodpecker hole. Nest is a cup of bark, moss and grass and is lined with hair. Lays five to six eggs, white, and rather sparsely speckled red-brown. The female alone incubates, although the incubation period is not known. Both parents tend the young which leave the nest after twenty days.

FOOD Chiefly insects.

DISTRIBUTION AND MOVEMENTS It is a resident species which is confined to Corsica.

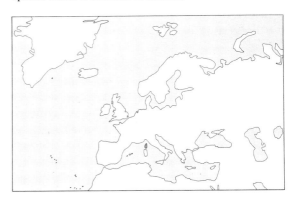

(Below) Male Corsican Nuthatch (bottom) and female (top). (Right) Areas where the Corsican Nuthatch may be seen all year round (orange)

The family Certhiidae or treecreepers contains six species. They are small brownish birds, with spotted and streaked upper parts and whitish underparts. Other distinguishing features are the thin, pointed decurved bill, the sharp, curved claws and the pointed, fairly stiff tail. The small size and habit of creeping mouselike about tree trunks are also distinctive: like the nuthatches they like to clamber up tree trunks and, although less frequently, over rocky surfaces or on the underside of branches. Occasionally they even move down the tree trunk head first like the nuthatches. The stiff tail is used as a support when climbing.

After exploring a tree in search of insects, they flutter down—their flight is brief and undulating—to a neighbouring tree and begin to climb to the top. Treecreepers frequent deciduous and coniferous woodland as well as parks and well-wooded gardens.

The nest is built in crevices in the bark of trees, in creepers, sometimes also in cracks in walls or between rocks or, more rarely, in nest boxes. The nest is lined with soft materials such as moss, plant wool, feathers and bits of bark. The number of eggs in the clutch varies from three to nine, averaging seven, which are white with red-brown markings.

Treecreepers are found only in the northern hemisphere. Five of the six species are found only in the Old World, but the sixth, the Treecreeper *Certhia familiaris,* occurs both in Eurasia and in North America. As might be expected from such a widely distributed species, several geographical races or sub-species exist. The Treecreeper varies not only in morphological characteristics, and especially in coloration, but also in its choice of habitat: it is present in widely varying types of woods and forests. In areas where it overlaps with a very similar species, the Short-toed Treecreeper *C. brachydactyla,* it prefers mountains and coniferous forests, leaving the plains and deciduous woodland to the latter species. This division of habitat may be observed in much of continental Europe.

(Right) Treecreeper *Certhia familiaris* by its nesting site. (Facing page and preceeding page, p. 115) Treecreepers: the English name aptly describes its habit of creeping mouse-like on tree trunks

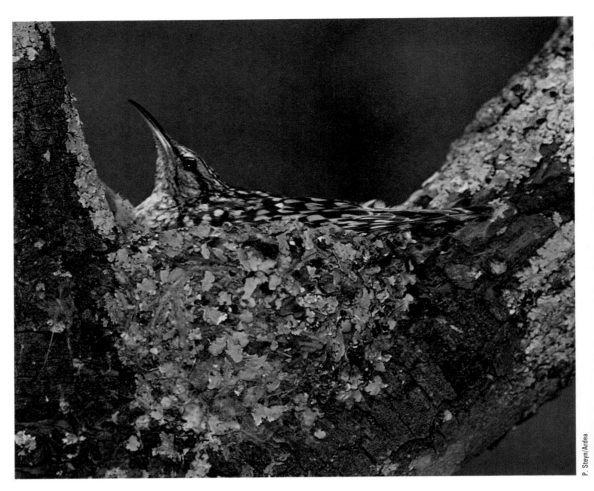

P. Steyn/Ardea

(Right) Spotted Treecreeper *Salpornis spilonota* from Africa and southeast Asia. (Below) World distribution of the family Certhiidae

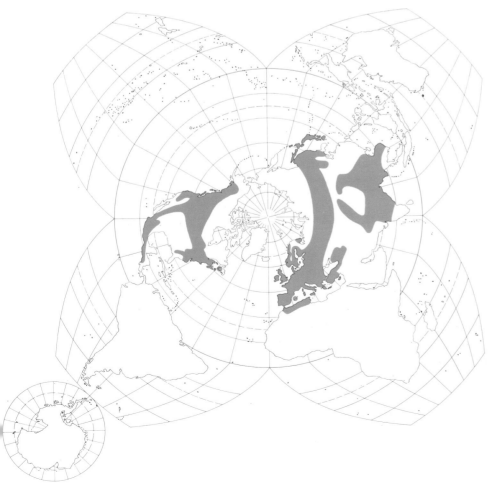

The Spotted Treecreeper *Salpornis spilonota* of the monotypic genus *Salpornis* inhabits Africa and southeast Asia. The remaining three species are exclusively Asiatic: the Himalayan Treecreeper *C. himalayana*, which has a long bill and is found, despite its name, from Turkestan to western China and Burma as well as in the Himalayas: the Brown-throated Treecreeper *C. discolor* and Stoliczka's Treecreeper *C. nipalensis* which are both present in eastern Asia.

Those populations which spend at least part of the year in cold climates are often exposed to inclement weather. Because of their small size their heat loss is rapid and extensive, in spite of the insulation provided by their feathers. Often, therefore, especially when the nights are cold in the winter, they huddle for shelter in their nests, in other natural cavities or even, if nothing better can be found, in cracks in the bark of trees, where they frequently fall into a state of semi-torpor. Some populations which inhabit high mountain areas move to lower altitudes in the winter.

The songs of the treecreepers consist of a monotonous repetition of feeble notes, varying, however, quite considerably between species and thus affording easy identification. The differing songs of the Treecreeper and Short-toed Treecreeper, which share much the same range in central and eastern Europe, are particularly useful in distinguishing these two species.

Treecreeper
Certhia familiaris

French: GRIMPEREAU DES BOIS
Italian: RAMPICHINO ALPESTRE
Spanish: AGATEADOR NORTENO
German: WALDBAUMLAUFER

HABITAT Coniferous and mixed woodland: also parks and gardens in Britain, but only mountainous areas in the south of its range.

IDENTIFICATION Length: 12 cm. Very similar to Short-toed Treecreeper: these two species are the only small brown land birds of Europe with curved bills. Upper parts light brownish-red with whitish markings; rump light buff-brown; head darker with clearly-marked forehead; white eyestripe. Underparts silky white. Bill brown above, whitish beneath. Juveniles have more coarsely-marked upper parts and rufous spotting on the underparts.

The long, sharp claws enable it to cling even to smooth bark, and it clambers up trees in a spiral, sometimes making short hops and holding its tail rigid against the bark.

CALL Call is a prolonged 'tsii': song a 'tee-tee-litidee'. Both are high pitched.

REPRODUCTION From April onwards. Nests in trees behind loose bark, in crevices in trees, behind ivy and other creepers or, rarely, in a crevice in a wall. Both sexes build the nest which is a loose cup of twigs, roots, moss and grasses. Eggs: usually six, sometimes three to nine, white, finely freckled dark red-brown or mottled purplish to brownish. The female alone incubates for fourteen to fifteen days. The young remain in the nest for sixteen to seventeen days and are tended by both parents.

FOOD Insects and larvae; also molluscs and seeds.

DISTRIBUTION AND MOVEMENTS Breeds from Scandinavia, Britain, Ireland, central France and the Pyrenees east across Eurasia to China and Japan. Also breeds south to the Caucasus, Iran and the Himalayas, and in Central and North America. Northernmost populations and those living at high altitudes are partially migratory. In Britain and Ireland is widely distributed resident breeder although sparse in the Scottish islands.

SUB-SPECIES *C. f. macrodactyla*: western, central and southern Europe. *C. f. britannica*: Britain and Ireland. *C. f. corsa*: Corsica. Other sub-species are present in Asia and America.

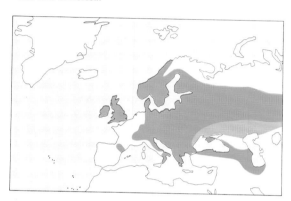

(Left) Wintering areas (magenta) and areas where the Treecreeper may be seen all year round (orange)

French: GRIMPEREAU DES JARDINS
Italian: RAMPICHINO
Spanish: AGATEADOR COMUN
German: GARTENBAUMLAUFER

Short-toed Treecreeper
Certhia brachydactyla

HABITAT Woodland, gardens, parks and other areas with scattered trees. Remains at lower altitudes than the Treecreeper.

IDENTIFICATION Length: 12 cm. Difficult to distinguish from Treecreeper although has brownish flanks. Upper parts brown streaked with greyish or rufous-white markings, tinged buff on rump and upper-tail coverts. Whitish or rufous-grey eyestripe; throat and upper breast white; belly greyish; flanks and under-tail coverts tinged rufous-grey. Legs brownish.

Climbs over the trunks and branches in a spiral, with feet wide apart, supported by the sharp, stiff tail-feathers. Occasionally seen in an upside-down position. At the top it spreads its wings and drops straight to the bottom of another tree. When alarmed, freezes in position and clings to the bark of the tree.

CALL A single loud 'tsee'. Song is louder and less high-pitched than the Treecreeper's.

REPRODUCTION From late March. Nests in crevices like the Treecreeper. The nest is made of twigs, bark and other plant material, and is lined with hair and feathers. Eggs: six or seven, white with dark red-brown blotching concentrated mostly in a band at the larger end. The female alone incubates for fourteen or fifteen days. Both tend the young who remain in the nest for fifteen to sixteen days.

FOOD Insects, larvae and small molluscs: also seeds.

DISTRIBUTION AND MOVEMENTS Breeds throughout continental Europe eastwards to Asia Minor. Also breeds in northern Africa. Has occurred as a vagrant to Britain.

SUB-SPECIES *C. b. megarhynchos:* western Europe. *C. b. dorotheae:* Cyprus.

(Right) Areas where the Short-toed Treecreeper may be seen all year round (orange)

Eric Hosking

The family Emberizidae includes not only the buntings, but also species such as the tanagers, cardinals and grosbeaks which were previously given family status in some classifications. However despite certain strikingly different external features, the brilliant South American tanagers, the Neotropical honeycreepers, the cardinals, grosbeaks and buntings all share so many characteristics that there is no alternative to placing them all in the same family.

However, there are some species which probably only remain in the family because too little is known about them to determine what their real position should be. This applies, for instance, to the Plush-capped Finch *Catamblyrhynchus diadema*. It is an unusual species which has a conical bill and is present in the Andes in South America.

The origins of the Emberizidae are considered to be almost certainly American, perhaps even Neotropical. However, the genus with the most species of European birds, *Emberiza*, is now found only in the Old World. The sub-families of the

Emberizidae are the Emberizinae or buntings and American sparrows; the Cardinalinae or cardinal-grosbeaks; the Thraupinae or tanagers and honeycreepers; and lastly two sub-families containing one species each; the Catamblyrhynchinae or Plush-capped Finch and the Tersinae or Swallow-Tanager.

The sub-family Emberizinae contains, besides the true buntings, numerous other species which are grouped in various exclusively American genera. These species, especially in the United States, are for the most part commonly called sparrows, although they have nothing in common with the true sparrows of the family Ploceidae. Members of this sub-family are small birds, mainly terrestrial in behaviour. Their food consists basically of seeds and other vegetable matter which they pick up off the ground. Many are found in grasslands or scrub; others prefer open woodland or the edges of forests. In general, they avoid dense, tall vegetation. Even within these limitations, however, they are found in greatly varying

(Above) Corn Bunting *Emberiza calandra* feeding its young. This plump, brown species is the largest bunting present in Europe, and may often be seen on farmland in Britain

121

H. Mickelsson

S. Roberts/Ardea

A. Blomgren

(Above) Snow Buntings *Plectrophenax nivalis*. (Above right, top) Reed Bunting *Emberiza schoeniclus*: the male in breeding plumage is easily distinguished by his all black head with white moustachial streak. (Above right, bottom) Rustic Bunting *Emberiza rustica*: it sometimes raises its crest feathers. (Facing page) Yellowhammer *Emberiza citrinella* at the nest

climates; from hot and dry to cold and damp, and from sea level to the most barren mountain peaks. The Snow Bunting *Plectrophenax nivalis* nests in the far north of Greenland and is, indeed, the most northerly dwelling land bird.

With such a wide distribution, the habits of the different species of the Emberizinae or buntings and American sparrows also vary considerably. The song, for example, may be loud and musical or very weak and so high-pitched as to be barely audible to the human ear.

Some species are extremely shy, others very confiding, such as the House or Striped Bunting *Emberiza striolata*. As its name implies it frequently nests on or in houses. By contrast the physical characteristics of the Emberizinae are fairly homogeneous. The legs are of medium length, the claws strong; the tail may be rather long, square, graduated or even slightly forked. The bill is short, conical, and, in the typical buntings of the genus *Emberiza*, has a swelling inside the upper mandible which is useful for crushing the harder seeds.

A typical member of the sub-family is the Reed Bunting *Emberiza schoeniclus* which is found throughout Europe. Depending upon the sub-species, the bill may be small and slender, almost like that of an insect-eater, or heavy and thick.

The wings are long and pointed in those species which migrate, and short and rounded in the majority of the sedentary species. They have nine primaries although a tenth outermost primary, rudimentary and concealed, is sometimes present. The male is generally more brightly coloured than the female. In shape they resemble finches of the family Fringillidae.

The typical nest is cup-shaped, and is constructed from small roots and grasses and sometimes with mosses and lichens. It is usually built on or near the ground, well concealed in vegetation. Some species nest in hollow trees or among rocks. Incubation is usually carried out by the female alone. There are about forty species present in the Old World: twenty-nine belong to the genus *Emberiza* which is typically Palearctic. However, the House or Striped Bunting *E. striolata*, has penetrated the Ethiopian region where a further seven species of the same genus are also found.

The American sparrows are far more numerous, both in the number of species and genera than their Old World relatives. They number about a hundred and fifty species and fifty genera, although many of the genera are monotypic. Distributed virtually throughout the Americas, some of these species have been the subject of detailed studies. The Song Sparrow *Melospizia melodia* is particularly well known. The White-throated Sparrow *Zonotrichia albicollis* occurs as a vagrant in western Europe.

J. Grahn

The tanagers, placed in the sub-family Thraupinae, are a group typical of the Neotropical avifauna; they are among the most common and brightly-coloured birds of the region. There are about two hundred and thirty species, which vary in size from eleven to twenty-one centimetres and display an extraordinary range of coloration. Except for the few species which penetrate to the temperate or cold regions of North America, the sexes have similar coloration and there is no seasonal variation of the vivid plumage. The genus *Tanagra* contains the most species and other genera, well-known to aviculturists are *Thraupis*, *Ramphocelus*, *Chlorospingus*, and *Chlorochrysa*. The Scarlet Tanager *Piranga olivacea* from North America occurs as a vagrant to Europe. It is one of the four tanagers which occurs north of Mexico. It inhabits woodland, particularly mature oak forests. The male's plumage is bright red, the female's olive-green. Tanagers often gather together in small groups to roost on trees or in bushes; some species remain paired all the year round and in these cases the male will sometimes feed the female, even outside the nesting season. The majority build a cup-shaped nest high up in tall trees, and although the nest may sometimes be situated in low bushes it is never normally on the ground.

Some species build domed nests with a side entrance. The Palm Tanager *Thraupis palmarum* nests in hollow trees while the Blue-Grey Tanager *T. episcopus* sometimes occupies the nests of other birds, hatching their eggs together with its own and bringing up the 'adopted children' with its own family. There are usually two eggs per clutch, often brightly coloured, but some species lay four or five eggs. The female alone incubates, but the male brings food; only in a few cases is the incubation period longer than two weeks. The young hatch almost naked.

The sub-family Cardinalinae, the cardinals and grosbeaks, are passerines which inhabit North, Central and South America. The Cardinal *Cardinalis cardinalis* is a typical and well-known member of this sub-family. The Cardinal is present in the United States and Central America, and the male has entirely red coloration, apart from a black bib. The Cardinal may frequently be observed in gardens, parks and suburbs. Like other members of this family the bill is stout and there is a crest on the head.

Similar species, also with a robust bill and a crest, occur in South America, while others nest almost as far as the Arctic. Among these are the Rose-breasted Grosbeak *Pheucticus ludovicianus*, which is black and white with a pink patch on the breast, and species such as the Orange-breasted Bunting *Passerina leclancheri* and the Painted Bunting *P. ciris*.

The remaining sub-families Catamblyrhynchinae and Tersinae contain only one species each: the Plush-capped Finch *Catamblyrhynchus diadema* and the Swallow-Tanager *Tersina viridis* respectively. Both occur in South America, although the Swallow-Tanager is also found in Central America.

(Left) Male Black-headed Bunting *Emberiza melanocephala*. (Below) Rose-breasted Grosbeak *Pheucticus ludovicianus* (left) and Cardinal *Cardinalis cardinalis* (right). (Facing page) Lapland Bunting *Calcarius lapponicus* and (below) world distribution of the family Emberizidae

J. S. Wightman/Ardea

Kinne/Photo Researchers

French: BRUANT PROYER
Italian: STRILLOZZO
Spanish: TRIGUERO
German: GRAUAMMER

Corn Bunting
Emberiza calandra

HABITAT Open, dry countryside, steppes and farmland.

IDENTIFICATION Length: 18 cm. Largest of all the buntings: upper parts greyish-brown, striped brown-black; pale supercilium, rufous chin; underparts yellowish-brown streaked black on sides of throat, breast and flanks. Flight feathers brown-black with buff borders. Lacks wing-bars: most distinctive feature of this species is its high-pitched song. Sexes similar. Juveniles have paler upper parts with wide rufous borders, rufous throat, whiter belly with more streaking on flanks; rufous, more clearly-marked borders on wings and tail.

CALL A short, rasping 'tchip'; also a softer 'tcree' or 'sree'. The song has been likened to the sound made by shaking a bunch of keys: a high-pitched, jangling 'tic-tic'.

REPRODUCTION From late April. The female builds the nest on the ground, among grasses or herbage although sometimes over a metre off the ground in thick bushes or hedgerows. The nest is a bulky and loosely made cup of grasses which is lined with finer grasses, roots and hair. The female lays four to six eggs, sometimes one to seven, which vary in coloration: whitish tinted bluish, purple or buff with grey or purple-grey blotching and darker streaks. The female alone incubates, for twelve to fourteen days. The young are tended mainly by the female and leave the nest after nine to twelve days. Generally two broods over most of the range, but sometimes a third.

FOOD Mainly vegetable matter. Hunts on the ground for seeds, buds and berries. Also feeds on insects, larvae, spiders, molluscs and earthworms.

DISTRIBUTION AND MOVEMENTS Breeds in Europe and western Asia, including Britain and Ireland, south into northern Africa and the Middle East. Partially migratory and winters in the south of the breeding range or just beyond. In Britain it is a widespread breeder in England (although absent from much of southwest England) and Scotland. However, it is virtually absent from Wales and scarce in Ireland. Essentially sedentary. and although some may migrate, adequate evidence is lacking. Recorded in very small numbers as a passage visitor in autumn and spring.

SUB-SPECIES *F.c. buturlini:* Asia.

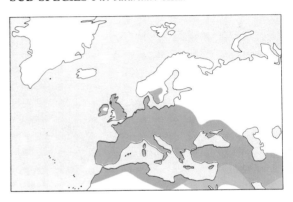

(Right) Wintering areas (magenta) and areas where the Corn Bunting may be seen all year round (orange)

Grey-necked Bunting
Emberiza buchanani

French: BRUANT A COU GRIS
Italian: ZIGOLO COLLOGRIGIO
German: STEINORTOLAN

HABITAT Dry, open country with sparse vegetation, rocky outcrops and stony countryside.

IDENTIFICATION Length: 15 cm. Very similar to Ortolan and Cretzschmar's Buntings. Adult male has greyish head; back, rump and upper-tail coverts brown with narrow dark streaking on back; throat rusty-white with white moustachial stripe; breast and belly rusty-brown shading off gradually towards under-tail coverts. Wings grey-brown, tail dark brown. Similar to Cretzschmar's Bunting, but that species has grey extending to chest.

CALL Emits a 'sip' and 'choup'. Song resembles that of the Ortolan Bunting but is longer with a rising inflection.

REPRODUCTION From May. Female builds a cup-shaped nest of grass and leaves. It is situated on the ground and sheltered by herbage. Eggs: usually five, white tinged pale or buff with sparse purple-grey markings. The female alone incubates but further information is not available.

FOOD Seeds and insects.

DISTRIBUTION AND MOVEMENTS Breeds from the Persian Gulf and southern shores of the Caspian east to western Pakistan and China.

SUB-SPECIES Sub-species are present throughout the range.

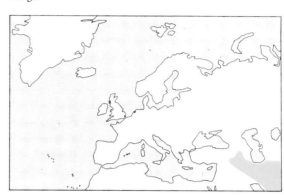

(Below) Male Grey-necked Bunting (foreground) and female. (Left) Breeding areas (yellow) of the Grey-necked Bunting

French: BRUANT JAUNE
Italian: ZIGOLO GIALLO
Spanish: ESCRIBANO CERILLO
German: GOLDAMMER

Yellowhammer
Emberiza citrinella

HABITAT Farmland, hedgerows and forest borders.

IDENTIFICATION Length: 16 cm. Along with the Yellow Wagtail is one of the most yellow birds present in Europe. Head lemon-yellow with dark stripes on crown, through eye and moustache. Rump yellow-chestnut. Underparts yellow; flight-feathers brown-black, outer-tail feathers brown-black with conspicuous white borders. Bill bluish-brown, legs pale pinkish-brown, iris deep brown. Female and juvenile are less yellow.

CALL The usual call is a grating 'twee-tik', and the song is popularly known as a phrase sounding like a 'little bit of bread and no cheese', with the 'cheese' extended.

REPRODUCTION From late April. Nest is a cup of grass, moss and stems which is usually located on the ground hidden in vegetation. However, it may be built in a thick bush about a metre off the ground. Eggs: three to five, white tinted with bluish or grey. Faintly marked with pale purplish scrawls and blotches. The female alone incubates for eleven to fourteen days: both tend the young.

FOOD Chiefly vegetable matter.

DISTRIBUTION AND MOVEMENTS Breeds in Europe from Scandinavia, Britain, Ireland and northern Spain east to northern USSR and Siberia and south to the Mediterranean area, Black Sea and Iran. Northern populations are migratory and winter in the south of the breeding range and beyond. In Britain and Ireland it is a widespread and numerous resident breeder, although absent from the Outer Hebrides and Shetland. Status as a winter and passage visitor is obscure: migrants of unconfirmed origin (probably northern Europe) occur.

SUB-SPECIES *E.c. caliginosa*: Britain and Ireland except southeast England. *E.c. citrinella*: southeast England and remaining parts of western Europe. *E.c. erythrogenys*: eastern Europe and Asia.

(Below) Male Yellowhammer (top) and female (bottom). (Right) Breeding areas (yellow), wintering areas (magenta) and areas where the Yellowhammer may be seen all year round (orange)

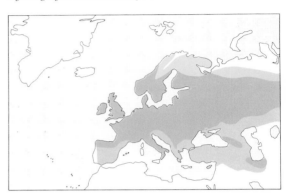

Pine Bunting
Emberiza leucocephala

HABITAT Open woodland, scrubland and cultivated areas. Often found near fresh water.

IDENTIFICATION Length: 16 cm. Adult male has striking head pattern: sides of crown black; centre of crown and cheeks white; neck chestnut. White stripe below eye widening over ear coverts and bordered blackish-brown at base of neck. Mantle and scapulars streaked black, with chestnut markings and yellowish-brown borders; chestnut rump; upper-tail coverts chestnut with white tips. Upper breast and flanks chestnut; centre of breast and belly pure white. Male's plumage duller in winter. Legs yellowish-brown; iris dark brown. Females: like male, but crown streaked black with brown borders. Resembles the female Yellowhammer but white instead of yellow.

CALL Resembles that of the Chaffinch.

REPRODUCTION From May onwards. Nests on the ground or among grasses. Nest is a cup of dry grass which is lined with hair and fine grass. Eggs: four to six, ground-colour pale blue and faintly marked with purplish-grey scrawling. Incubation carried out by female alone; exact period not known.

FOOD Seeds and insects.

DISTRIBUTION AND MOVEMENTS Breeds in the USSR east across Siberia, to western China. Migratory and winters in Central Asia and India. Accidental in western Europe including Britain.

SUB-SPECIES A sub-species is present in China.

French: BRUANT A CALOTTE BLANCHE
Italian: ZIGOLO GOLAROSSA
Spanish: ESCRIBANO DE GMELIN
German: FICHTENAMMER

(Above) Male Pine Bunting (foreground) and female.
(Below) Male Siberian Meadow Bunting (foreground) and female

Siberian Meadow Bunting
Emberiza cioides

HABITAT Mainly mountain slopes with scattered bushes or trees; also scrub and grassy areas.

IDENTIFICATION Length: 16 cm. Crown and nape dark chestnut-pink with brown-buff borders to feathers. Mantle and scapulars chestnut-brown streaked black; rump and upper-tail coverts chestnut with buff tips; chin and throat pale ash-grey: flanks buff-chestnut; breast, belly and under-tail coverts buff; tail-feathers chestnut with brown borders.

CALL Resembles that of Yellowhammer.

REPRODUCTION Mid-April onwards. Lays three to six eggs. The nest, made of grasses and lined with horsehair and small roots is situated in a bush or on the ground. May be double brooded, but further details are lacking.

FOOD Seeds and probably insects.

DISTRIBUTION AND MOVEMENTS Breeds from Turkestan east to China and Japan. Accidental in Europe.

SUB-SPECIES Sub-species are present in Asia.

French: BRUANT DES PRES
Italian: ZIGOLO MUCIATTO ORIENTALE
Spanish: ESCRIBANO DE BRANDT
German: WIESENAMMER

(Right) Reed Bunting *Emberiza schoeniclus* at the nest. (Below) Cirl Buntings *Emberiza cirlus*: the male feeds the female on the nest

Andy Davies

Eric Hosking

Eric Hosking

M. D. England/Ardea

(Above) Male Yellow-breasted Bunting *E. aureola* at the nest. (Left) Rock Bunting *E. cia*. The Yellow-breasted Bunting is easily identified, as its English name indicates, by its bright yellow breast and also by the black head. The Rock Bunting's striking head pattern, grey with three black stripes, is a distinguishing feature

French: BRUANT FOU
Italian: ZIGOLO MUCIATTO
Spanish: ESCRIBANO MONTESINO
German: ZIPPAMMER

Rock Bunting
Emberiza cia

HABITAT Rocky and stony hillsides and mountainous regions. Also vineyards and gardens.

IDENTIFICATION Length: 16 cm. Distinguished by silver-grey throat and head, with narrow dark streak on crown extending to nape. Only other buntings with a grey throat is the House Bunting. Whitish stripe over eye, black eyestripe, black moustachial stripe. Upper parts reddish-brown striped brown-black except for rump. Underparts cinnamon-red; axillaries white; flight-feathers brown-black bordered brownish-buff; tail-feathers brown, central ones edged rufous, outer ones partly white. Bill blue-grey, legs pinkish-brown. Female: like male, but paler with more brown coloration and more streaked.

CALL A sharp 'tsiit'. Song is a high pitched and buzzing 'zi-zi-ziir'.

REPRODUCTION From early April. Nests in a cavity among rocks or in a wall: also among stones under low bushes. Builds a cup-shaped nest of grasses, bits of bark and moss. Eggs: four to six, pale grey, purplish or whitish with brown hair-streaks and some small brown or purplish-grey spots. The female alone incubates for twelve to thirteen days; the young are fed by both parents and leave the nest after twelve or thirteen days.

FOOD Chiefly seeds; also insects.

DISTRIBUTION AND MOVEMENTS Breeds in mountainous areas from Iberia, southern France and Germany east through southern Europe and Asia to China and the Himalayas. Also breeds in northwest Africa. Basically sedentary. In Britain it is a rare vagrant, but as it is imported here as a cage-bird some records may be of individuals which have escaped from captivity.

SUB-SPECIES *E.c. africana:* southern Spain and northwest Africa. *E.c. pragesi:* Crimea, Caucasus, Transcaucasia and northeastern Turkey.

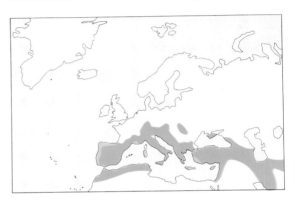

(Left) Male Rock Bunting (foreground) and female. (Above) Breeding areas (yellow), wintering areas (magenta) and areas where the Rock Bunting may be seen all year round (orange)

French: BRUANT CENDRE
Italian: ZIGOLO CINEREO
Spanish: ESCRIBANO CINEREO
German: KLEINASIATISCHE AMMER

(Right) Male Cinereous Bunting (foreground) and female. (Facing page. left) Breeding areas (yellow), areas where the Cinereous Bunting may be seen all year round (orange) and on passage (pink)

Cinereous Bunting
Emberiza cineracea

HABITAT High rocky slopes up to the tree line: also arid areas.

IDENTIFICATION Length: 16 cm. Resembles a grey Yellowhammer. Head, cheeks and throat pale lemon-yellow, suffused grey on crown; back grey-brown and variably streaked. Wings brown with paler borders to coverts and secondaries; tail brown with paler outer feathers. Rump, upper breast and flanks pale ash-grey. Legs straw-coloured. Female and juvenile are browner than the male with some streaking at sides of neck and base of throat.

CALL Emits a 'kip'. Song consists of three long and two short notes.

REPRODUCTION Builds its nest on the ground among rocks. Eggs: three, white tinged blue-grey with black-brown scrawls. No further information on reproduction is available.

FOOD Mainly seeds.

DISTRIBUTION AND MOVEMENTS Breeds in Turkey, the Middle East and east to Iran. Winters in southern Asia Minor, Arabia and East Africa. Accidental in southeastern Europe.

SUB-SPECIES *E.c. semenowi*: Asia.

Cretzschmar's Bunting
Emberiza caesia

HABITAT Rocky regions: also semi-desert areas.

IDENTIFICATION Length: 16 cm. The male resembles the male Ortolan Bunting but may be easily distinguished by blue-grey, not olive, head and breast and rust-coloured, not yellow, throat. The two females are less easily distinguished, but the female Cretzschmar's Bunting has no yellow coloration on the throat. Juveniles are even more difficult to tell apart: as a general rule juvenile Cretzschmar's Buntings are buffer than juvenile Ortolans and differ from juvenile Rock Buntings in having a pinkish bill.

CALL Call is a loud 'styip' which is similar to that of Ortolan but briefer. Emits a typical bunting song: 'tsee-tsee-tsee'.

REPRODUCTION From mid-April. Nests on the ground by herbage. Nest is a cup of plant stems which is lined with roots, grass and hair. Eggs: four to six, white tinged pale bluish or greyish with fine purplish markings. Double brooded. Further information is unavailable.

FOOD Probably mainly seeds.

DISTRIBUTION AND MOVEMENTS Breeds in Greece, Asia Minor and the Middle East: also breeds on Cyprus and Corfu. Accidental elsewhere in Europe including Fair Isle in Britain.

French: BRUANT CENDRILLARD
Italian: ORTOLANO GRIGIO
Spanish: ESCRIBANO CENICIENTO
German: ROSTAMMER

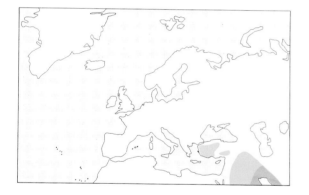

(Below) Male Cretzschmar's Bunting· (right) and female (left). (Left) Breeding areas (yellow), wintering areas (magenta) and areas where Cretzschmar's Bunting may be seen on passage (pink)

French: BRUANT ORTOLAN
Italian: ORTOLANO
Spanish: ESCRIBANO HORTELANO
German: GARTENAMMER

Cirl Bunting
Emberiza cirlus

French: BRUANT ZIZI
Italian: ZIGOLO NERO
Spanish: ESCRIBANO SOTENO
German: ZAUNAMMER

HABITAT Areas with scattered vegetation, hedgerows and farmland.

IDENTIFICATION Length: 17 cm. Adult male: forehead and crown olive-green streaked black and tinged brown; mantle and scapulars chestnut with buff-grey borders; rump olivaceous-brown; upper-tail coverts brown streaked black; yellowish above and below eye; black streak through eye. Dark crown and throat distinguish it from the Yellowhammer. Underparts: upper breast olive-green; sides of breast chestnut; centre of breast, belly and under-tail coverts yellow; flanks buff with dark brown streaks; flight-feathers black-brown. Female is duller and she also lacks the male's dark head pattern.

CALL A thin 'seet' which is higher pitched than the Yellowhammer's. The song consists of a shrill and trilling repetition of metallic notes. Also rarely emits a song similar to the Yellowhammer's.

REPRODUCTION From mid-May. The nest is a cup built by the female of roots, grass and moss and is lined with finer grasses and hair. It is usually above the ground in thick bushes, hedgerows or on a low branch of a tree. Eggs: three to four, ground-colour, bluish or greenish with black, purple or grey streaks. Incubation is carried out by the female alone for eleven to thirteen days. The young are tended mainly by the female, and leave the nest after eleven to thirteen days. Two broods, sometimes three.

FOOD Mainly grain and seeds; also berries and insects.

DISTRIBUTION AND MOVEMENTS Breeds from southern England, France and southwest Germany south through Mediterranean Europe to Asia Minor. Resident, although there is some post-breeding dispersal. In Britain it is a scarce and locally distributed resident breeder, virtually confined to counties south of the Thames. Vagrant to Scotland and Ireland.

SUB-SPECIES *E.c. nigrostriata:* Corsica and Sardinia.

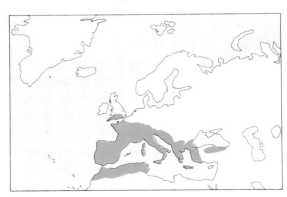

(Above left) Male Cirl Bunting (foreground) and female. (Right) Areas where the Cirl Bunting may be seen all year round (orange)

Ortolan Bunting
Emberiza hortulana

HABITAT Open, hilly countryside, often also in plains, gardens and hedgerows. Also frequents cultivated areas.

IDENTIFICATION Length: 17 cm. Head, neck and upper breast greyish-green; throat and moustachial stripe pale yellow; distinctive yellow eye-ring. Upper parts brown streaked blackish, rump buff streaked brown; breast and belly cinnamon-red. Bill brownish-pink; legs pink; iris brown. Female and juvenile more brownish and lighter with dark streaks on the breast.

CALL A weak 'zit' and also a piping 'tsseu'. Song is a sad 'zeu-zu'.

REPRODUCTION From May onwards. The female builds the cup-shaped nest of grasses and roots. It is lined with fine roots and hair, or rarely feathers. Nests on the ground in grass or under a bush. Four to six eggs are laid, sometimes three and rarely seven, varying in colour from bluish-white to pinkish-grey, sprinkled with grey speckles and streaks. The female alone incubates for eleven to fourteen days. The young are fed by both parents and leave the nest after ten to fifteen days. Double brooded.

FOOD Insects, larvae and seeds.

DISTRIBUTION AND MOVEMENTS Breeds from Scandinavia, Germany, France and Iberia east through Eurasia to Afghanistan. Also breeds in the Middle East. Winters in some areas of the Mediterranean, eastern tropical Africa and Arabia. In Britain it is an annual passage visitor in small numbers to the east coast (principally Norfolk and Fair Isle). Also occurs on passage to Ireland.

Yellow-breasted Bunting
Emberiza aureola

French: BRUANT AUREOLE
Italian: ZIGOLO DAL COLLARE
Spanish: ESCRIBANO AUREOLADO
German: WEIDENAMMER

HABITAT Open woodland and scrub.

IDENTIFICATION Length: 14 cm. Distinguished by white wing patches which are conspicuous in flight, and narrow white shoulder-patch; the wing pattern is similar to that of Chaffinch. Male has dark brown head and back, buff rump; underparts bright yellow with a characteristic narrow chestnut breast band, streaked flanks. In summer plumage the black head and breast band contrast with the yellow underparts. In winter black and chestnut markings appear faded, but it is still distinguishable from other buntings by the wing pattern and the pectoral band.

CALL The usual call is a short 'zeepp', also a soft, trilling 'trssseet'. Song is like that of Ortolan Bunting, but higher-pitched and quicker.

REPRODUCTION From June. Nests near the ground in low bushes or in areas covered with tall vegetation. The nest is made from grasses, lined with finer grasses and hair. Four or five eggs are laid, rarely six, ground-colour generally green or olive, mottled or lightly spotted dark brown and ash-grey. The female alone incubates for about thirteen days.

FOOD Insects and larvae: also seeds, rice and other vegetable matter.

DISTRIBUTION AND MOVEMENTS Breeds in northeastern Europe from Finland east across the USSR. Winters in tropical Asia. Rare vagrant to Britain and Ireland.

SUB-SPECIES A sub-species is present in eastern Asia.

(Below) Male Yellow-breasted Bunting (foreground) and female. (Left) Breeding areas (yellow) of the Yellow-breasted Bunting

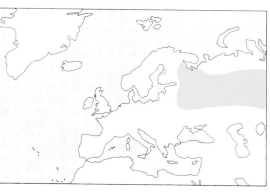

(Facing page, near left) Male Ortolan Bunting (top) and female (below). (Above) Breeding areas (yellow) and areas where the Ortolan Bunting may be seen on passage (pink)

French: BRUANT RUSTIQUE
Italian: ZIGOLO BOSCHERECCIO
Spanish: ESCRIBANO RUSTICO
German: WALDAMMER

Rustic Bunting
Emberiza rustica

HABITAT Marshy areas with shrubby undergrowth, swamps, forest edges and clearings.

IDENTIFICATION Length: 14 cm. Distinguished from Reed Bunting by white throat and eyestripe and chestnut breast band. Upper parts brown, streaked black. The male has blackish crown (brownish in winter) and cheeks. Female and male in winter plumage have black parts browner.

CALL The call-note is a 'tik-tik' and a 'tseep-tseep-tseep'. Song is brief and warbling and reminiscent of a Robin's.

REPRODUCTION From late May. Nests on the ground in herbage or in a shrub near the ground. The nest is a cup of grasses and moss which is lined with finer grass, hair and roots. Eggs: four or five, pale bluish and heavily speckled with greyish or olive. The female alone incubates for twelve or thirteen days.

FOOD Seeds.

DISTRIBUTION AND MOVEMENTS Breeds in northeast Europe east across the USSR to Kamchatka. Winters in north-central China and Japan. It is a vagrant to Britain, recorded chiefly on the east coast. Has occurred in Ireland.

SUB-SPECIES A sub-species is present in eastern Asia.

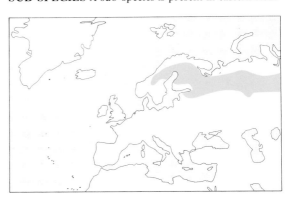

(Below) Male Rustic Bunting (foreground) and female. (Right) Breeding areas (yellow) of the Rustic Bunting

Yellow-browed Bunting
Emberiza chrysophrys

French: BRUANT A SOURCILS
JAUNES
Italian: ZIGOLO DAL
SOPRACCIGLIO GIALLO
Spanish: ESCRIBANO CEJIGUALDO
German: PRACHTAMMER

HABITAT Taiga and woodland.

IDENTIFICATION Length: 16 cm. Best distinguishing feature is the yellow 'eyebrow', not however always clearly visible in the field. The male in summer plumage has black head and cheeks; as well as the yellow eye-stripe, there is a white streak of varying size on the crown. Back and scapulars cinnamon-coloured, streaked dark. Rump and upper-tail coverts red-brown with pale borders. Wings brown, also with pale borders; underparts pale: yellowish-white with streaking on sides of neck and upper breast and on part of flanks and undertail coverts. Female in summer like male, but duller; underparts have greyish tinge.

CALL Song resembles a delicate, soft, musical whistle.

REPRODUCTION Eggs: usually four, greyish with brownish markings. No further information is available.

FOOD Seeds and insects.

DISTRIBUTION AND MOVEMENTS Nests in central eastern Siberia and winters in China. Accidental in Europe.

(Right) Male Yellow-browed
Bunting (foreground) and
female

Little Bunting
Emberiza pusilla

HABITAT Tundra, often close to water. Also cultivated areas.

IDENTIFICATION Length: 13 cm. Smallest bunting of northern Eurasia. Its brown plumage and small size make it inconspicuous; it is easily mistaken for female Reed Bunting, although it is smaller and more brightly coloured. May be distinguished by its chestnut coloured temples and cheeks. Brown upper parts with black streaks; off-white underparts with fine, black streaks. The male differs from the female in having more vivid coloration and its chestnut crown is edged with black.

CALL A 'tsesw' like the Reed Bunting's. Also a distinctive alarm note 'tep-tep'. Song is brief and twittering.

REPRODUCTION From June onwards. Nests on the ground, often hiding the cup-shaped nest in a hollow among vegetation. Eggs: generally four or five, rarely up to seven, pale greenish, grey or pink with sparse blackish markings. Both sexes incubate for eleven or twelve days and both tend the young.

FOOD Mainly seeds.

DISTRIBUTION AND MOVEMENTS Breeds from Scandinavia east to Siberia. Winters in northeast India and eastwards into southern China. Is a vagrant to Britain and Ireland which has been recorded annually in recent years: over-half the records are from Fair Isle.

French: BRUANT NAIN
Italian: ZIGOLO MINORE
Spanish: ESCRIBANO PIGMEO
German: ZWERGAMMER

(Above) Male Little Bunting.
(Left) Breeding areas (yellow)
of the Little Bunting

French: BRUANT ROUX
Italian: ZIGOLO RUTILO
Spanish: ESCRIBANO
HERRUML ROSO
German: ROTELAMMER

Chestnut Bunting
Emberiza rutila

HABITAT Forest edges, marshy ground and fresh water margins.

IDENTIFICATION Length: 14 cm. Slightly smaller than the Yellowhammer. The male is unmistakable because of its uniform, chestnut-coloured head, throat, and upper parts. Remaining underparts yellow; dark streaks on its flanks. Female's head and throat are chestnut-coloured, with brownish-grey borders; back is olive-brown with blackish streaks. Underparts yellowish.

CALL A harsh 'tioioi-tioio-tioi-si-si' which closely resembles the call of the Yellow-breasted Bunting.

REPRODUCTION From late May. The cup-shaped nest is built on low branches and it is lined with rootlets. Eggs: four greyish-white streaked with brown-sepia are laid. The female mainly incubates. Probably double brooded.

FOOD Mainly seeds; also insects in the summer.

DISTRIBUTION AND MOVEMENTS Breeds in eastern Siberia and winters in southeast Asia. Accidental in Europe in France and the Netherlands.

(Below) Male Chestnut Bunting (top) and female (below)

Red-headed Bunting
Emberiza bruniceps

HABITAT Scrub and steppes, and often by fresh-water.

IDENTIFICATION Length: 16 cm. Male's striking plumage is distinctive: chestnut head, throat and upper breast; greenish-yellow nape, mantle and scapulars. Rump greenish: brown upper-tail coverts with yellow margins. A yellow streak often separates the chestnut coloration of the ear-coverts from the throat; the remaining underparts are yellow.

CALL A lively series of harsh, strident notes.

REPRODUCTION From May onwards. It lays three to five greyish-white eggs tinged with blue or greenish coloration with brown or purple markings. Further information is lacking.

FOOD Like that of other buntings.

DISTRIBUTION AND MOVEMENTS Breeds in the southeast USSR and southern Asia. Winters in India. Accidental in France, Britain and the Netherlands although these records may be of individuals which have escaped from captivity. However some Fair Isle autumn records may be genuine.

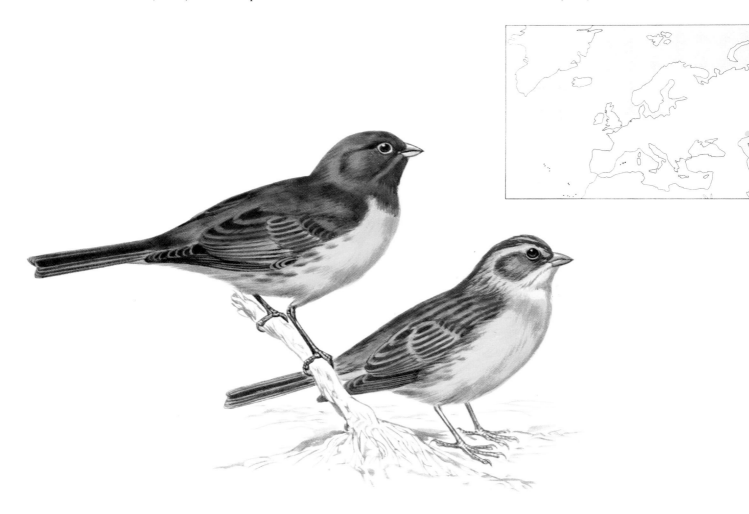

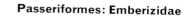

(Left) Male Red-headed Bunting (foreground) and female. (Facing page) Breeding areas (yellow) of the Red-headed Bunting

Black-faced Bunting
Emberiza spodocephala

French: BRUANT MASQUE
Italian: ZIGOLO MASCHERATO
Spanish: ESCRIBANO
    ENMASCARADO
German: MASKENAMMER

(Below) Male Black-faced Bunting (right) and female (left)

HABITAT Forest edges and areas with scattered trees.

IDENTIFICATION Length: 14 cm. A medium sized bunting with inconspicuous coloration: grey head, neck and upper breast with a few black speckles. Rust-brown upper parts with dark streaks on the back; brown wings with olive margins to the feathers. Olive-brown rump and upper-tail coverts. Yellowish underparts; brown bill, often with a pale base to the mandible; light brown legs. The female is a paler, more subdued version of the male: its brownish head is streaked and its underparts are dirty yellowish-white.

CALL Emits a high-pitched buzzing song.

REPRODUCTION Its nest is situated on the ground or slightly above the ground in thick vegetation. In some cases such as the Oriental sub-species *E.s. sordida* there are said to be concentrations of nests, with as little as half a metre between the nests thus creating the appearance of proper colonies. Eggs: usually five pale blue eggs are laid.

FOOD Seeds and insects.

DISTRIBUTION AND MOVEMENTS Breeds from central Siberia east to Japan and south to China, Korea and parts of Manchuria. Winters in southeast Asia. Accidental in Europe in Germany.

SUB-SPECIES Sub-species are present in Asia.

French: BRUANT MELANOCEPHALE
Italian: ZIGOLO TESTANERA
Spanish: ESCRIBANO
CABECINEGRO
German: KAPPENAMMER

Black-headed Bunting
Emberiza melanocephala

HABITAT Scrub and hedgerows: also vineyards, olive groves and gardens.

IDENTIFICATION Length: 16 cm. Slightly larger than the Yellow Bunting. In summer plumage male may be distinguished by its black hood and by the bright yellow coloration extending from its chin and forming a collar at the nape; uniform, reddish-brown mantle; its tail is black-brown without any white. Distinguished from Cirl Bunting by all-black head and from Yellow-breasted by lack of the dark breast band. In the winter its head is brownish, and rufous fringes veil the brown coloration of its upper parts. Females and juveniles are darker, with olive-brown streaks on the upper parts.

CALL Emits a harsh 'zeet'. Song is more melodious than that of most buntings: a 'chit-chit'.

REPRODUCTION From mid-May. Nests in thick cover one to three metres off the ground. Nest is a cup of grass and leaves, lined with hair and finer grasses. Eggs: four or five, rarely six or seven, pale bluish speckled with purple-grey or brownish markings which may be concentrated at the larger end. The female alone incubates for about fourteen days: she alone tends the young.

FOOD Besides seeds, it also consumes insects in the summer.

DISTRIBUTION AND MOVEMENTS Breeds from eastern Italy east across the Balkans to Asia Minor and Iran. Winters in northern and central India. Has been recorded as a vagrant in Britain although some may have been escapes from captivity. Most records of the Black-headed Bunting are from May and June, although they occur in widely scattered localities.

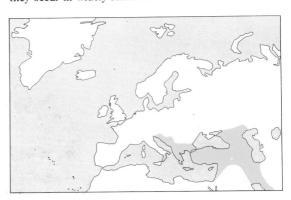

(Below) Male Black-headed Bunting (foreground) and female. (Right) Breeding areas (yellow) of the Black-headed Bunting

(Left) The male Pine Bunting *Emberiza leucocephala* may be identified by the distinctive brown and white pattern on the head. (Below) The Snow Bunting *Plectrophenax nivalis* is a winter visitor to parts of Britain, and breeds locally in northeast Scotland

I. Neufeldt/Ardea

T. Marshall/Ardea

French: BRUANT DES ROSEAUX
Italian: MIGLIARINO DI PALUDE
Spanish: ESCRIBANO PALUSTRE
German: ROHRAMMER

Reed Bunting
Emberiza schoeniclus

(Above) Male Reed Bunting (right) and female (left). (Right) Breeding areas (yellow), wintering areas (magenta) and areas where the Reed Bunting may be seen all year round (orange)

HABITAT Reed beds, marshes, lakes, wet moorland and, more recently, in drier bushy country.

IDENTIFICATION Length: 15 cm. Male: distinctive black head and throat; white moustachial stripe and white half-collar on nape and the sides of neck. Black upper parts with wide rufous borders; grey rump with reddish streaks; off-white underparts with fine brown and black stripes on the flanks. Black flight feathers with reddish-yellow margins; brown median tail feathers with lighter brown margins; the remaining tail feathers are black with brown margins and the outer two pairs are partly white. Deep brown bill, legs and iris. Female: streaky reddish-brown. Juveniles: like females but more heavily streaked on the upper parts. Hops and runs rapidly on the ground. It is sociable and spends the night in communal roosts.

CALL Most frequent call is a 'tseep'. Song is a squeaky and stacatto 'tweek-tweek'.

REPRODUCTION From late April onwards. It nests on the ground or just above it, usually near water. The well hidden nest is a cup of grass and moss with a soft lining of plant fibres and hairs. The female builds the nest and it is situated in a grass or rush clump or in a bush up to a metre off the ground. There are usually four or five eggs per clutch, though there may be six or occasionally seven. They are pinkish-brown, brownish-grey or reddish, with ash grey and deep brown blotches and scribbles and brownish tinges. Incubation is carried out mainly by the female for twelve to fourteen days. The young are fed by both parents and leave the nest

after ten to thirteen days, but stay close by to be fed until they can fly with reasonable confidence. Normally double, sometimes treble brooded.

FOOD Mainly seeds, but also molluscs and insects.

DISTRIBUTION AND MOVEMENTS Breeds through most of Europe, northern and central Asia and eastwards as far as the Kamchatka peninsula and northern Japan. Also south to Asia Minor, Syria, Iran and Turkestan. Also breeds locally in northwest Morocco. It is generally resident, but the northernmost populations are migratory and winter in the south of the breeding range and beyond. In Britain it is a widespread resident breeder and a winter visitor.

SUB-SPECIES *E. s. schoeniclus:* northern Europe south to France and east to central USSR. *E. s. witherbyi:* Portugal, the coasts of Spain and southern France, the Balearic Islands and Sardinia. *E. s. intermedia:* Sicily, Italy, eastern and southeastern Europe. Other sub-species are present throughout the range.

French: BRUANT DE PALLAS
Italian: MIGLIARINO DEL PALLAS
O POLARE
Spanish: ESCRIBANO DE PALLAS
German: PALLAS-ROHRAMMER

Rose-breasted Grosbeak
Pheucticus ludovicianus

HABITAT Bushy areas often close to water: also edges of woods, gardens and parks.

French: GROS-BEC À
POITRINE ROSE
Italian: BECCOGROSSO
PETTOROSEO
Spanish: PICOGORDO
PECHIRROJO
German: ROSENBRUSTKERN-
KNACKER

Pallas's Reed Bunting
Emberiza pallasi

HABITAT Low-lying areas and tundra.

IDENTIFICATION Length: 15 cm. Similar to the Reed Bunting. In summer the male's head, chin, throat and upper breast are black; upper parts and scapulars are almost black with narrow, ochre-coloured borders to the feathers. White collar, moustachial stripe and underparts. Pale grey or off-white rump and upper-tail coverts. Dark wings. The female is very difficult to identify in the field: the narrow collar is grey with very faint brown streaks; brown ear-coverts; otherwise very like the female Reed Bunting.

CALL Its song sounds almost like a cricket—'tsee-tsee-tsee-tsee'—and is reminiscent of the Willow Tit's song.

REPRODUCTION Very little information is available, but it is believed to nest on the ground, laying white eggs with black blotches.

FOOD Probably mainly seeds and insects.

DISTRIBUTION AND MOVEMENTS Breeds in eastern Siberia, Mongolia and possibly parts of Manchuria. It winters further south in Mongolia, China and Korea. Accidental in Denmark and on Fair Isle.

SUB-SPECIES Sub-species are present in Asia.

IDENTIFICATION Length: 20 cm. Male is unmistakable in breeding plumage: black and white with a reddish breast. Remaining underparts white. Black head, throat, neck and back; black wings with two white bars. White rump and black tail with white patches. In flight its white rump and the coloration of its wings are conspicuous. The female is brown with a broad white eyestripe and a pale stripe on the crown. She also has two white wing-bars and the underparts are pale brownish-white with widely spaced dark stripes. In winter the male's head and back become browner so that in some cases it looks like the female, but the coloration of its tail and wings remain unchanged and there is always a trace of pink on its breast. Immatures have striped head and heavy bill: predominantly brown upper parts and whitish underparts. Breast tinged yellow.

CALL Call is a metallic 'keek'.

REPRODUCTION Its nest is made of grass, leaves, etc., and it is usually situated on a low tree or bush. There are between three and five white or very pale blue eggs which are rarely speckled. There are usually two clutches.

FOOD Seeds, berries, fruit and insects.

DISTRIBUTION AND MOVEMENTS It is a North American species and nests from British Columbia to Nova Scotia, and south to the central United States. It winters in Central and South America. It is accidental in Europe, and has occurred a handful of times as a vagrant to Britain and Ireland.

(Above left) Pallas's Reed Bunting. (Above) Female Rose-breasted Grosbeak (top) and male

French: BRUANT LAPON
Italian: ZIGOLO DI LAPPONIA
Spanish: ESCRIBANO LAPÓN
German: SPORNAMMER

Lapland Bunting
Calcarius lapponicus

HABITAT Open ground, tundra and marshy areas. In winter frequents coasts and moors.

IDENTIFICATION Length: 15 cm. Male: black head with bright chestnut nape and neck; yellowish or greyish-brown back, rump and scapulars with black streaks. Cream-coloured supercilium extends to the side of the neck. Brown streaks on the flanks; the remaining underparts are yellowish-white; black flight feathers; chestnut and black wing coverts with white tips. Brown tail feathers with reddish borders, the outer two pairs being partly white or yellowish. Brownish-yellow bill with a black tip; brown legs and iris. In winter it loses the black of the head and more closely resembles a female. Some chestnut remains on nape. Female: like the male in winter plumage, but with less black on its head and very little chestnut on the nape. Juveniles: buff upper parts with broad black streaks; white patches on the ears; yellowish-white underparts with black streaks on the breast and flanks. Pale central crown stripe.

It is a wary species, and crouches down on the ground when danger threatens. It runs quickly, with occasional short hops. Flight is undulating.

CALL Similar to the Skylark's, but with shorter phrases: 'tee-too-ree-tee-too'. Chief call is a flat and trilling 'ticky-tic'.

REPRODUCTION From late May. Nests in depressions in the ground, sometimes in the side of a bank or tussock. The cup-shaped nest is built by the female alone out of grass and moss, and is lined with finer grasses, hair and feathers. There are from two to seven eggs, with the average clutch numbering five or six.

They have blackish streaks and reddish-brown blotches on a background colour ranging from greenish-grey to olive-brown. Incubation takes ten to fourteen days and is carried out by the female, sometimes with the help of the male. The young are fed by both parents and leave the nest after eight to ten days. There is probably only one clutch per year.

FOOD Mainly seeds: also sometimes feeds on insects and larvae.

DISTRIBUTION AND MOVEMENTS Breeding distribution circumpolar in arctic and subarctic areas of northern Europe, north America and northern Asia. It is a migrant and travels south to winter in the central and northeastern United States, the southern USSR and northern China. The wintering range of European breeding populations is not definitively established. In Britain it is a scarce passage and winter visitor, particularly to the east coast.

SUB-SPECIES Sub-species are present in Asia and northern North America.

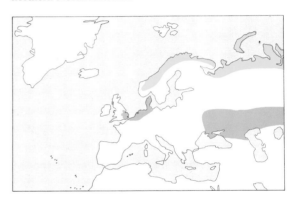

(Below) Male Lapland Bunting (right) and female (left). (Right) Breeding areas (yellow) and wintering areas of the Lapland Bunting (magenta)

Snow Bunting
Plectrophenax nivalis

French: BRUANT DES NEIGES
Italian: ZIGOLO DELLE NEVI
Spanish: ESCRIBANO NIVAL
German: SCHNEEAMMER

HABITAT Tundra, rocky coasts and mountain tops. In winter found mainly on coasts, also inland in hilly regions.

IDENTIFICATION Length: 16 cm. Male has very distinctive black and white coloration in breeding plumage. Pure white upper parts, head and neck: black mantle; black primaries with a white base; secondaries mostly white with black patches at the tips. Black bill and legs; brown iris. Winter plumage more brown: upper parts, head, breast and flanks are reddish-brown. Female: brown-grey upper parts; rufous crown and sides of the head with black flecks. Underparts white with greyish patches on the sides of the breast; brown wing coverts with white and rufous margins; there is less white on the flight and tail feathers. Juveniles: brown wings, rufous head and breast band; creamy-white underparts. In winter it is sociable and forms large flocks on favoured coastlines where the white on the flying wing is described by observers as reminiscent of falling snow flakes.

CALL Song is loud, sweet and somewhat repetitive. Emits a large variety of notes; over twenty have been described. These include a soft 'twee', a mournful 'tew' and a 'chis-eck'.

REPRODUCTION From late May. Nests in crevices among rocks or a hole in a wall or old building. The nest is a cup of dry grass, moss and lichen and is lined with finer grasses, hair, wool and feathers. Eggs: four to six, rarely eight, which are pale blue or green-blue with brown or purple-grey markings. Incubation takes ten to fifteen days and is carried out by the female alone. The young which are tended by both parents, leave the nest after ten to fourteen days.

FOOD Mainly seeds; also molluscs and insects and their larvae.

DISTRIBUTION AND MOVEMENTS Breeding distribution circumpolar in arctic and sub-arctic regions of Eurasia and North America south to continental coasts of the Arctic ocean, Scotland and Scandinavia. Northernmost populations winter south to central Europe and Asia and the northern United States. Other populations are mainly resident. In Britain is confined as a breeding bird, in very small and variable numbers, to a handful of the highest Scottish peaks. It is a winter visitor and passage migrant to the east coast and some inland districts: these individuals originate from Greenland as well as Scandinavia. *P.n. insulae* is said to have occurred at Fair Isle and the Outer Hebrides.

SUB-SPECIES *P.n. nivalis*: through the range except for Iceland and Siberia. *P.n. insulae*: Iceland.

(Above) Male Snow Bunting (foreground) and female. (Below) Breeding areas (yellow), wintering areas (magenta) and areas where the Snow Bunting may be seen all year round (orange)

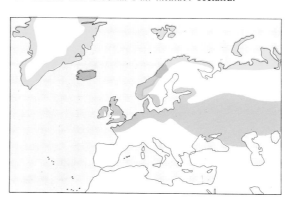

French: BRUANT RENARD
Italian: PASSERELLA ILIACA
Spanish: CHINGOLO ZORRUNO
German: FUCHSAMMER

Fox Sparrow
Passerella iliaca

HABITAT Wooded regions and areas with bushy vegetation. Also sometimes found on cultivated land, parks and gardens.

IDENTIFICATION Length: 18 cm. Resembles a large House Sparrow. Brown or grey-brown on the upper parts: whitish underparts with dark streaks. Tail long, and both tail and rump are a conspicuous rufous colour. The sexes are alike: juveniles resemble adults.

CALL Its call note consists of a loud 'chaka' or 'smack' and a thin, long drawn out 'tseeeep'. Its song is variable but usually melodious and includes variations on the note 'wee-ee'.

REPRODUCTION The nest is a mass of grass, stalks, moss, leaves and small roots, lined with finer plant materials, feathers and hair. It is situated on the ground or in the shelter of a branch and sometimes may be built in a low bush. Three to five eggs are laid with heavy red-brown markings on a pale ground colour. Incubation takes twelve days.

FOOD Seeds and insects.

DISTRIBUTION AND MOVEMENTS Breeds throughout North America; only the northernmost populations migrate to the southern United States and northern Mexico. Accidental in Europe in Ireland, Germany, Italy and Iceland.

SUB-SPECIES There are numerous sub-species in North America.

Song Sparrow
Melospiza melodia

French: BRUANT CHANTEUR
Italian: MELOSPIZA MELODIA
Spanish: CHINGOLITO MELODIO
German: SINGAMMER

HABITAT Open ground with scattered bushes, also marshes and hedgerows.

IDENTIFICATION Length: 18 cm. Coloration varies highly according to geographical location though its basic pattern does not change. The most widespread type of coloration consists of rufous-brown upper parts and white underparts. It has brown streaks (which may be darker or lighter in tone) on its face, the sides of the crown, back, throat, breast and flanks. There are three deeper brown, or sometimes black, markings in the centre of its upper breast which merge into a single, larger marking which is clearly visible even at a distance. A larger sub-species with grey coloration on its head, face and back is found in the Aleutian Islands in Alaska. In the desert regions of southwest North America, the predominant coloration is so pale as to be almost sand-coloured.

CALL Call is a hissing 'sst'. Also emits an alarm note 'kenk'. Emits a wide variety of song notes.

REPRODUCTION The nest is concealed in the grass, on the ground or in low bushes. It is made of stalks, leaves and other plant materials. Incubation is carried out by the female only and takes, on average, about twelve days. This species has two or three clutches per year.

FOOD Seeds and insects.

DISTRIBUTION AND MOVEMENTS Breeds in North America from Alaska and northern Canada south to central Mexico and adjacent islands. The northern-most populations winter south to Florida and Mexico. Accidental in Europe in Britain on only a handful of occasions.

SUB-SPECIES Many sub-species are present in North America.

French: BRUANT ARDOISÉ
Italian: JUNCO COLOR LAVAGNA
Spanish: JUNCO PIZARROSO
German: WINTERAMMER

Slate-coloured Junco
Junco hyemalis

(Above) Male Slate-coloured Junco (left) and female

HABITAT Mixed and coniferous forests; also forest clearings and parkland.

IDENTIFICATION Length: 16 cm. Predominantly grey. Grey-black upper parts, head, neck, throat, upper breast, flanks, wings and central tail feathers: only the belly and outer tail feathers are white. The sexes are similar in coloration, although the females tend to be slightly paler. Pale pinkish bill, brown iris and flesh-coloured legs. Juveniles are a little browner and may have a few streaks on the breast and flanks.

CALL Call note: variations on 'chiirp'. Song consists of a series of slow but very melodious notes—'cheep-cheep'—which sometimes end in a trill or gentle warbling.

REPRODUCTION Nests on the ground in the shelter of a tree trunk or rock. The cup-shaped nest is made of woven grasses and small roots, lined with hair and fine plant materials. There are four to six eggs per clutch with dense red and purple speckles on a pale blue, pale green or pale grey ground colour. Incubation takes eleven to thirteen days. In some cases there are two clutches a year.

FOOD Insects, seeds and grains.

DISTRIBUTION AND MOVEMENTS Breeds in North America from Alaska and northern Canada south to the prairie provinces and Applachian mountains. It winters from southern Canada to Mexico and countries around the Gulf of Mexico. Accidental in Ireland, Italy, Britain and Iceland.

SUB-SPECIES There are several sub-species in North America.

White-throated Sparrow
Zonotrichia albicollis

HABITAT Coniferous forests and bushy areas.

IDENTIFICATION Length: 18 cm. Slightly larger than the House Sparrow. White stripe on the crown, white throat and yellow spot in front of the eye are the most conspicuous features. White supercilium and wing-bars. There is a black stripe on the side of its crown and another black stripe through its eye. Remainder of the head grey. Rufous-chestnut nape, back, rump, wings and tail, with dark streaks on its back. Blackish bill and flesh-coloured legs. The sexes are alike. Juveniles have rufous, black-flecked streaks on the head.

CALL Various calls including a 'cheep' note. Monotonous and repetitive song: 'peeto-tee'.

REPRODUCTION It builds its nest out of grass and leaves on the ground or occasionally on a thick clump of grass. It lays four or five very pale blue or green eggs with dark speckles and markings. The female alone incubates the eggs for twelve days.

FOOD Seeds and insects.

DISTRIBUTION AND MOVEMENTS Breeds in the coniferous forests of Canada and northern United States. Winters south of the breeding range to northern Mexico. Accidental in Europe in Britain and Ireland.

French: TOHI COMMUN
Italian: PIPILO OCCHIROSSI
German: GRUNDRÖTEL

Rufous-sided Towhee
Pipilo erythropthalmus

HABITAT Bushes, forest edges, scrub and parks.

IDENTIFICATION Length: 21 cm. Larger, and in particular longer, than a sparrow. Black head, neck, breast, back, rump, wings and tail; reddish flanks; white markings on the remaining underparts. Female: similar, but with reddish-brown coloration in place of the black. Black bill; brownish legs; the iris ranges from red-brown to off-white depending on the sub-species.

CALL Emits a call 'chee-wink' or 'toh-wee-ee'. The song is highly varied and consists of the repetition of one or two loud notes followed by trills.

REPRODUCTION The nest is constructed of a variety of plant materials and is lined with finer grass. It is usually situated on the ground but is sometimes found slightly off the ground in a bush. Four to six white eggs with reddish-brown speckles are laid. Incubation takes twelve to fourteen days.

FOOD Seeds, insects and berries.

DISTRIBUTION AND MOVEMENTS A North American species which breeds from Canada south to Florida and Guatemala. Winters in the south of the breeding range. Accidental in Europe in Britain.

(Above) Male Rufous-sided Towhee (foreground) and female. (Below) White-throated Sparrow

French: BRUANT À COL BLANC
Italian: ZONOTRICHIA
         COLLOBIANCO
Spanish: CHINGOLO GORGIBLANCO
German: WEISSKEHLAMMER

149

French: TANGARA ROUGE
Italian: TANAGRA ESTIVA
Spanish: CANDELO UNICOLOR
German: SOMMERTANGARE

Summer Tanager
Piranga rubra

(Above) Male Summer Tanager (top) and female

HABITAT Wooded areas: often found by rivers.

IDENTIFICATION Length: 19 cm. Adult male: uniform pinkish-scarlet coloration all the year round. The female has greenish upper parts, golden-yellow underparts, slightly darker wings than its back and no distinctive markings. In winter plumage, juvenile males resemble females but their plumage is more orange. Conical, pointed off-white bill. The only species for which it could be mistaken is the Scarlet Tanager *Piranga olivacea* (which has also occurred as a rare vagrant in Europe), though the latter's wings are invariably darker than the rest of its plumage—the male's wings being black and the female's dark brown. It prefers a solitary existence, hidden among trees.

CALL Distinctive call 'peet-oosk-took'.

REPRODUCTION It builds a nest of stalks, leaves, and bark on branches about three metres above the ground. It lays three to seven pale green or pale blue eggs with brown and pale grey blotches and speckles.

FOOD Insects, other small invertebrates, berries and fruit.

DISTRIBUTION AND MOVEMENT Breeds from California, Nebraska and the central-eastern United States south to central Mexico. Winters from southern Mexico to northern South America. Accidental in Europe in Britain.

FAMILY PARULIDAE: Wood Warblers

The family Parulidae is typical of the New World, and together with other groups such as tanagers, honeycreepers, cardinal-grosbeaks and the American orioles of the family Icteridae constitute the group of American passerines which are distinguished by having nine primaries.

Members of the family Parulidae or wood warblers are small arboreal birds which at their largest are only slight bigger than a House Sparrow. They are compactly built species with rounded wings. The neck is short, the tail of medium length and the bill is usually slender and pointed, although some species have heavy, broad bills. The males, and sometimes both sexes, are often brilliantly coloured, with various combinations of yellow, orange, black and white. Some species have partly red or blue plumage while others have more or less uniform brown, grey or olive coloration. Sexual dimorphism is most common in species distributed in the northernmost areas, and they also show marked seasonal dimorphism. Males and females of the more tropical species, on the other hand, have vivid coloration at all seasons.

This family is the New World ecological counterpart of the Old World families Sylviidae and to an extent Turdidae. Most species feed on insects but many supplement their diets with berries, fruit and other vegetable matter. The habitat is varied: wood warblers are found in coniferous, deciduous or tropical forests, in swamps and marshes, in open ground with scattered bushes or even deserts.

This high level of diversity is also apparent in their nesting habits. The nests may be built on the ground, among bushes, on climbing plants or high up in trees. The Prothonotary Warbler *Protono-*

K. Maslowski/Photo Researchers

(Above) Female American Redstart *Setophaga ruticilla* in winter plumage and (right) male American Redstart. (Preceding page) Yellow Warblers *Dendroica petechia* at the nest

J. S. Dunnint/Photo Researchers

taria citrea nests in tree holes, while various members of the genus *Parula* build their nests among clumps of hanging lichen, moss or similar plants. The eggs are usually white with a varying amount of speckles, although occasionally without any markings. Tropical species lay an average of two to four eggs per clutch and more northerly species lay from three to five, or very occasionally six.

The family is distributed from Alaska and northern Canada to southern parts of South America. It includes about one hundred and thir-

teen species grouped in twenty-six genera. Over half the genera are predominantly North American or West Indian and the remainder are essentially tropical or occur in both North and South America. As a rule, the northern species travel considerable distances on migration.

Twenty-seven species belong to the predominantly North American genus *Dendroica*, five of which are found exclusively in the West Indies. The Yellow Warbler *D. petechia* and its numerous sub-species are among the most widely distributed American species, nesting from North America to

(Left) Black and White Warbler *Mniotilta varia* and (below) female Yellowthroat *Geothlypis trichas*

S. Roberts/Ardea

(Above) The Blackpoll Warbler *Dendroica striata* usually builds its nest among the low branches of young conifers. (Below) World distribution of the family Parulidae and (below right) Wilson's Warbler *Wilsonia pusilla* from North and Central America

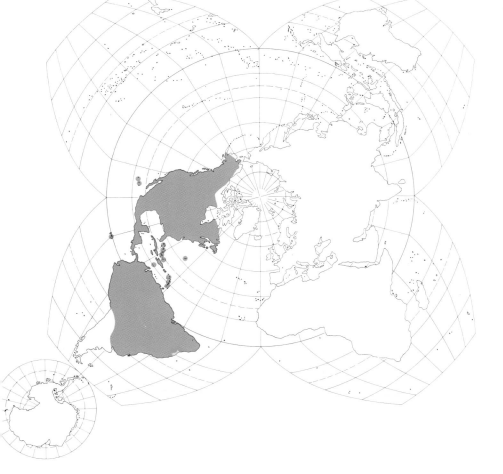

northern parts of South America. Species of the genus *Dendroica* also eat more fruit than any other members of the family, feeding almost entirely on fruit and berries during the winter. Kirtland's Warbler *D. kirtlandii* is one of the rarest birds in the world, nesting only in a limited area of dense coniferous woods of central Michigan. This species also has the unenviable claim to fame of having the smallest distribution area of any non-island species.

Another important genus is *Vermivora* with eleven species. The essentially tropical genus *Basileuterus* (twenty-two species) is found from Mexico to Argentina. The Black and White Warbler *Mniotilta varia* from North America has adapted to a way of life reminiscent of the Tree-creeper.

The American Redstart *Setophaga ruticilla* also belongs to this family. It owes its name to the coloration of its tail which reminded the early North American settlers of the European Redstart. The ten species of the tropical genus *Myioborus* resemble those of the genus *Setophaga*, except that both sexes have brilliantly coloured plumage. Bright red appears in the plumage of three Central American species: the Red-faced Warbler *Cardellina rubrifrons*, the Red Warbler *Ergaticus ruber* and the Pink-headed Warbler *E. versicolor*. Among the species inhabiting swamps and water-meadows are the yellowthroats of the genus *Geothlypis* which have black facial masks of various sizes. The largest species is the Yellow-breasted Chat *Icteria virens*, but its inclusion in this family is not recognized by all authorities because of its resemblance to the family Mimidae.

The three species of the genus *Seiurus* are among the few species with terrestrial habits in this predominantly tree-dwelling group. They build their spherical nests—which bear a slight resemblance to those of the ovenbirds of the family Furnariidae from tropical regions of the New World—on the ground. Confusingly enough one member of this genus—*S. aurocapillus*—is known as the Ovenbird.

J. Simon/Bruce Coleman

Parula Warbler
Parula americana

HABITAT Wooded areas, often close to water.

IDENTIFICATION Length: 11 cm. Upper parts, including the head, are blue-grey with a distinctive olive-yellow triangle on the upper part of its back. Yellow throat, breast and flanks with a conspicuous dark breast band. A pale, incomplete eye-ring is visible from close to. There are two white wing-bars. The remaining underparts are white. Female's coloration is duller, with little or no blue-grey or deep brown on the breast. Juveniles have greyer upper parts and lack the triangle found in adults.

CALL Call is a weak 'cheep' like that of many other members of the family Parulidae. Song: a series of buzzing notes ending in an upward trill.

REPRODUCTION The nest is a small, basket-like structure containing between three and seven white eggs with brown speckles. The nest is suspended among moss and lichens and other parasitic plants growing on trees. The eggs are incubated by the female alone for a fortnight, although some authorities maintain that the male also incubates.

DISTRIBUTION AND MOVEMENTS Breeds in North America from southeast Manitoba and Nova Scotia, south to Texas and Florida. Winters from Mexico and Florida south to Nicaragua and the Antilles. Accidental in Britain.

French: FAUVETTE NOIRE ET
BLANCHE
Italian: PARULA BIANCA E NERA
Spanish: NIOTILTA VARIA
German: KLETTERWALDSÄNGER

Black and White Warbler
Mniotilta varia

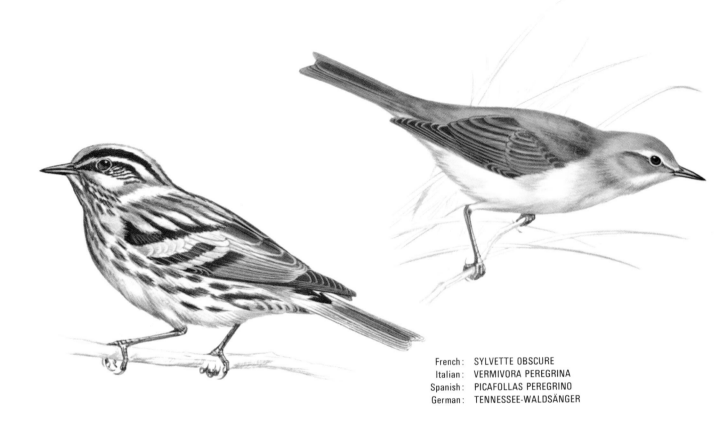

French: SYLVETTE OBSCURE
Italian: VERMIVORA PEREGRINA
Spanish: PICAFOLLAS PEREGRINO
German: TENNESSEE-WALDSÄNGER

(Above) Black and White
Warbler (left) and
Tennessee Warbler (right)

HABITAT Forested areas.

IDENTIFICATION Length: 14 cm. Black and white streaks on the upper parts and the underparts, especially the flanks and breast. A double white wing-bar is conspicuous. The female's plumage is similar, but the streaks are less distinct, particularly on its underparts. She also lacks the male's black throat. Juveniles are patterned brownish-black and dirty white instead of black and white. The Black and White Warbler may be confused with the Blackpoll Warbler *Dendroica striata*, though the latter has a black crown extending to its eye.

CALLS Calls include a weak 'tseep' and a louder 'chink'. Its rather high-pitched song consists of a repetition of the note 'wee-zee-ee'.

REPRODUCTION The carefully lined, cup-shaped nest is constructed out of leaves, grasses, strips of bark, and other plant material. It is usually built on the ground next to a tree trunk or log. Four or five white or creamy-white eggs with brown spots or blotches are laid. Incubation takes about ten days.

FOOD Mainly insects.

DISTRIBUTION AND MOVEMENTS Breeds in North America from Mackenzie eastwards to New-foundland and south as far as Texas. It winters from the southern United States south to Columbia and Venezuela. Accidental in Britain.

Tennessee Warbler
Vermivora peregrina

HABITAT Deciduous and coniferous woods.

IDENTIFICATION Length: 13 cm. Adult male: grey crown and nape, with streaks on its head. Slightly olive-tinged back, rump, wings and tail. White underparts and supercilium. Female's plumage resembles the male's but is more subdued in coloration; underparts are slightly yellowish. Juveniles and adults in winter plumage have browner buff-yellow upper parts and a few spots on the throat, breast and flanks; supercilium a dirty shade of yellow. Black bill and legs; brown iris.

CALL Song consists of high-pitched but not very musical notes which are repeated at variable speeds.

REPRODUCTION The nest is made of moss, lined with grasses, small roots and fur, and is usually situated on the ground, in the shelter of a bush, in a damp area. There are between four and seven white eggs per clutch with brown speckles.

FOOD Mainly insects and other small invertebrates.

DISTRIBUTION AND MOVEMENTS Breeds in North America, particularly in the eastern United States. Winters in Central America and in northern South America. Accidental in Iceland, Greenland and Fair Isle.

Myrtle Warbler
Dendroica coronata

French: FAUVETTE COURONNÉE
Italian: PARULA CORONATA
Spanish: PICAFOLLAS CORONADO
German: KRONWALDSÄNGER

HABITAT Mixed and coniferous forests.

IDENTIFICATION Length: 15 cm. Blue-grey upper parts with dark streaks. Rump, centre of the crown and a patch on the bend of its wing are yellow. White underparts heavily streaked on the breast and flanks; two white wing-bars, white supercilium, and white markings on the outer tail feathers. Black lores, cheeks and ear-coverts. Females and juveniles in winter plumage are dark brown rather than blue-grey; adult males have more subdued plumage in the autumn. Blackish bill and legs. At all ages in all seasons yellow rump is the most reliable field mark.

CALL Call notes: a rather loud 'sheek' and a melodious, weaker 'tseet-tseet'.

REPRODUCTION The cup-shaped nest is made of pine needles and grass and is lined with hair and feathers. It is usually situated at least three metres above the ground and contains between three and five off-white eggs with various dark markings. The markings are concentrated mainly at the blunt end. Incubation takes twelve or thirteen days.

FOOD Insects; also seeds and berries.

DISTRIBUTION AND MOVEMENTS Breeds in North America from northern Alaska east to Labrador and south to the northern United States. Winters from the southern United States to the West Indies, Mexico and Panama. Accidental in Britain on only a few occasions.

(Above) Female Myrtle Warbler (top) and male (bottom)

157

French: FAUVETTE À GORGE NOIRE
Italian: PARULA GOLANERA
Spanish: DENDROICA PAPINEGRA
CARIGUALDA
German: GRÜNER WALDSÄNGER

Black-throated Green Warbler
Dendroica virens

French: SYLVETTE RAYÉE
Italian: PARULA DI BLACKPOLL
German: STREIFEN-WALDSÄNGER

(Above) Black-throated Green Warbler (left) and Blackpoll Warbler (right)

HABITAT Mainly coniferous forests.

IDENTIFICATION Length: 13 cm. Olive green upper parts with dark grey wings and tail. Two pale wing-bars and yellow face. Black throat and upper breast and dark streaks on the flanks; remaining underparts are creamy-white. Female's coloration greyer. Both females and juveniles have yellow coloration which is drabber than that of the males. Black bill and dark brown legs.

CALL Emits a 'seek'. Song consists of a 'see-ee-ee'.

REPRODUCTION The cup-shaped nest is positioned on a branch or between forked branches, from one to twenty-five metres above the ground. It is made of spiders' webs, pieces of bark, grass, moss and lichen, and is lined with hair. There are four or five off-white eggs per clutch.

FOOD Almost exclusively insects.

DISTRIBUTION AND MOVEMENTS Breeds across Canada south to the central and south eastern United States. It winters in Central America. Accidental in Europe in Germany.

SUB-SPECIES Sub-species are present in America.

Blackpoll Warbler
Dendroica striata

HABITAT Coniferous forests.

IDENTIFICATION Length: 14 cm. Smoke-grey nape, back, wings and tail with two white wing-bars and black streaks on the back and rump. White head and underparts with streaked flanks. All black crown. In winter male has olive-coloured upper parts, straw-coloured underparts, streaks on the back and yellowish wing-bars. The female is finely streaked.

CALL Call note: a simple 'seet'. Song consists of a long, shrill succession of notes.

REPRODUCTION The nest is made from a variety of materials and is usually situated in young conifers not far above the ground. The eggs are evenly covered with brown spots and markings on a white, pale green or very pale yellow ground. The female is fed by the male during incubation which takes about eleven days.

FOOD Insects, seeds and berries.

DISTRIBUTION AND MOVEMENTS Breeds across northern North America south to central British Columbia, central Ontario and the northeastern United States. Winters in northern South America. Accidental in Britain on several occasions.

French: SYLVETTE JAUNE
Italian: PARULA GIALLA
German: GOLDWALDSÄNGER

French: FAUVETTE À BAVETTE JAUNE
Italian: PARULA GOLAGIALLA
Spanish: AMARILLITO DE VIRGINIA
German: GELBKEHLCHEN

Yellow Warbler
Dendroica petechia

(Above left) Female Yellow Warbler (top) and male. (Above right) Male Yellowthroat (foreground) and female

HABITAT Forested areas, often by water. Also frequents parks, gardens and suburban areas.

IDENTIFICATION Length: 13 cm. Pale greenish-yellow upper parts; yellow underparts with reddish streaks on the flanks, throat and upper breast. However, there is great variety in the coloration of individuals of this species, depending on their geographical location, particularly in regard to the extent and vividness of yellow coloration. Females usually have olive-brown upper parts, including the crown, and pale yellow underparts. Blackish bill and dark grey legs.

CALL A series of shrill, whistling notes 'seet-seet'.

REPRODUCTION The cup-shaped nest is lined with soft grasses and plant down and is situated in the fork or branches of a tree, not far above ground level. There are between three and six white or very pale green eggs with brown speckles and markings. Incubation takes about eleven days.

FOOD Mainly insects; possibly also berries.

DISTRIBUTION AND MOVEMENTS Breeds in most areas of North America. It winters in South America as far south as Brazil and Peru. Accidental in Europe in Britain.

SUB-SPECIES There are several sub-species in North America.

Yellowthroat
Geothlypis trichas

HABITAT Marshy areas and woodland by water.

IDENTIFICATION Length: 14 cm. Olive-green upper parts with a black mask from the forehead to the sides of the neck, separated from the crown by a narrow white border. Yellow throat and breast, and remaining underparts very pale grey. The female's coloration is similar, but she lacks the black mask and the yellow of the throat extends only to the centre of the upper breast. Black bill and dark, flesh-coloured legs.

CALL Call note: a clear 'chic'. The song is varied and includes a loud, clear 'weechee-weechee'.

REPRODUCTION The fairly large nest is made of small pieces of reed, grass, leaves and moss and is lined with fine plant materials. It is situated on the ground or just above it, and contains between three and six cream-coloured eggs with dark markings. Incubation takes eleven to thirteen days.

FOOD Almost exclusively insects.

DISTRIBUTION AND MOVEMENTS Breeds in most parts of North America and winters in the southern United States, the Bahamas, the West Indies, Mexico and Costa Rica. In Europe it has occurred on only one occasion in Britain.

SUB-SPECIES Sub-species are present in North America.

Northern Water Thrush
Seiurus noveboracensis

American Redstart
Setophaga ruticilla

French: GRIVE DES RUISSEAUX
Italian: SEIURO O TORDO
 D'ACQUA
 SETTENTRIONALE
Spanish: FALSO BISBITA
 CORONADO
German: DROSSELWALDSÄNGER

French: FAUVETTE À QUEUE
 ROUSSE
Italian: CODIROSSO AMERICANO
Spanish: COLIRROJO AMERICANO
German: AMERIKANISCHER
 ROTSCHWANZ

(above) Northern Water Thrush (left). (Above right) Male American Redstart (top) and female

HABITAT Damp, marshy woodland and areas by water.

IDENTIFICATION Length: 16 cm. Somewhat similar to a thrush: olive-brown upper parts, a grey line over its eye, pale grey underparts. Black streaks on the throat, breast, part of its abdomen and flanks. Dark bill and iris; light flesh-coloured legs. In habits more terrestrial than other members of the family.

CALL Call consists of a sharp, explosive 'speek', similar in tone to that of the Grey Wagtail. Its loud song includes a characteristic 'choo-choo-choo' note.

REPRODUCTION The nest is built on the ground in the shelter of a bank or, more frequently, in a hole in a rotting tree. It is made of peat moss, leaves and moss. There are three to six eggs which are usually white with brown speckles and markings.

FOOD Insects (mainly aquatic) which it sometimes catches as it wades in the water: also spiders and occasionally seeds.

DISTRIBUTION AND MOVEMENTS Breeds from Alaska and Canada to the northern United States. Winters mainly in Central America and northern South America. Accidental in Europe in France and Britain.

SUB-SPECIES There are several sub-species in North America.

HABITAT Woodland, gardens and parks.

IDENTIFICATION Length: 14 cm. Black upper parts, face, throat, breast and flanks. Wing-bar, outer tail feathers, sides of the breast and flanks are bright orange. Its remaining underparts are white. In the winter, females and immature birds have pale grey upper parts (darker on the wings and tail), white underparts and yellow coloration where the males are orange. Black bill and legs.

CALL The call is a clear 'seet'. Emits a short, shrill, repetitive whistling song.

REPRODUCTION The nest is situated in the fork of a branch up to seven metres off the ground. It is made of plant down, strips of bark, grasses and small roots woven and bound together with spiders' webs and lined with soft materials. There are two to five cream-coloured eggs with the brownish speckles frequently concentrated at the blunt end. Incubation takes about twelve days.

FOOD Berries and seeds: also insects which it captures in flight like a flycatcher.

DISTRIBUTION AND MOVEMENTS It nests in Alaska and northern Canada south across much of the United States. Winters from southern California and Cuba south through Central America to Ecuador and Brazil. Accidental in Britain, Ireland and France.

FAMILY VIREONIDAE: Vireos

Vireos are small birds, not generally more than fifteen cm long, with fairly uniform coloration. Species of the family generally have greyish or olive-green upper parts and whitish underparts. The sexes are similar, and neither adults nor juveniles have conspicuous streaks or markings. The family Vireonidae contains approximately forty species which are distributed in North, Central and South America.

Vireos inhabit forest and brush: they hunt for insects and small fruit in the foliage. However only a few species, such as the Red-eyed Vireo *Vireo olivaceus*, live in tall trees. Vireos sometimes hang upside down, like tits, and in this position they search under the leaves for insects. Vireos rarely feed on the ground. They resemble some American wood warblers, but may be distinguished by their manner of feeding. While vireos search carefully and deliberately for their insect prey, the wood warblers dart quickly and nervously.

The songs of the species of this family are not varied nor particularly musical: they are, however, frequently insistent and repeated unlike the songs of the warblers of the families Sylviidae and Parulidae which are highly varied, delicate and melodious.

Vireos' nests are cup-shaped structures which are situated in the fork of a bush or tree. The nest is carefully constructed from a variety of plant materials, and is similar in structure to the nest of the Golden Oriole. Three or four eggs are laid in the temperate zones, and only two or three in the tropics. The eggs are generally white or pinkish with some light speckling. The males of many species assist the female with incubation which takes twelve to sixteen days.

The Yellow-throated Vireo *V. flavifrons* is frequently a victim of the parasitic Brown-headed Cowbird *Molothrus ater* of the family Icteridae. Like many of the cuckoos, the Brown-headed Cowbird is a brood parasite and lays its eggs in the nests of other birds and leaves them to hatch and tend its young. The Yellow-throated Vireo, in response to this incursion, will sometimes lay a new lining over the eggs – including the intruder's eggs, and start all over again. She is able to distinguish the eggs of the Brown-headed Cowbird as they do not mimic her own eggs in coloration.

Species of the family are allocated, according to different authorities, to between two and seven genera. Within this family, two distinct groups are clearly apparent: the true North American vireos and the Neotropical species of the genus *Hylophilus* which are known as greenlets. The Red-eyed Vireo is a vagrant to Britain from North and South America. Like other vireos it has a heavier bill than the warblers. Northern species of the family are migratory.

(Above) Red-eyed Vireo *Vireo olivaceus*: like other vireos it has a heavier bill than the warblers. (Below) World distribution of the family Vireonidae

K. Maslowski/Photo Researchers

French: VIRÉO À OEIL ROUGE
Italian: VIREO OCCHIROSSI
Spanish: VIREO OJIRROJO
German: ROTAUGENLAUBWÜRGER

Red-eyed Vireo
Vireo olivaceus

HABITAT Forests with dense undergrowth, wooded parkland and suburban areas with abundant trees.

IDENTIFICATION Length: 15 cm. Dark grey crown and nape and black-bordered white eyestripe are its most conspicuous features. Olive face, back, rump, wings and tail. Bluish-grey bill and legs. Reddish eyes—hence its English name—are also noticeable. The male courts the female by fluttering his half-open wings and singing.

CALL Call note: a mournful 'kwee-ee-ee'. Song is similar to that of the American Robin with a series of short, monotonous, repeated phrases with intermittent pauses.

REPRODUCTION The neat, cup-shaped nest is made of lichen and other material and is situated in a fork or branches of a tree up to eighteen metres above the ground. It is lined with spiders' webs and lichen and is well camouflaged. There are between three and five white eggs marked with a few brown and black speckles. Incubation takes eleven to fourteen days and is carried out by both male and female.

FOOD Mainly insects, spiders and other small invertebrates. It also consumes small quantities of berries and fruit.

DISTRIBUTION AND MOVEMENTS Breeds from British Columbia south to Florida and the coast of the Gulf of Mexico. Migrates across Central America and the West Indies to winter in the Amazon basin in South America. Has occurred as a rare vagrant to Britain and Ireland.

FAMILY ICTERIDAE: Blackbirds and allies

J. R. Simon/Bruce Coleman

The family Icteridae contains eighty-seven species which vary greatly: they may be terrestrial or arboreal, solitary or gregarious. They also vary considerably in size from fifteen to fifty-three centimetres. However, they share a number of common characteristics such as their conical, pointed bills which vary in length, but which are never much longer than their heads. The Icteridae includes some large species such as oropendolas and caciques which have a shield or visor extending from the upper mandible of the bill.

The coloration of members of this family may be entirely black or there may be striking areas of brown, red or yellow plumage. Streaking is rare and is mainly confined to females or to both sexes in meadow and savannah-dwelling species such as those of the genus *Sturnella* and the Bobolink *Dolichonyx oryzivorus*.

Sexual dimorphism is present especially among the northernmost species. The Bobolink which migrates further than any other member of the family, displays marked seasonal dimorphism. In certain species, males and females also differ in size.

Few species have adapted to such a variety of conditions as members of this family. Their social structure and nesting habits are extremely varied. They feed on plants and living creatures in varying proportions depending on the season and on the species concerned, although some species are omnivorous.

Species of the genus *Quiscalus*, which includes the Common Grackle *Q. quiscalus*, have powerful structures inside their upper mandibles and their bills are controlled by special muscles enabling them to crush even the hardest nut shells.

Cowbirds of the genera *Molothrus*, *Tangavius*, and *Scaphidura* are primarily insect-eaters, but also consume seeds on the ground and owe their common name to their habit of hunting for parasites on the backs of cows and other domestic stock. On the other hand, the predominantly arboreal species of the family, such as the American orioles, caciques and oropendolas, feed mainly on fruit or suck nectar from flowers. However, they also eat insects and small invertebrates, particularly when feeding their young.

There is even greater variety in the breeding habits of members of this family. Some members of the family live in flocks and colonies throughout the year while others lead solitary lives. Some species nest in huge colonies, others flock only in winter, while still others nest in isolation. One very interesting feature, although not restricted to this family, is the marked incidence of polygamy, particularly in those species which nest in colonies. Some genera are normally monogamous; others, like the cowbirds, definitely promiscuous. Polygamy may be habitual or occasional, and may sometimes, given the varying ratio of males to females within the colony, produce polyandry.

Furthermore there are some species, for example

(Above) Yellow-headed Blackbird *Xanthocephalus xanthocephalus*. It has occurred as a vagrant in Denmark and Sweden from North America

(Above) Yellow Oriole *Icterus nigrogularis* from Central and South America and (above right) Western Meadowlark *Sturnella neglecta*. (Below) World distribution of the family Icteridae

most of the cowbirds, in which parasitism is the rule. Cowbirds build no nest but lay their eggs in the nests of other species, whose rightful owners act as foster-parents. Parasitism may be specific – that is, the parasite may lay its eggs in the nest of one particular species – or less selective, when the choice of nest to be exploited depends mainly on what is available. The only non-parasitic cowbird, the South American Bay-winged Cowbird *Molothrus badius*, is capable of building its own nest, but seldom does so, preferring to occupy the abandoned nests of other birds or to evict the legitimate owners of newly-built nests. Parasitic members of this family, especially the cowbirds, normally choose species of the same size or smaller. Careful observation of the Brown-headed Cowbird *M. ater* has established that it chooses its victim in advance, surreptitiously watching the nest-building process, sometimes for several days. It refrains from laying its own eggs before the chosen victim does: only when this takes place does the Brown-headed Cowbird lay its egg, removing one egg only of the rightful owner from the nest. As with cuckoos, the cowbird egg hatches before those of its hosts. The Brown-headed Cowbird is, as previously mentioned a brood parasite of the Red-eyed Vireo. However, their parasitism is not as highly developed as that of other groups such as the cuckoos: for example, there is no egg mimicry.

Other species build well-camouflaged nests on the ground or suspend them from marsh reeds; this includes several species of blackbird. The oropendolas of Central and South America construct penduline or basket-shaped nests.

Yellow-headed Blackbird
Xanthocephalus xanthocephalus

French: CAROUGE À TÊTE JAUNE
Italian: ITTERIDE TESTAGIALLA
Spanish: TORDO MEJICANO
        CABECIGUALDO
German: GELBKOPFSTÄRLING

HABITAT Reed-beds, swamps and other damp areas.

IDENTIFICATION Length: 26 cm. Neck, head and upper breast yellow; lores and remaining plumage smoky black, except for some white patches on the wing and an ochre-yellow patch on the under-tail coverts. In autumn and winter the yellow is sprinkled with black. Female and immature males brownish, except for yellow face, throat and upper breast; the rest of the breast is brown streaked with white. Bill and legs black.

CALL The call note is a low 'cra-a-ack'. The song, which varies considerably between individuals, is a series of cacophonous, liquid and clicking notes.

REPRODUCTION Nesting is colonial, with thirty or so nests in a few square yards among reeds. The nest is cup-shaped, attached to the reed-stems and lined with grasses, at a height of a few centimetres to a metre above the water. It contains three to five eggs, grey or pale green, with varying darker markings.

FOOD Seeds and insects.

DISTRIBUTION AND MOVEMENTS Breeds mainly in the central plains of North America from southwest Canada to northern Mexico. Winters in the southwestern United States as far as southern Mexico. Accidental in Europe in Denmark and Sweden.

(Above) Male Yellow-headed Blackbird (top) and female

French: GOGLU
Italian: BOBOLINK
Spanish: CHARLATÁN
German: REISSTARLING

French: TROUPIALE DE
BALTIMORE
Italian: ITTERO DI BALTIMORA
Spanish: TURPIAL DE BALTIMORE
German: BALTIMORE-TRUPIAL

Bobolink
Dolichonyx oryzivorus

Baltimore Oriole
Icterus galbula

(Above) Male Bobolink (top)
and female. (Above right)
Male Baltimore Oriole (top)
and female

HABITAT Cultivated areas: also water-meadows and damp areas.

IDENTIFICATION Length: 20 cm. A small, black, semi-glossy bird, with white lower back and rump and white stripe from back to shoulder. Nape ochre-yellow. Female light buff-brown with wide dark brown streak above eye and a narrower stripe through eye; streaking and spotting on back, on rump and on flanks brown; wings and tail brown with pale borders to the feathers. Tail feathers pointed. In winter plumage the male, though similar to the female, appears darker. Bill short and conical.

CALL The call-note of the male is a repeated 'chow', that of the female a rapid 'queek'. In flight also emits a 'pink' and a 'cheeteeta'. The song is a succession of loud, clear notes of varying pitch.

REPRODUCTION Nests on the ground among grasses: lays four to seven eggs, pale grey and light buff, in a hollow coarsely lined with stems.

FOOD Seeds and insects.

DISTRIBUTION AND MOVEMENTS Breeds from southern Canada south into the northern-central United States from California to New Jersey. Winters in South America in Bolivia, Brazil and Argentina. Rare vagrant on several occasions to Britain.

HABITAT Open woodland: also frequents wooded suburban areas.

IDENTIFICATION Length: 21 cm. Black head, upper breast, upper two-thirds of back, wings and tail. White wing-bar and white fringes to secondaries; remaining plumage, including shoulder-patches and all but the base of outer tail feathers, clear bright orange. Female olive with spotting on the back. Tail light brown, underparts also pale, but the plumage of the female varies considerably. Juveniles have upper parts similar to females, much paler orange underparts and a hint of black on throat and upper breast. In winter plumage adult males resemble females.

CALL Call of the Baltimore Oriole is a characteristic 'uutlee'.

REPRODUCTION There are four to six eggs, ground colour pale grey, with dark spotting and marking of varying intensity; they are incubated for at least twelve days.

FOOD Insects and fruits.

DISTRIBUTION AND MOVEMENTS Breeds east of the Rocky Mountains, from Canada south to the states bordering Gulf of Mexico. Winters from southern Mexico to Colombia. Accidental in Europe in Britain and Iceland.

FRINGILLIDAE: Finches

R. Vaughan/Ardea

The problem of classifying many of the small to medium-sized passerines with conical bills is a controversial one, as indeed has been noted in reference to the family Emberizidae. Some authorities have combined the family Emberizidae with the Fringillidae, while others have included chaffinches, goldfinches and like in the family Emberizidae. In this encyclopedia a widely accepted classification is used and the family Fringillidae is treated as consisting of the sub-families Fringillinae or chaffinches or Old World seedeaters and Carduelinae or goldfinches and allies. There are one hundred and twenty-five species in the family, all but three belonging to the sub-family Carduelinae.

Members of the family Fringillidae are basically seedeaters and arboreal in habit. They vary a good deal in coloration and some are quite vividly coloured. Sexual dimorphism may be more or less marked, as may seasonal changes of plumage. The bill, adapted for crushing hard seeds or extracting them from their shells, is robust, generally swollen at the base and more or less conical in shape. However, it varies considerably in size depending on the genus. The cardueline finches of the genus *Carduelis* have the most slender bills which are also very pointed: the hawfinches and grosbeaks of the genera *Coccothraustes*, *Mycerobas*, *Eophona* and *Hesperiphona* have a huge, almost pyramidal bill, which recalls that of a parrot. In this large bill the muscles, and in particular the muscles of the mandible, are well developed. The muscles of the head and neck are also generally stronger, and the force exerted by, for example, the Hawfinch *Coccothraustes coccothraustes*, is enough to crush an olive stone.

(Above) Brambling *Fringilla montifringilla*: the orange-buff breast and shoulders are distinctive. However the best field mark of the Brambling is the white rump which is conspicuous as it flies away

167

The most specialised bill of all in this family, however, is that of the crossbills of the genus *Loxia*, in which the tips of the mandibles cross over one another at an angle, producing an instrument particularly well adapted for extracting the seeds from the cones of pines and other conifers. This structure gives the crossbills a unique, and almost deformed appearance, and allows them, by making seeds in cones available, to exploit a food source which is not available to many other species.

The reproductive behaviour of the species of the family, in contrast with the striking differences in their feeding habits, is relatively uniform. The cup-shaped nest is carefully constructed from plant

material interwoven with feathers, hair, spiders' webs and so forth. The exterior often resembles the bark of trees so closely, with its cladding of mosses and lichens, that it is almost invisible from below. Although usually solitary nesters, some finches, especially some of the cardueline finches, nest in loose colonies in which several nests are found in a relatively limited area. In such cases territorial behaviour is reduced or at least circumscribed to the immediate vicinity of the nest, which may be on the ground, but is more often built in trees, sometimes at a considerable height. However the nest may also be situated among rocks.

The ground colour of the eggs is pale blue or bluish with varying degrees of brown or reddish markings. In a few cases the eggs may be tinged greenish, brownish or olive, as with the Chaffinch *Fringilla coelebs* and Brambling *F. montifringilla*. The average number of eggs in a clutch is five, but this may vary, even within a particular species, depending on the latitude. The different species of crossbills lay three or four eggs; they also have the most irregular nesting habits. The incubation period is from ten to fourteen days, but accurate information is not available even for some such common species as the Citril Finch *Serinus citrinella* or the White-winged Crossbill (sometimes called the Two-barred Crossbill) *Loxia leucoptera*.

The distribution of this family extends over the greater part of the temperate regions of Eurasia, Africa and the Americas, although some species breed in arctic or sub-arctic regions or else in the tropics or sub-tropics. The highest-breeding passerine is possibly the Red-breasted Rosefinch *Carpodacus puniceus*, which nests up to 6,000 metres above sea level in the mountains of central Asia. The origins of the family are undoubtedly in the Old World; only at a later date did they 'invade' the Americas where a single genus, *Spinus* (included

by some authorities in *Carduelis*), has undergone adaptive radiation.

The sub-family Fringillinae contains three species, which differ from the cardueline finches in some anatomical details, such as having no crop, and in some of their habits. These three species are the Eurasian Chaffinch *Fringilla coelebs* with several well-differentiated sub-species, especially in the Canary Islands. The Canary Island Chaffinch *Fringilla teydea* which, although it closely resembles some races of the Chaffinch, does not hybridise with them and is therefore considered to be a separate species. The third and last species is the Brambling *F. montifringilla* a highly migratory

(Right) Siskin *Carduelis spinus*: the black chin and crown distinguishes the male from other yellow-green finches. (Below) Female Serin *Serinus serinus*. (Facing page, far left) Chaffinch *Fringilla coelebs*. (Facing page, top left) Crossbill *Loxia curvirostra*. (centre left) Greenfinch *Carduelis chloris* and (bottom left) Pine Grosbeak *Pinicola enucleator*

species found in the north of Europe and Asia, and is considered the northern equivalent of the Chaffinch.

The sub-family Carduelinae, or goldfinches and allies contains many genera. In species of the genus *Serinus*, the general coloration is yellowish or light green, greyish or almost white with more or less conspicuous streaking and in some cases black

areas. The species of this genus occur in the Ethiopian region, in Madeira, the Canaries and the Azores, in the Mediterranean region and in the southern Palearctic. Originating from the Canaries is the Canary *Serinus canaria*, from which the numerous varieties of domestic canary are descended. Other species in this genus are the Serin *S. serinus* and the Cape Siskin *S. totta*

About thirty species are classed in the genera *Carduelis* and *Acanthis*. These include the true goldfinches, greenfinches, siskins, redpolls and linnets. The plumage is often streaked and the coloration varies; sexual dimorphism is reduced. Species of the genus *Leucosticte* are birds of high mountain: the plumage is dark, even almost black, contrasting with deep pink and silver markings. The genus includes the Rosy Finch *L. arctoa* which is found in Eurasia and North America. The four species of the genus *Rhodopechys* are found in plains, arid land and even desert areas in North Africa and Asia.

The mainly Asiatic genus *Carpodacus* comprising the rosefinches numbers about twenty species. Species of this genus include the Common Rosefinch or Scarlet Grosbeak *C. erythrinus* which is the most common and widespread rosefinch of Europe. Other species include the Sinai Rosefinch *C. synoicus* of the Middle East and the Great Rosefinch *C. robicilla*, a large and red species, which inhabits the Caucasus.

The bullfinches belong to the genus *Pyrrhula*. There are six species, of which the most common is the European Bullfinch *P. pyrrhula*.

(Above) Goldfinch *Carduelis carduelis* with young at the nest: the red face and yellow wing-bars make it easily identifiable (Left) World distribution of the family

Chaffinch
Fringilla coelebs

HABITAT Hedges, woodland gardens and cultivated land: frequent in town suburbs.

IDENTIFICATION Length: 15 cm. Forehead black, crown and neck slate-blue, back and scapulars chestnut-brown. Lower back and rump yellowish-green; sides of head and of neck, throat and breast pink. Belly and under-tail coverts whitish; flight-feathers black, partly white at base. White shoulder patch, white wing-bar and white in tail combined with slate-blue head and nape make the male easily identifiable. However coloration varies according to the sub-species. Female: upper parts yellowish-brown; sides of head and underparts pale grey-brown, tinged whitish on chin, throat and belly; wings and tail browner; wing coverts less white. White shoulder patch is conspicuous and helps to distinguish the female from other brown finches. Juveniles: as female, with whitish patch on nape, brownish-green rump.
Undulating and bounding flight, characteristic of the finches. Often seen in company with other finches.

CALL Most common call is a 'pink-pink'. In flight emits a subdued 'tseep'. The song consists of a vigorous and rattling succession of notes, ending with a 'tick'. Both call and song vary considerably according to the sub-species.

REPRODUCTION From April onwards. The male chooses the nesting site but leaves the actual building of the nest to the female. It is a deep cup of lichens, grass, roots and feathers lined with plant down and roots. The nest is usually situated in a fork of a tree from three to twelve metres above the ground. The female lays four or five eggs, greenish or light blue with purplish, red-brown mottling or dark markings. Incubation is carried out almost entirely by the female and lasts for ten to fourteen days; the young leave the nest after another thirteen or fourteen days. Usually double brooded.

FOOD Mainly seeds: also consumes fruit and sometimes invertebrates.

DISTRIBUTION AND MOVEMENTS Breeds virtually throughout Europe and western Asia east to Siberia. Also breeds south to northern Africa, the Middle East and Iran. Northern populations are migratory, wintering in the south of the breeding range and beyond. In Britain and Ireland it is an abundant and widespread resident breeder in all counties except Shetland. The sub-species *F.c. gengleri* is resident and endemic to Britain and Ireland. Also occurs as a winter and passage visitor from northern Europe.

SUB-SPECIES *F.c. coelebs:* continental Europe, Asia Minor and the Near East. *F.c. gengleri:* Britain and Ireland. *F.c. schiebeli:* Crete. *F.c. solomkoi:* Crimea and Caucasus. Other sub-species are present in Asia and Africa.

French: PINSON DES ARBRES
Italian: FRINGUELLO
Spanish: PINZÓN VULGAR
German: BUCHFINK

(Below) Male Chaffinch (left) and female. (Left) Breeding areas (yellow), wintering areas (magenta), areas where the Chaffinch may be seen all year round (orange) and on passage (pink)

French: PINSON DU NORD
Italian: PEPPOLA
Spanish: PINZÓN REAL
German: BERGFINK

Brambling
Fringilla montifringilla

(Above) Male Brambling (foreground) and female. (Right) Breeding areas (yellow), wintering areas (magenta) and areas where the Brambling may be seen on passage (pink)

HABITAT Birch woods and scrub in taiga. In winter frequents more open country.

IDENTIFICATION Length: 15 cm. Crown, sides of head and of neck and upper back brilliant black, bordered rufous. Lower back and rump white; the white rump is the most conspicuous field mark of this species. Under-tail coverts bordered rufous; throat and breast orange-red. Flanks spotted black; belly white; flight-feathers black fringed white and yellowish. Bill yellow; legs brownish-pink; iris brown. In spring the black becomes brighter and the orange is yellower. Female: duller in coloration with the black replaced by dark brown; sides of head greyer; orange paler and less extensive. Juveniles similar to female but with yellowish-white rump and belly. Often seen together with Chaffinches.

CALL The typical call is a harsh, stacatto 'tswek'. Flight-note is a 'chuc-chuc'. The song is a grating, monotonous, repeated 'dzwee', interspersed with a few brief, twittering notes.

REPRODUCTION From mid-May. Breeds in coni-ferous and birch forests, nesting in trees at a height of two to eight metres. Eggs: six or seven light blue tinged with pink with small line scribblings and blotching. The female alone incubates for eleven or twelve days. The young are fed by both parents, and leave the nest after about twelve days.

FOOD Seeds, fruit and insects.

DISTRIBUTION AND MOVEMENTS Breeds in northern Eurasia from Scandinavia east to Kamchatka. Winters south to northwest Africa, the Mediterranean islands, Iraq and northern India. Occurs in Britain and Ireland as a passage and winter visitor in varying numbers and is widespread except in northern Scotland and Ireland where it occurs only irregularly. Bred once in Scotland in 1920 and is reported to have bred there more recently but these records are unconfirmed.

Citril Finch
Serinus citrinella

French: VENTURON MONTAGNARD
Italian: VENTURONE
Spanish: VERDERÓN SERRANO
German: ZITRONENGIRLITZ

HABITAT Mountainous areas with scattered conifers: also open rocky ground.

IDENTIFICATION Length: 12 cm. Forehead yellowish-green; top of head, nape and sides of neck bluish-grey. Mantle and scapulars olive-green, lightly streaked dark brown; rump greenish-yellow. Underparts yellowish-green, tinged yellow on belly and under-tail coverts. Flanks brownish; grey tinge on breast. Flight-feathers brown-black, edged green and whitish. Colour of bill varies between yellowish-brown and grey, lower mandible paler. Legs vary from blackish-grey to yellowish-pink.

Female duller and less streaked. Juveniles have upper parts rufous-grey-brown, streaked brown-black. Underparts vary from brownish-grey to yellowish, with dark streaking; belly and under-tail coverts pale yellow. Like other finches, flight of the Citril Finch is noticeably dancing and bounding.

CALL A short, slightly nasal call often repeated in flight: 'tket'. Song resembles the Siskin's, but has more harsh notes.

REPRODUCTION From April onwards. Nests in a tree from two to four metres off the ground. The female builds the nest which is a cup of grasses, roots and lichen lined with fine materials such as plant down and feathers.

Eggs: four or five, rarely three, greenish-blue, speckled and spotted brown-black and red-brown.

FOOD Chiefly seeds; also small insects.

DISTRIBUTION AND MOVEMENTS Breeds in mountainous, forested areas of southern Europe from Spain east to Austria and southern Germany. Resident, but wanders to lower levels in winter. Accidental in Britain in Norfolk on one occasion.

SUB-SPECIES *S.c. corsicana*: Corsica and Sardinia.

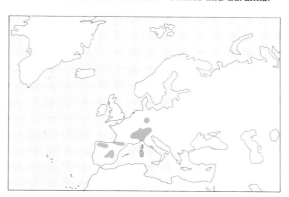

(Below) Citril Finch (right) and the sub-species *S.c. corsicana*. (Left) Areas where the Citril Finch may be seen all year round (orange)

French: SERIN À FRONT ROUGE
Italian: VERZELLINO TESTAROSSA
German: ROTSTIRNGIRLITZ

Red-fronted Serin
Serinus pusillus

HABITAT Scrubby and grassy hillsides: occasionally forested or rocky areas.

IDENTIFICATION Length: 13 cm. One of the most distinctive finches present in Europe. Adult male has black head, neck and upper breast except for forehead and crown which are a vivid and conspicuous red. Back and scapulars brown-black with ochre borders to the feathers; upper-tail coverts orange-red. Wing-coverts brown-black, fringed bright yellow; white patch on tips of primaries. Tail and flight feathers black, edged yellowish, remaining underparts yellow with black centres to the feathers. Bill and legs black. Female has less red on head.

CALL A trilling, descending 'tserup'. Song resembles the Goldfinch's.

REPRODUCTION From May. Nests on the ground in low cover: also on rock ledges. Nest is a bulky cup of grasses and stems, lined with wool, hair and feathers. The female alone builds the nest. Eggs: usually five or six, occasionally four to seven, pale blue with a varying amount of reddish-brown or lilac markings. The female alone incubates for twelve or thirteen days, although both sexes tend the young.

FOOD Chiefly seeds.

DISTRIBUTION AND MOVEMENTS Breeds from Turkey and the Middle East north to the Caspian and Caucasus and east to Tibet.

(Above) Male Red-fronted Serin (top) and female. (Right) Wintering areas (magenta) and areas where the Red-fronted Serin may be seen all year round (orange)

174

Serin
Serinus serinus

HABITAT Woodland edges, orchards, town parks and gardens. Commonly seen in suburban areas.

IDENTIFICATION Length: 11 cm. Smallest of the widespread European finches. Forehead and nape greenish-yellow striped brown-black, as is yellow back. The rump is conspicuously greenish-yellow; is striped brown and tinged rufous on flanks; belly whitish; flight and tail feathers brown-black edged greenish; wing coverts lightly tipped pale. Bill brown, paler on lower mandible; legs deep brown; iris brown-black. Female as male, but less yellow and more striped on breast and head; rump paler. Juveniles: upper parts rufous, striped deep brown; rump pale, streaked; underparts rufous striped brown, except for belly and chin.

CALL Emits a 'ticht'. Song is jingling and resembles the Corn Bunting's.

REPRODUCTION From March onwards. Nest is situated in a bush or tree one to five metres off the ground in a fork or on the tip of a branch. The female builds the cup-shaped nest of roots, moss and lichens, lined with hair, feathers and plant down. Eggs: usually four, sometimes three or five, pale blue or sometimes light green, speckled and marked with purplish or red brown. The female incubates, although the male is said to sometimes assist, for thirteen days. Both tend the young.

FOOD Seeds.

DISTRIBUTION AND MOVEMENTS Breeds in western and central Europe although gradually extending its range northwards, from Iberia east to the Ukraine and north to southern Sweden. Also breeds in northern Africa and Asia Minor. In Britain became a more frequent vagrant in the 1960's and this resulted in a pair breeding for the first time in 1967. However the expected subsequent colonisation has not materialised.

French: SERIN CINI
Italian: VERZELLINO
Spanish: VERDECILLO
German: GIRLITZ

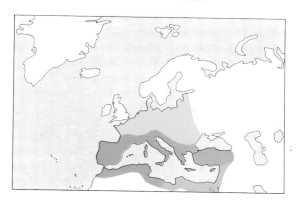

(Below) Male Serin (right) and female. (Left) Breeding areas (yellow), wintering areas (magenta) and areas where the Serin may be seen All year round (orange)

(Above) Hawfinch *Coccothraustes coccothraustes* and (above right) Goldfinch *Carduelis carduelis*. The Hawfinch's large bill is distinctive while the Goldfinch's red face makes it easily identifiable. (Right) The Redpoll sub-species *Acanthis flammea cabaret* which breeds in Britain, Ireland and the Alps

B. Bevan/Ardea

L. Lee Rue/Bruce Coleman

(Above) Male and female
Bullfinches *Pyrrhula pyrrhula*
at the nest. (Left) Female
Pine Grosbeak *Pinicola
enucleator*

French: CHARDONNERET
Italian: CARDELLINO
Spanish: JILGUERO
German: STIEGLITZ

Goldfinch
Carduelis carduelis

HABITAT Forest edges and areas with scattered trees and bushes, including orchards, gardens and parks. Also frequents farmland.

IDENTIFICATION Length: 12 cm. An easily recognised species due to conspicuous red face and yellow wingbars. Both male and female have a black line around base of bill. Rear part of crown and nape black; sides of nape, ear coverts and lower throat white. Upper parts buff-brown, rump white. Underparts brown, often with some yellow markings on sides of breast; centre of breast white; wing coverts black and bright yellow. Juveniles: lack red and upper parts greyish-brown; underparts whitish.

During courtship the male sways his body from side to side and holds the wings out spread, vibrating them rapidly. Flight is notably dancing.

CALL Call is a harsh 'geez'. Song is a twinkling, liquid 'tsweet-witt-witt'.

REPRODUCTION From late April onwards. Nest is built in a tree at the end of branches, occasionally also in hedgerows or shrubs. It is constructed by the female, occasionally assisted by male, of roots, grasses, moss, lichens and with wool. Eggs: three to seven, bluish-white with some red-brown spotting and streaking, sometimes very dark. The female, fed by the male, incubates for twelve or thirteen days. The young leave the nest after thirteen or fourteen days. Normally two broods, sometimes three.

(Right) Breeding areas (yellow), wintering areas (magenta), areas where the Goldfinch may be seen all year round (orange) and on passage (pink)

FOOD Chiefly seeds, particularly of thistles; also insects and larvae.

DISTRIBUTION AND MOVEMENTS Breeds from southern Scandinavia, Britain, Ireland and Iberia east through Eurasia to Siberia. Also breeds in northwest Africa, the Mediterranean islands and Asia east to northern India. Partially migratory: northern populations winter in southern parts of the breeding range. In Britain and Ireland it is a fairly numerous and widely distributed resident and migrant breeder, although sparse in the north.

SUB-SPECIES *C.c. carduelis:* most of Europe. *C.c. britannica:* Britain and Ireland. *C.c. parva:* southern France, Iberian peninsula, Balearic Islands, northern Africa, Canary Islands, Madeira, Azores. *C.c. tschusii:* Corsica, Sardinia and Sicily. *C.c. balcanica:* the Balkan peninsula. Other sub-species are present in the Near East and Asia.

Greenfinch
Carduelis chloris

French: VERDIER
Italian: VERDONE
Spanish: VERDERÓN COMÚN
German: GRÜNFINK

HABITAT Gardens, wooded countryside, parks and orchards.

IDENTIFICATION Length: 14 cm. Largest yellow-green finch present in Europe. Upper parts brownish-green, yellower on rump; brownish moustachial streak. Ear coverts, sides of neck and flanks brownish-green. Underparts yellowish-green tinged from grey to greenish-yellow on belly; lower belly and under-tail coverts greyish. Flight feathers brown-black fringed grey and yellow-green; outer borders of primaries yellow. Bill pale pink with brown tip; legs pale flesh-colour. In summer the green and yellow are brighter.

Female has browner upper parts and greyer under-parts; there is less yellow on primaries and tail feathers. Juveniles: as female, but upper parts clearly streaked brown; rump brown, streaked; underparts more yellow-ish-grey, streaked brown; wing coverts brown. Flight of the Greenfinch is undulating. Does not venture far from trees. Male seeks to attract female by hopping, with one wing raised, head erect, mouth open and tail spread.

CALL The main call is a 'cheep' or 'cheek', especially in flight. Song is a series of twittering notes ending in a nasal 'scaar'.

REPRODUCTION From late April. Nests in hedge-rows, bushes and small trees, in a fork of branches or against the trunk. The nest is bulky cup of grasses, plant stems and moss, lined with plant fibres, roots and feathers. The female lays four to six eggs, light bluish-white with brownish-red spots and blotches or purplish markings. The female alone incubates for about twelve to fourteen days. The young are fed by both adults and remain in the nest for thirteen to sixteen days. Two broods, rarely three.

FOOD Chiefly seeds: also insects.

DISTRIBUTION AND MOVEMENTS Breeds from Scandinavia, Britain, Ireland and Iberia east across Eurasia to the Urals and Iran. Also breeds in northwest Africa and the Middle East. Introduced to Australia and New Zealand. Generally resident, but more northerly populations move in winter to central and western Europe and to the Mediterranean. In Britain and Ireland is a numerous and widespread breeding bird and winter visitor in varying numbers.

SUB-SPECIES *C.c. aurantiiventris:* southern Europe and northwest Africa. *C.c. turkestanicus:* Crimea, Caucasus and western Asia.

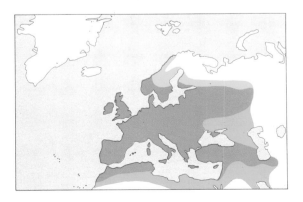

(Above) Female Greenfinch (top) and male. (Left) Breeding areas (yellow), wintering areas (magenta) and areas where the Greenfinch may be seen all year round (orange)

179

French: TARIN DES AULNES
Italian: LUCHERINO
Spanish: LÚGANO
German: ERLENZEISIG

Siskin
Carduelis spinus

HABITAT Coniferous or mixed woods.

IDENTIFICATION Length: 12 cm. Male: crown black (tipped grey in autumn). Chin also black, and the black chin and crown distinguish the Siskin from all other yellow-green finches. Rump, eyestripe, neck and breast yellowish. Belly grey-white, yellow wing-bar. Outer tail feathers black and yellow. Bill brownish; legs grey or brown; iris brown-black. Female is grey with no black on the head, and whitish, streaked underparts. Distinguished from Serin at all ages by the yellow patches at the base of the tail.

CALL Emits a 'tsuu'. Song is a sweet, musical twittering.

REPRODUCTION From April onwards. Nests high up in trees, usually near the end of a branch. Nest is a small compact cup of twigs, grass and moss, and is lined with hair, wool, feathers and plant down. Eggs: three to five, rarely two or six, light blue with rufous, lilac or pinkish spotting. The female incubates for eleven to fourteen days. Both tend the young which leave the nest after thirteen to fifteen days.

FOOD Chiefly seeds, but comes into gardens to feed on peanuts in February and March.

DISTRIBUTION AND MOVEMENTS Breeds in western Eurasia from Scandinavia, Britain and Ireland east to Siberia. Also breeds southwards, although discontinuously, to the Pyrenees, Alps and northern Iran: also in Japan. Breeds outside the normal range following eruptions. Migratory, and winters in the Mediterranean basin, southwest Asia and southern China. In Britain it is a resident breeder which is widely distributed in the Scottish Highlands but more locally elsewhere in Scotland: also breeds locally over much of Ireland. It has now begun to breed fairly regularly in England and Wales. British and Irish birds are probably resident, although some may move south in winter. Also a winter visitor from the continent.

(Above) Male Siskin (left) and female. (Right) Breeding areas (yellow), wintering areas (magenta) and areas where the Siskin may be seen all year round (orange)

Redpoll
Acanthis flammea

French: SIZERIN FLAMMÉ
Italian: ORGANETTO
Spanish: PARDILLO SIZERÍN
German: BIRKENZEISIG

HABITAT Northern forests, especially birch and conifer forests; also regions with alder, willow and juniper. May be observed in large gardens and on watersides in winter, often in company with Siskins and Goldfinches.

IDENTIFICATION Length: 13 cm. Forehead and crown crimson. Conspicuous black chin distinguishes it from the Linnet and Twite. Upper parts grey-brown with or without buff or whitish borders. Pink breast and rump with little or no dark streaking are distinctive. Under-tail coverts brown fringed yellowish; faint pale eyestripe, pinkish cheeks; flanks pale pink and yellowish streaked black. Belly white; flight and tail feathers brown, bordered whitish or pink; wing coverts brown; bill yellow, tipped deep brown; legs brown. Flight agile and undulating; gregarious.

CALL In flight the call-note is a characteristic high-pitched and metallic 'church-uch', and a rapid, sustained twittering. When alarmed it utters an anxious 'tsweet'. The song is a series of short trills which is based on the call-note.

REPRODUCTION From late April. Nests in a bush or tree, sometimes high in a tree but at other times near the ground. Pairs may nest near each other in loose association. The nest is an untidy cup of dry twigs, small roots and grass. It is lined with plant down, feathers and hair. Five or six eggs are laid, occasionally three to seven, pale blue with pale pink or lilac spotting and streaking. The female alone incubates for ten to thirteen days; the young are fed by both parents. They leave the nest after eleven to fourteen days.

FOOD Mainly seeds: also insects.

DISTRIBUTION AND MOVEMENTS Breeds from Greenland, Iceland, Scandinavia, Britain and Ireland east across the whole of northern Eurasia. Also breeds in northern North America as far south as Newfoundland and southern Canada. Winters in the south of the breeding range and beyond to south-central Europe, Japan and the northern United States. Fairly numerous and widely distributed breeder over most of Britain and Ireland with most birds migrating southwards to the continent in the winter. Their place is taken by an influx of northern birds which winter mainly on the east coast of Britain, although locally elsewhere in highly variable numbers.

SUB-SPECIES *A.f. flammea*: northern Eurasia and North America. *A.f. islandica*: Iceland. *A.f. cabaret*: Britain, Ireland and the Alps. *A.f. rostrata*: Greenland.

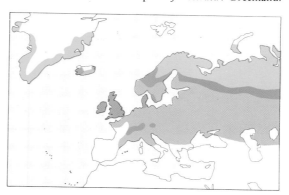

(Below) Redpoll (left) and the sub-species *A.f. cabaret* (right). (Left) Breeding areas (yellow), wintering areas (magenta) and areas where the Redpoll may be seen all year round (orange)

French: SIZERIN BLANCHÂTRE
Italian: ORGANETTO ARTICO
Spanish: PARDILLO DE HORNEMANN
German: POLARBIRKENZEISIG

Arctic Redpoll
Acanthis hornemanni

HABITAT High arctic tundra: generally breeds further north than the Redpoll.

IDENTIFICATION Length: 13 cm. Rump pure white and unstreaked, tinged pink in adult male; remaining upper parts, including upper-tail coverts, have white or buff margins to the feathers. Sides of neck and flanks white with a few black streaks; white streak over eye; ear coverts buff; crown crimson. Under-tail coverts white, usually lacking dark streaks; remaining underparts white; cheeks, throat and breast pale pink. In general, appears paler than the Redpoll, especially on the head and back: wing-bars are also whiter.

CALL Voice resembles the Redpoll's, but notes are not as rapidly repeated.

REPRODUCTION From late June onwards. Nest is a cup of grass and twigs which is lined with feathers, hair and plant down. The nest is situated in a low tree or bush, or sometimes on the ground in the shelter of a rock. Eggs: usually four or five, similar to the Redpoll's, but larger and paler. Incubation takes approximately eleven days, and the young leave the nest after eleven to twelve days.

FOOD Mainly seeds and insects.

DISTRIBUTION AND MOVEMENTS Breeds in northern Eurasia and northern North America; also in northern Greenland. Undertakes irregular movements in winter to the Baltic area, northern Mongolia and the northern United States. Vagrant to Britain, occurring most regularly in autumn at Fair Isle, sometimes elsewhere in winter.

SUB-SPECIES The sub-species *A.h. exilipes* is present in northern Eurasia. The nominate sub-species *A.h. hornemanni* breeds in northern North America and Greenland.

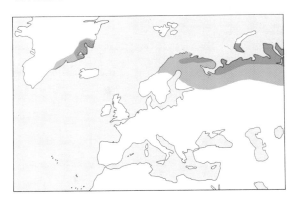

(Right) Wintering areas (magenta) and areas where the Arctic Redpoll may be seen all year round (orange)

Linnet
Acanthis cannabina

French: LINOTTE MÉLODIEUSE
Italian: FANELLO
Spanish: PARDILLO COMÚN
German: BLUTHÄNFLING

HABITAT Areas with low trees and bushes including hedgerows, orchards, large gardens and heathland. In winter found in more open country such as farmland.

IDENTIFICATION Length: 13 cm. Most common species of the genus *Acanthis* present in Europe. Prominent white wing-patch and reddish breast make the male in breeding plumage easily distinguishable. Top of head streaked brown-black and rufous, greyer on sides and on neck. Upper parts red-brown, variably streaked brown-black, paler on rump; throat yellowish, streaked blackish; breast pinkish. Flanks streaked red-brown; belly whitish, under-tail coverts yellowish streaked black. Tail feathers brown-black, the central pair fringed yellowish, the others edged white. Bill brown, greyish at base of lower mandible. Legs brownish-pink.

Female as male, but lacks the red. She is also more strongly streaked and darker above; streaked brown-black on breast and flanks. Juveniles: as female, but with uniform yellowish-white throat and finer streaking on upper parts; bill greyish.

CALL Habitual call is a rapid 'chii-cit' like the Green-finch's. Song is a twittering mixture of various notes.

REPRODUCTION From mid-April. Nests in rank hedges or thick vegetation, not far off the ground. The nest is a bulky cup of grass stems and moss and is lined with hair and wool. Eggs: four to six, ground colour white tinged bluish, finely marked with pale pink or purple. The female alone incubates for ten to fourteen days. Both tend the young which leave the nest after about fourteen days. Two broods, occasionally three.

FOOD Chiefly seeds: also some insects.

DISTRIBUTION AND MOVEMENTS Breeds from Scandinavia, Britain, Ireland and Iberia east across Eurasia to Siberia and south to Asia Minor and Iran. Also breeds in northern Africa, Madeira and the Canary Islands. Winters in the south of the breeding range, but more northerly populations winter south to Egypt and northern India. Absent from Shetland and Outer Hebrides, otherwise it is a widespread and numerous resident breeder in Britain and Ireland. Also a passage migrant and winter visitor in large numbers, probably from northern Europe.

SUB-SPECIES *A.c. cannabina*: most of Europe, northern Africa and western Siberia. *A.c. autochthona*: Scotland. *A.c. bella*: Asia Minor and central Asia. Other sub-species are present in Maderia and the Canary Islands.

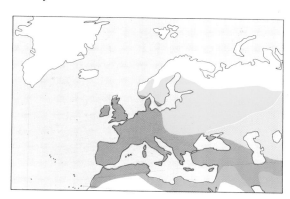

(Below) Male Linnet (top) and female. (Left) Breeding areas (yellow), wintering areas (magenta), areas where the Linnet may be seen all year round (orange) and on passage (pink)

French: LINOTTE À BEC JAUNE
Italian: FANELLO NORDICO
Spanish: PARDILLO PIQUIGUALDO
German: BERGHÄNFLING

Twite
Acanthis flavirostris

HABITAT Open and rocky country, usually at high altitudes. Winters on lower open ground, especially near coasts.

IDENTIFICATION Length: 13 cm. Upland counterpart of the Linnet: both species have a white wing patch but the Twite has featureless brown plumage apart from its pink rump. Brown upper parts streaked black as are the brown breast and flanks. Belly, under-tail coverts and axillaries white, tinged buff; tail feathers brown-black. Bill pearl-grey, tinged lemon-yellow; legs and iris dark brown. Juveniles: margins of feathers of crown and nape slightly greyer, not buff; rump paler, with no pink; ear coverts, throat and breast more strongly streaked.

CALL Call is a characteristic 'twaa-et'. Song: a musical twittering like the Linnet's.

REPRODUCTION From late April. Nests in loose colonies on the ground under low cover, in hollows in banks or on rock ledges. Nest is built entirely by the female of grasses, twigs and moss, lined with hair and wool. Eggs: usually five or six, blue, with light pinkish or red-brown streaking. The female alone incubates for ten to thirteen days. The young are tended by both parents and remain in the nest for fifteen days. Frequently double brooded.

FOOD Chiefly seeds: also insects and their larvae.

DISTRIBUTION AND MOVEMENTS Breeds discontinuously in Asia from Turkey to China and north to the USSR. Isolated breeding populations are present in northwest Europe in Britain, Ireland and Norway. Winters in breeding range, but sometimes moves southwards: most European birds are partly or completely migratory. Widespread breeding bird in Scotland but restricted to the Pennines in England. Found mainly in coastal areas of the north and west in Ireland. Winter visitor to east and southeast coasts of England.

SUB-SPECIES *A.f. flavirostris*: Scandinavia. *A.f. pipilans*: Britain and Ireland. *A.f. brevirostris*: Caucasus and eastern Turkey, northwestern Iran. Other sub-species are present in Asia.

(Right) Breeding areas (yellow), wintering areas (magenta) and areas where the Twite may be seen all year round (orange)

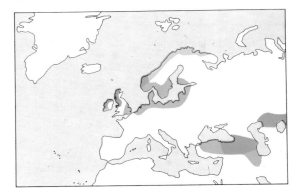

Crimson-winged Finch
Rhodopechys sanguinea

French: BOUVREUIL À AILES ROSES
Italian: TROMBETTIERE ALIROSSE
German: ROTFLÜGELGIMPEL

HABITAT Rocky mountain country, sometimes with scattered scrub, not usually lower than fifteen hundred metres except in winter when it feeds on cultivated fields at lower altitudes.

IDENTIFICATION Length: 16 cm. Resembles a large Trumpeter Finch, with clay-brown upper parts and rufous-brown underparts. Deep pink coloration on wings, cheeks and tail; forehead and crown black. Females similar to males, but forehead and crown are dark brown, not black, and general coloration more subdued. Bill yellow-brown, legs blackish. On the ground moves with great agility.

CALL Voice resembles the Linnet's: emits a twittering call.

REPRODUCTION From early April. Breeds on mountainsides on the ground in a crevice or hollow. The nest is a shallow cup of plant stems and grasses, lined with finer plant materials. Eggs: four or five, pale blue sparsely marked with brown. The female alone incubates for twelve days: both parents tend the young.

FOOD Probably mainly seeds.

DISTRIBUTION AND MOVEMENTS Breeds in northern Africa, Turkey and Asia. An essentially resident species, performing only movements to lower altitudes in winter.

SUB-SPECIES *R.s. aliena*: northern Africa.

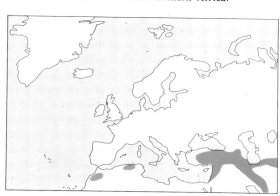

(Below) Male Crimson-winged Finch (left) and female. (Left) Areas where the Crimson-winged Finch may be seen all year round (orange)

French: BOUVREUIL GITHAGINE
Italian: TROMBETTIERE
Spanish: CAMACHUELO
TROMPETERO
German: WÜSTENGIMPEL

Trumpeter Finch
Rhodopechys githaginea

(Above) Male Trumpeter Finch (left) and female. (Right) Areas where the Trumpeter Finch may be seen all year round (orange)

HABITAT Deserts; arid areas and steppe: also rocky hill areas.

IDENTIFICATION Length: 13 cm. In shape resembles a Sparrow but with a more stumpy bill. Male: sandy-brown coloration, tinged pink on rump, wings, face and underparts. In the breeding season the bill, normally pale horny-yellow, turns scarlet. Female is duller, like the male in winter plumage: mainly grey with pinkish tinge and contrasting dark wing tips. Juveniles lack the pink.

Although a confiding bird, it is difficult to observe because its colouring blends so well with the surroundings.

CALL Emits a brief, nasal 'trumpeting' call—hence its English name.

REPRODUCTION From March onwards. Nests on the ground, in rock crevices or under a low plant. The nest is a cup of grass, stems and twigs and is lined with wool and hair. Lays on average five light blue eggs, with sparse blackish speckling.

FOOD Seeds.

DISTRIBUTION AND MOVEMENTS Breeds in the Canary Islands, northern Africa and Asia Minor eastwards to Afghanistan. Accidental in Malta, Britain and Italy, and has recently been proved breeding in Spain.

SUB-SPECIES Sub-species are present in Asia.

Pallas's Rosefinch
Carpodacus roseus

French: ROSELIN ROSE
Italian: CIUFFOLOTTO SCARLATTO
DEL PALLAS
Spanish: CAMACHUELO ROSÉO
German: ROSENGIMPEL

HABITAT High forest and scrub.

IDENTIFICATION Length: 15 cm. Intermediate in size between Common and Great Rosefinches. Male is generally pinkish, except on nape and back which are rufous-brown with darker markings, and on the wings and tail which are blackish-brown. Whitish-streaked centres to feathers of head, cheeks and throat. Wing coverts are tipped pale, forming two indistinct wing-bars. Female has much more subdued coloration: upper parts, including part of head, more brownish; resembles female Common Rosefinch but with pinkish-red on forehead, throat and upper breast as well as part of rump. Tail long and slightly forked.

CALL Rather silent, but emits a brief, soft whistle.

REPRODUCTION Very little is known of the breeding of this bird, except that the young hatch towards the end of June and probably leave the nest about the middle of July.

FOOD Probably mainly seeds.

DISTRIBUTION AND MOVEMENTS Breeds in Siberia and central Asia, up to about latitude 66° north. Also nests on the island of Sakhalin and in central and northwestern parts of the Altai mountains. In winter moves to lower altitudes and further south into China. Accidental in eastern Europe in Hungary, and also wanders to the western USSR.

SUB-SPECIES A sub-species is present in Asia.

(Above) Male Pallas's Rosefinch (top) and female

French: ROSELIN TACHETÉ
Italian: CIUFFOLOTTO SCARLATTO
MAGGIORE
German: KAUKASUS-KARMINGIMPEL

Great Rosefinch
Carpodacus rubicilla

(Above) Male Great Rosefinch (top) and female. (Right) Wintering areas (magenta) and areas where the Great Rosefinch may be seen all year round (orange)

HABITAT Rocky slopes and scrub.

IDENTIFICATION Length: 20 cm. The largest rosefinch present in Europe. Male is easily distinguished by white spots on red crown, breast and flanks. General coloration deep pinkish-red with brown back and wings and blackish tail. Bill horn-coloured: legs black. Female grey-brown, with clearly visible spots and streaks on throat and belly.

CALL Fairly loud song, consisting of an intermittently repeated whistle.

REPRODUCTION Probably from June. Nests low in a shrub or on the ground among rocks. The cup-shaped nest is made of twigs, roots, grass and moss and is lined with wool and hair. Eggs: four or five, light blue like those of other rosefinches with dark markings at the larger end. Further information is unavailable.

FOOD Seeds and berries.

DISTRIBUTION AND MOVEMENTS Breeds in Asia Minor and the Caucasus east across Afghanistan to China.

SUB-SPECIES Sub-species of the Great Rosefinch are present in Asia.

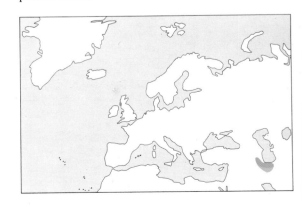

Common Rosefinch
Carpodacus erythrinus

French: ROSELIN CRAMOISI
Italian: CLUFFOLOTTO SCARLATTO
Spanish: CAMACHUELO CARMINOSO
German: KARMINGIMPEL

HABITAT Forest edges, scrub, gardens and cultivated areas.

IDENTIFICATION Length: 14 cm. Is the most common and widespread rosefinch present in Europe. Very round head and large brown bill. Male has bright crimson head, breast and rump; lower belly white, wings and tail brown. Pale double wing-bar. Female and juveniles brown and rufous like Corn Buntings, but more slender, with streaked breasts and a faint pale double wing-bar. Also known as the Scarlet Grosbeak.

CALL Emits a 'twee-eek'. Song consists of a clear 'piu-vu'.

REPRODUCTION From mid-May. Nests in a shrub or low in a tree. The nest is a loosely constructed cup of plant stems and grass, lined with hair and feathers, which is built by the female alone. Normally lays five eggs that are light blue spotted with black. Incubation by the female alone for twelve to fourteen days. The young are fed by both parents.

FOOD Seeds and grain.

DISTRIBUTION AND MOVEMENTS Breeds from Germany and Scandinavia east across Eurasia. Also breeds southwards to eastern Turkey. Winters in India and southeast Asia. In Britain it is recorded as an annual visitor in very small numbers to Fair Isle. Vagrant elsewhere in Britain and Ireland.

SUB-SPECIES *C.a. kubanensis*: Asia Minor, Caucasus and northern Iran. Other sub-species are present in Asia.

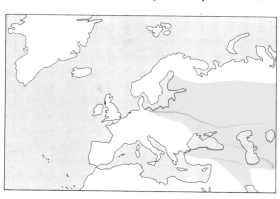

(Above) Male Common Rosefinch (right) and female. (Below) Breeding areas (yellow) and areas where the Common Rosefinch may be seen on passage (pink)

French: DURBEC DES SAPINS
Italian: CIUFFOLOTTO DELLE
PINETE
Spanish: CAMACHUELO PICOGRUESO
German: HAKENGIMPEL

Pine Grosbeak
Pinicola enucleator

HABITAT Northern coniferous and birch forests.

IDENTIFICATION Length: 20 cm. Largest finch present in Europe. Large bill, flat head and fairly long tail; male has neck, breast and rump pale pinkish-red, belly white. Wings and tail brown: tail is forked. Head deep pink: double white wing-bar. Female is golden greenish-bronze where male is pinkish-red. Juveniles as female.

Flight undulating. Usually very confiding; particularly sociable in winter.

CALL Call is a loud trisyllabic whistle. Song is also loud and whistling, and combines a variety of notes.

REPRODUCTION From late May. The nest is built by the female of small twigs, and is lined with roots, grass and moss. Four eggs are laid, sometimes three or five, deep blue, spotted or blotched black or purple-brown: markings are often concentrated at the large end. Incubation by female alone, fed by male, lasts thirteen to fourteen days. Young are fed by both parents.

FOOD Chiefly seeds and berries: also insects.

DISTRIBUTION AND MOVEMENTS Breeds from Scandinavia east across northern Eurasia to Kamchatka and southwards into Mongolia. Also breeds from Alaska to Newfoundland south into the northeastern United States, and in mountainous areas of western North America. Partially migratory, wintering south of the breeding range. Is a rare vagrant to Britain.

SUB-SPECIES *P.e. enucleator*: Scandinavia and the northern USSR. Other sub-species are present in Asia.

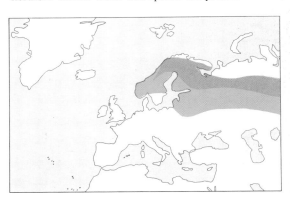

(Below) Male Pine Grosbeak (top) and female. (Right) Wintering areas (magenta) and areas where the Pine Grosbeak may be seen all year round (orange)

R. T. Smith/Ardea

David Sewell

(Above) The Crossbill *Loxia curvirostra* is the most common and widespread crossbill and is found mainly in coniferous forests, particularly spruce and fir. (Left) Greenfinch *Carduelis chloris:* its heavy bill is a distinguishing feature

191

French: BECCROISÉ PERROQUET
Italian: CROCIERE DELLE PINETE
Spanish: PIQUITUERTO LORITO
German: KIEFERNKREUZSCHNABEL

Parrot Crossbill
Loxia pytyopsittacus

(Right) Areas where the Parrot Crossbill may be seen all year round (orange)

HABITAT Northern coniferous forests.

IDENTIFICATION Length: 17 cm. Slightly larger than the Crossbill, with a rounder and more heavily built bill which makes it look more like a parrot. Like other crossbills the mandibles cross over. Its plumage is similar to that of the Crossbill from which it can be distinguished by its heavier bill. Seen much more frequently in pine forests than other crossbills.

CALL Like the Crossbill's, but somewhat louder and deeper.

REPRODUCTION Usually from late March. Nests in conifers from three to fourteen metres above the ground. Its nest is like the Crossbill's but more solidly built. It is made of grass, pine needles, moss and twigs, lined with fine grasses, lichen, feathers and bark. There are two to four eggs per clutch, or very occasionally five. They are larger than the Crossbill's, but with similar coloration. Incubation is carried out by the female alone for fourteen to sixteen days.

FOOD Mainly various types of pine seeds: also berries.

DISTRIBUTION AND MOVEMENTS Breeds from Scandinavia east to the northern USSR. It is a resident but sometimes eratically migratory and has reached central and western Europe during the winter. In Britain it is a very rare vagrant, but occasionally errupts and may then occur in some numbers. It is a matter of debate as to whether the crossbills of Scotland are a sub-species of the Crossbill *Loxia curvirostra* or a race of the Parrot Crossbill.

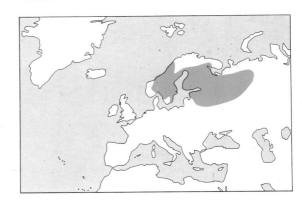

Crossbill
Loxia curvirostra

HABITAT Coniferous forests: occasionally seen in villages and towns.

IDENTIFICATION Length: 16 cm. Most common and widespread crossbill. Male: brick-red body with small brown markings, except for the rump which is more brightly coloured. Brown sides of the head; greyish belly and undertail coverts; greyish-white underwing; black-brown flight feathers and tail feathers with pale borders. Brown bill, legs and iris. Female: olive-coloured upper parts; yellow rump; greenish-grey sides of the head; yellowish-grey underparts. Juveniles: green-grey with dark streaks. Distinctive criss-cross motion of the mandibles (hence its English name) as it extracts seeds from fir, pine, spruce and larch cones. Tail, like that of other crossbills, is forked.

CALL Emits a characteristic metallic 'jip'. Song is a series of staccato, bell-like notes which are based on the call note.

REPRODUCTION Breeding season highly variable, beginning in January and extending to July. Breeds in conifers from two to twenty metres off the ground. The nest is built well above the ground of twigs, moss, lichen and wool and is lined with fine grasses, hair and feathers. Eggs: three or four, sometimes two or five with purplish-grey, red-brown or black-brown speckles on a grey, greenish-white or bluish ground. Incubation by the female alone takes fourteen to sixteen days. The young leave the nest after seventeen to twenty-two days, although they are dependent upon the parents for another three or four weeks.

FOOD Normally seeds, but also feeds on buds, fruit and grubs.

DISTRIBUTION AND MOVEMENTS Breeds from Scandinavia east across Eurasia to the Pacific. Also breeds locally south into Britain, Ireland, Iberia, northern Africa, southern Europe and Asia Minor discontinuously east to the Himalayas. Also breeds in North America. In Eurasia northern populations move erratically in some numbers in irruptive movements. At these times it may appear in widespread areas of Britain and even penetrate as far as Ireland. There is evidence of a return movement in spring, but some birds will remain to breed in the year following an irruption. In one case, at least, in the Breckland of East Anglia a population was established in 1920 that has persisted to the present day. In Scotland the population is resident, and distinctive enough to merit sub-specific status.

SUB-SPECIES *L.c. scotica*: nothern Scotland. *L.c. corsicana*: Corsica. *L.c. balearica*: the Balearic Islands. *L.c. guillemardi*: Cyprus. *L.c. mariae*: southwestern Crimea. There are other sub-species in the Philippines, North and Central America, Asia and northern Africa.

French: BECCROISÉ DES SAPINS
Italian: CROCIERE
Spanish: PIQUITUERTO COMÚN
German: FICHTENKREUZSCHNABEL

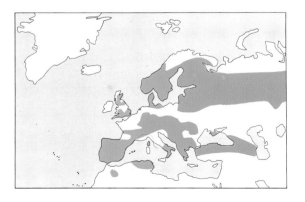

(Above) Male Crossbill (top) and female. (Left) Areas where the Crossbill may be seen all year round (orange)

French : BECCROISÉ BIFASCIÉ
Italian : CROCIERE FASCIATO
Spanish : PIQUITUERTO FRANJEADO
German : BINDENKREUZSCHNABEL

White-winged or Two-barred Crossbill
Loxia leucoptera

HABITAT Coniferous forests, especially larch forests.

IDENTIFICATION Length: 14 cm. Resembles the Crossbill, but smaller. It can be identified by its two white wing-bars, even in flight. Adult males: bright red coloration, brighter than the Crossbill's. Primaries with pinkish-white margins and white tips. Bill less heavy than the Crossbill's. Juveniles and adult females: yellowish-white margins to the wing feathers; juveniles have smaller wing-bars than adults. Females are paler than the female Crossbill.

CALL A dry 'cheef-cheef' and a melodious 'pee-eet'. Its song is clearer, louder and more varied than the Crossbill's: consists of almost canary-like trills.

REPRODUCTION From late March. Nests in trees, particularly cedars: its nest is smaller than the Crossbill's. It is built on a foundation of twigs, of grass, lichen, moss and leaves, lined with roots, feathers and lichen. Eggs: three or four, rarely five which are pale blue or greenish-white with dark purple spots and speckles usually concentrated at the larger end. The length of incubation is not known.

FOOD Mainly the seeds of various conifers, particularly larches.

DISTRIBUTION AND MOVEMENTS Breeds in northern Europe, northern and central Asia, North America and the West Indies. It is resident but sometimes wanders south in the winter, reaching southern Scandinavia, the Baltic provinces and the northern United States. Occasionally it travels to parts of western Europe and Japan. In Britain it is a rare vagrant usually recorded at the same time as invasions by the Crossbill. In Ireland it is exceptionally rare.

SUB-SPECIES *L.l. bifasciata*: Europe. The nominate sub-species is present in North America.

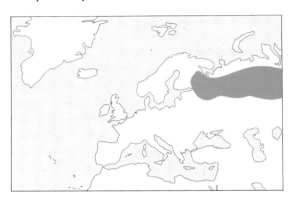

(Below) Male White-winged Crossbill (top) and female. (Right) Areas where the White-winged Crossbill may be seen all year round (orange)

Bullfinch
Pyrrhula pyrrhula

French: BOUVREUIL PIVOINE
Italian: CIUFFOLOTTO
Spanish: CAMACHUELO COMÚN
German: GIMPEL

HABITAT Woodland, scrub, orchards and gardens.

IDENTIFICATION Length: 15 cm. Adult males: conspicuous shiny blackish-blue crown: grey-blue mantle and scapulars slightly tinged with yellowish-brown or occasionally pink. White rump; blackish-blue upper-tail coverts. Underparts: sides of the neck, throat, breast and flanks pink: this coloration combined with the black cap make the Bullfinch easily identifiable.

Females: head pattern like the male's: grey-brown back of the neck; dark yellowish-brown mantle, scapulars and back tinged with grey; blackish-blue upper-tail coverts; white rump and axillaries; pinkish-brown ear-coverts, sides of the neck and underparts; wings and tail like the male's. Juveniles: like adult females, but with brown head and mantle; white rump.

CALL A low, chirping 'dev'. This is also the basis of its squeaky song.

REPRODUCTION From late April. Breeds in a bush or shrub, usually one or two metres off the ground. Nest is a loose structure of twigs, moss and lichen, lined with roots and hair. The nest is built by the female. There are usually four or five, occasionally six or seven blue-green eggs with purplish-brown streaks and a few markings. Incubation takes twelve to fourteen days and is mostly carried out by the female: she is fed on the nest by the male. Both tend the young which remain in the nest for twelve to eighteen days.

FOOD Seeds: also shoots and buds.

DISTRIBUTION AND MOVEMENTS Breeds in the Azores, Britain and Ireland, Scandinavia, the northern USSR, the northern Iberian Peninsula, Italy and most of Europe east to Mongolia and Kamchatka. It is generally resident, but has been found accidentally south and east of its distribution area as far away as Korea, northern China and Japan. In Britain and Ireland it is a widespread and numerous resident breeder, except in the north and west.

SUB-SPECIES *P.p. murina*: the Azores. *P.p. pileata*: Britain and Ireland. Other sub-species are present in Asia.

(Right) Male Bullfinch (below) and female (top).
(Below) Breeding areas (yellow), wintering areas (magenta) and areas where the Bullfinch may be seen all year round (orange)

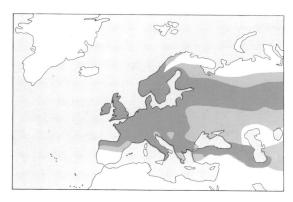

French : GROS-BEC
Italian : FROSONE
Spanish : PICOGORDO
German : KERNBEISSER

Hawfinch
Coccothraustes coccothraustes

HABITAT Broad-leaved and mixed woodland: also parks, gardens and other areas with scattered trees.

IDENTIFICATION Length: 18 cm. Largest European finch regularly present outside the northern conifer belt. Mainly chestnut plumage. Black bib and edging round the bill; yellowish-brown forehead and sides of the head. Red-brown nape; pinkish-grey bands at the back of the neck; deep brown mantle, back and scapulars; red rump; pale pinkish-brown breast. White wing patch. White belly and under-tail coverts. Short tail. Tail feathers: black base and white tips, with black and red outer borders. Its large bill is pale blue with a black tip in the spring and a light horn colour in the winter. Pinkish-grey legs turn bright pink in the spring. The female is paler and less reddish on the belly. Juveniles are more yellowish than chestnut, with dark spots on the flanks and a whitish belly.

Its flight is fast, high and undulating. It walks with an upright gait and hops energetically. It often joins flocks in the winter, but is extremely wary.

CALL Emits a harsh 'tic' and also a high-pitched 'tsep'. Song is weak and resembles the Bullfinch's: however it is rarely heard.

REPRODUCTION From late April. Nests in trees on low horizontal branches or against the trunks often close to the nests of other hawfinches. The nest is a cup of twigs, roots and lichen and is lined with roots, plant fibres and hair. There are four or five grey, bluish or sometimes yellowish eggs marked with grey-brown, red-brown, olive-brown or black blotches and scrawls. The female incubates, occasionally assisted by the male, for about thirteen days. Both tend the young which leave the nest after ten to thirteen days. Normally there is only one clutch.

FOOD Seeds, plant shoots and insects.

DISTRIBUTION AND MOVEMENTS Breeds from northwest Africa, Britain and Scandinavia east across Eurasia to Japan and south to Asia Minor, the Caucasus, northern Iran, Afghanistan and parts of Turkestan. In Britain it is a fairly widespread resident breeder in England, but is common nowhere. In Wales and Scotland it is regular but rare. And in Ireland the Hawfinch is no more than a vagrant, although it was once a regular visitor.

SUB-SPECIES *C.c. coccothraustes*: northern, southern and central parts of western Europe; southern Asia. *C.c. nigricans*: southeast USSR, the Crimea, the Caucasus and Transcaucasia. There are other sub-species in Asia and Africa.

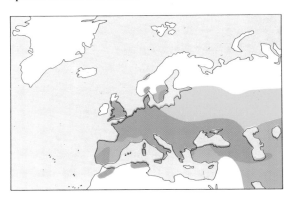

(Right) Breeding areas (yellow), wintering areas (magenta) and areas where the Hawfinch may be seen all year round (orange)

Evening Grosbeak
Hesperiphona vespertina

French: GROS-BEC ERRANT
Italian: BECCOGROSSO VESPERTINO
German: ABENDKERNBEISSER

HABITAT Coniferous and deciduous woods.

IDENTIFICATION Length: 21 cm. Overall appearance is reminiscent of the Hawfinch. Yellow forehead and streak above the eye; crown, tail and most of its wings are black; the rest of its head and neck are grey-brown shading into the bronze-yellow of its remaining plumage. Off-white secondaries. Female: dark, smoke-grey upper parts, light grey underparts with some white on the throat and rump. The large, conical bill is straw-coloured; flesh-coloured legs.

CALL Call note: a loud 'clee-ee-eer' and clee-eep. Its song is made up of brief warbling ending in a shrill whistle.

REPRODUCTION Its cup-shaped nest is built of plant material, and is situated in a conifer, between three and twenty metres above the ground. There are three or four pale blue-green eggs with pale brownish markings.

FOOD Seeds; it also occasionally feeds on insects.

DISTRIBUTION AND MOVEMENTS Breeds in North America as far south as the mountains of New Mexico. Generally resident. Very rare vagrant to Britain.

SUB-SPECIES Sub-species are present in North America.

(Left) Male Evening Grosbeak (top) and female

197

FAMILY ESTRILDIDAE: Waxbills

P. Blasedale/Ardea

(Above) Black-rumped Waxbill
Estrilda troglodytes

Many of the small, exotic species which are often kept as cagebirds belong to this family. There are one hundred and twenty-four species grouped in over twenty-five genera in the family Estrildidae. They are distributed in the Old World; from Africa to the Philippines, New Guinea, Australia and the Pacific Islands as far east as Fiji and Samoa.

Waxbills are small or very small birds, their average length being nine centimetres. They were once classed with sparrows and weavers of the family Ploceidae which they do, in fact, resemble in having a reduced, very small first primary. In other respects, however, they differ greatly from ploceoid birds, so it is preferable to allocate them to a separate family. The tail and legs vary in length but the bill is usually short and stout. It may be straight, curved or hooked. Plumage is usually a variety of bright colours, although some species are predominantly grey or brown. Most species are gregarious. Many waxbills are seed-eaters, although some feed on insects, nectar and buds.

The nests of waxbills are usually fairly bulky structures, securely wedged between branches, but not as carefully woven as weaver's nests. There are between four and six eggs per clutch, which both parents incubate for twenty-one days.

Although the droppings are not removed after the first week, the nestlings do not soil the nest because they defecate on the walls and their excreta dries rapidly.

The young mature quickly and many species are able to breed by the time they are three or four months old. Pair bonds appear to be fairly stable. Courtship displays vary from one species to another, but the tremor of half-open wings so common among birds of this order, especially small passerines, has not yet been observed. During courtship, the colourful parts of the plumage are displayed and the male often presents the female with a symbolic offering in the form of a blade of grass.

The family is usually divided into the following three tribes on the basis of their behaviour (especially their sexual habits): Estrildini, Erythrurini and Amadini.

Most species of the Estrildini tribe are African, two species are Asian and one is Australian, that is, the Red-browed Finch *Estrilda temporalis*. The African species provide an excellent example of adaptive radiation, some feeding exclusively on grain and others on insects or even nectar and pollen such as the Flowerpecker Weaver-Finch *Parmoptila woodhousei*. Some of the grain-eating species have

A. J. Deane/Bruce Coleman

Bruce Coleman

Bruce Coleman

(Above left) The Waxbill *Estrilda astrild* has a distinctive red bill. (Above) Red-cheeked Cordon-Bleu *Uraeginthus bengalus* (top) and Black-headed Munia *Lonchura malacca* (bottom). (Left) The Cut-throat *Amadina fasciata* is easily recognised by its striking red throat

Bruce Coleman

(Right) Zebra Finches *Poephila guttata* from Australasia. (Below) World distribution of the family Estrildidae

G. Pizzey/Bruce Coleman

average-sized bills while others have bills like the Hawfinch's which is adapted to crushing large, hard seeds. The best known genera of this group are *Estrilda*, *Spermophaga*, *Clytospiza*, *Cryptospiza*, *Hypargos* and *Pytilia*. The Waxbill *Estrilda astrild* is a very small finch-like species which has been introduced to Portugal.

The Erythrurini tribe also includes some familiar cage-birds. These are essentially Australasian species, such as the well-known Long-tailed Weaver-Finch *Poephila acuticauda* and the Zebra Finch *P. guttata*.

Amadini is the most homogeneous tribe. Most species are large and compactly built, with black and brown plumage combined with white and chestnut coloration and various markings and bars. They have comparatively large, lead-grey bills. Two species—the Cut-throat *Amadina fasciata* and the Red-headed Finch *A. erythrocephala*— have brilliant red coloration on the throat and head respectively. The Java Sparrow *Padda oryzivora* is the largest species. It originated in Java and Bali and is fourteen centimetres long, with grey plumage, black head, white cheek marking and red bill. It is now widely distributed, thanks to its introduction into much of southeast Asia and parts of East Africa. It is kept as a cage-bird in many parts of the world and has been bred in a number of colour mutations. The rare albino is most prized by breeders.

Black-rumped Waxbill
Estrilda troglodytes

French: BEC DE CORAIL
Italian: BECCO DI CORALLO
Spanish: AMPÉLIDO

HABITAT Semi-arid regions with sparse vegetation.

IDENTIFICATION Length: 10 cm. Sexes are alike: pale grey-brown upper parts tinged with pink and covered with fine, indistinct bars. Red streak across the eye. Black rump and upper-tail coverts. Black tail and off-white undertail. White margins to the outer tail feathers. Grey chin, throat and underparts tinged with pink; red coloration on the centre of the belly, especially in males. Dark red bill, blackish legs and reddish-brown iris. Lives in small flocks but breeds separately.

CALL When perching, its call note is a sort of 'chee-wee-ee'; in flight it emits a 'tyoup-tyoup-tyoup'. Song is repetitive and not melodious.

REPRODUCTION From June onwards. Its nest consists of a partly open spherical structure situated on the ground in the shelter of a bush or a tussock of grass. There are four to six white eggs which are thought to be incubated by the female only. Incubation takes about twelve days.

FOOD Almost exclusively seeds.

DISTRIBUTION AND MOVEMENTS It is an African species typical of the semi-arid belt south of the Sahara, from the Atlantic coast east to Uganda. It has been successfully introduced into Portugal.

SUB-SPECIES Sub-species are present in Africa.

201

PLOCEIDAE: Sparrows and allies

B. Bevan/Ardea

J. S. Wightman/Ardea

D. S. Frugis

(Above) House Sparrow *Passer domesticus* (top) and Snow Finch *Montifringilla nivalis* (below). (Above right) The sub-species *P.d. italiae* of the House Sparrow: it is an intergrade with the Spanish Sparrow *P. hispaniolensis*, and has a chestnut crown and blacker breast and whiter underparts than the House Sparrow

Opinion differs as to the number of sub-families which comprise this large family, but here the most widely adopted practice of dividing it into three sub-families is followed. These three are the Passerinae or sparrows, the Ploceinae or weavers and the Bubalornithinae or buffalo-weavers.

Species from ten to eighteen centimetres long are allocated to the sub-family Passerinae. Their plumage is mostly dull, being brown and/or grey, with the occasional addition of black or, less frequently, bright yellow coloration. They have thick, somewhat conical bills and feed mainly on cereals. In shape they resemble finches but may be distinguished by the tail which is not forked. Their bulky, feather-lined nests are generally spherical.

The genus *Montifringilla* is essentially Asiatic, but includes a species found also in the southern Alps of Europe—the Snow Finch *M. nivalis*. There are five species of the genus *Petronia* all of which are found in Africa, but three occur in Asia and one, the Rock Sparrow *P. petronia*, is also found in southern Europe, usually in rocky mountainous areas, on farmland or even near villages.

The genus *Passer* includes fifteen species, five of which are exclusive to Africa; the remainder are distributed in the Palearctic region and further east to southern Asia. The common House Sparrow *P. domesticus* is widely distributed, and is now found almost everywhere, even on many oceanic islands, thanks chiefly to human intervention. In North America several sub-species of the House Sparrow have already evolved. Italy has a sub-species of its own – which is regarded as a distinct species by some authorities—the Italian Sparrow *P.d. italiae*. It is not found in Corsica (where the typical European race occurs) or in Sardinia (where it has been replaced by a population of the Spanish Sparrow *P. hispaniolensis*). The Spanish

(Above left) Tree Sparrow *Passer montanus*. (Above right) House Sparrows *P. domesticus*. This small brown bird is a familiar sight in towns and cities

Sparrow is curious in some respects; its range extends to India and it hybridises with various races of the House Sparrow, including *P..d. italiae*.

Another widely distributed species, which has also been introduced into a number of countries, is the Tree Sparrow *P. montanus*, which originated in Eurasia. Most species of the genus *Passer* exhibit marked sexual dimorphism (with the exception of the Tree Sparrow). Many sparrows associate readily with humans and have adapted to live near houses, even in the largest and most bustling cities. Broadly speaking they are extremely sociable birds. The Spanish Sparrow is the most gregarious of all, with colonies of several hundred pairs nesting together, mainly in trees and bushes in cultivated and inhabited regions usually close to water.

The other genera of the subfamily are also very sociable. They are exclusively African; four species belong to the genus *Plocepasser*, two to the genus *Sporopipes*, two to the genus *Pseudonigrita* and one each to the genera *Histurgops* and *Philetarius*. The Social Weaver *Philetarius socius* is distributed in southwest Africa and builds an extraordinary communal nest. Apparently the various pairs build countless single nests side by side on a large acacia tree: these nests form an enormous conical structure riddled with holes. The most surprising thing is that all the members of the colony, both males and females, work together to repair and improve the structure which serves as admirable protection from the torrential rain of the rainy season. The pairs also maintain lasting relationships within the community.

There are about ninety species in the subfamily Ploceinae. They are known collectively as weavers, but include widow-birds and whydahs. The majority have brilliant red or yellow coloration on part of their plumage. All but five species (which occur in India and Malaysia) are African,

203

R. Kinne

(Right) Black-winged Red Bishops *Euplectes hordeaceus*. (Below) World distribution of the family Ploceidae

from south of the Sahara. The characteristic which they share is the elaborate structure of their nests.

The sub-family Ploceinae can be divided into two groups. One group constitutes the exclusively arboreal species, with areas of bright red and yellow coloration on their plumage, which build rather intricate hanging nests with tunnel entrances. The second group includes species such as queleas, widow-birds, bishops and fodies. The males (but not always the females) of these species are vividly coloured and often long-tailed. Apart from these two groups there are three monotypic genera. The most interesting of these is a small, yellowish bird the Parasitic Weaver *Anomalospiza imberbis*—about which little is known except that it parasitises the nests of warblers of the genus *Cisticola*. If the true widow-birds of the genus *Vidua* are excluded from the Ploceidae family, then the species is the only parasitic ploceoid. In fact the extremely close resemblance of the eggs and young (which have similar palate markings and nodules) of species of the genus *Vidua* may be a sign of great affinity rather than an unusual case of evolutionary convergence. It is thus acceptable to include the species of the genus *Vidua* in this family, and they are collectively known as the parasitic viduines. They inhabit Africa south of the Sahara.

There are only three species in the African sub-family Bubalornithinae: the Buffalo Weaver *Bubalornis albirostris*, the Red-billed Buffalo-Weaver *B. niger* and the White-headed Buffalo-Weaver *Dinemellia dinemelli*.

House Sparrow
Passer domesticus

French: MOINEAU DOMESTIQUE
Italian: PASSERA EUROPEA
Spanish: GORRIÓN COMÚN
German: HAUSSPERLING

HABITAT Cultivated land and built-up areas of all kinds, including city centres.

IDENTIFICATION Length: 14 cm. Grey crown, dark chestnut-coloured nape, black throat and off-white cheeks. Black, rufous and reddish streaks on its mantle; brownish-grey back, rump and upper-tail coverts; black streak through the eye; the remaining upper parts are off-white, tinged with reddish and grey coloration on the flanks. Black-brown flight feathers with reddish borders; black-brown wing coverts with rufous borders, the median coverts with off-white tips and the lesser coverts rich brown; black-brown tail feathers with reddish margins. Bill: black in summer and yellowish-brown in winter; pale brown legs and brown iris.

Females and juveniles lack the black throat and chestnut head pattern, their upper parts are a dirty brown and their underparts are greyish-white. Only distinctive feature is the pale wing-bar. The House Sparrow often bathes in water and scratches about in dry ground, making small holes. Its flight is rapid and direct.

CALL The basic call is a loud 'cheep' with variations. A double 'chiisck' is strung together as a song and often emitted in chorus.

REPRODUCTION From late April onwards; although the nesting period is highly variable. Nests in holes or cracks in buildings, among creepers or sometimes in trees. The nest is a round, domed structure with a side entrance which is built by both sexes. It is constructed of straw, plant fibres, dry grasses and rubbish such as string or paper. It is lined with hair and feathers. There are between three and five, or occasionally as many as eight eggs, ranging in colour from pure white to greenish-grey, with black-brown or olive and ash-grey spots. Eggs may vary in a clutch, some appearing whiter.

Incubation is carried out by both parents, although mainly by the female, for eleven to fourteen days. The young are fed by their parents, mainly on insects, and leave the nest after about fifteen days. Multi-brooded.

FOOD Mainly grain and other cereals; also seeds, young plants, fruit, earthworms and insects.

DISTRIBUTION AND MOVEMENTS Breeds throughout the Palearctic except for the northernmost regions. It has been introduced in to North and South America, Australia, New Zealand and some oceanic islands. In Britain and Ireland is a widespread resident breeder save only for the extreme west of Ireland, where it is absent from some desolate areas and islands.

SUB-SPECIES *P.d. domesticus:* most of Europe and northern Asia. *P.d. italiae* (uniform, chestnut-coloured crown without any grey coloration; whiter wing coverts: southeast France, Italy, Corsica and Crete. *P.d. biblicus* (paler): Asia Minor, Cyprus and central parts of western Asia. There are other sub-species in Asia and Africa.

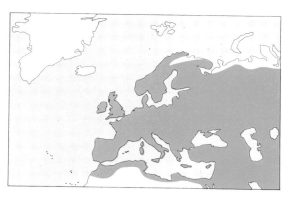

(Below) Male House Sparrow (right) and female (left).
(Left) Areas where the House Sparrows may be seen all year round (orange).

French: MOINEAU FRIQUET
Italian: PASSERA MATTUGIA
Spanish: GORRIÓN MOLINERO
German: FELDSPERLING

Tree Sparrow
Passer montanus

(Below) Breeding areas (yellow), wintering areas (magenta) and areas where the Tree Sparrow may be seen all year round (orange)

HABITAT Less associated with humans than the House Sparrow. Frequents open woodland and areas with scattered trees.

IDENTIFICATION Length: 14 cm. Deep chocolate-brown nape and crown distinguish it from the slightly larger House Sparrow. Yellowish-brown upper parts; black streaks on the mantle and scapulars; white sides of the head and neck with conspicuous black patch on the cheeks. Black chin; black on throat not as extensive as the House Sparrow's. White underparts, with greyish tinges on the upper breast and brownish tinges on the flanks; black-brown flight feathers with rufous margins. Juveniles: like adults (adult male and female are similar) but with a blackish-grey throat and patch on the cheek; reddish tips to the wing coverts.

CALL A characteristic 'chip-chip'. Generally similar to the House Sparrow's, but higher-pitched and harsher.

REPRODUCTION From April onwards. Nest is built in holes in trees, walls and roofs. Also nests in other birds' nests, nest boxes, pipes or in creepers. The nest is a loose domed structure of plant stalks and twigs. Eggs: four to six, rarely two to nine, white to to pale grey heavily marked with brown and grey. Both sexes incubate for eleven to fourteen days. The young are cared for by both parents and leave the nest after twelve to fourteen days.

FOOD Seeds, grain and insects.

DISTRIBUTION AND MOVEMENTS Breeds in most of Eurasia from Scandinavia, Britain, Ireland and Iberia east to the Pacific. Partially migratory: northern populations winter in the south of the breeding range and beyond. Introduced in the Philippines, the United States and Australia. In Britain it is a widespread and fairly numerous resident breeder, although thinly distributed and absent from some areas of the north and west. In Ireland it is of very local occurrence mainly in coastal areas.

SUB-SPECIES Sub-species are present in Asia.

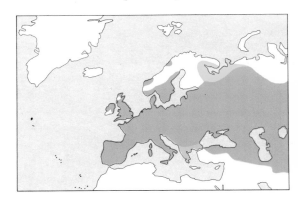

Spanish Sparrow
Passer hispaniolensis

French: MOINEAU ESPAGNOL
Italian: PASSERA SARDA
Spanish: GORRIÓN MORUNO
German: WEIDENSPERLING

HABITAT It is closely associated with man, particularly in villages and small towns; also found in wooded country, areas with scattered trees and cultivated land.

IDENTIFICATION Length: 14 cm. Male: chestnut-coloured crown, flanks covered with dense black streaks and a darker back than that of the House Sparrow. Its cheeks and belly are whiter than the House Sparrow's. Coloration varies somewhat from one sub-species to another, and hybrid populations can cause confusion, but on the whole its plumage has more sharply contrasting coloration than the House Sparrow's. The female is similar to the female House Sparrow, but has a darker back, more streaked flanks and white cheeks.

CALL Similar to the House Sparrow's but deeper.

REPRODUCTION From April onwards. It prefers to nest in trees, often in closely packed colonies. Its bulky spherical nest contains between four and seven very pale blue eggs with small, dark brown markings mainly concentrated at the blunt end. Their overall appearance is paler than those of the House Sparrow. Incubation takes about eleven days, and the young leave the nest after eleven to fifteen days.

FOOD It eats a variety of food but prefers seeds, grain and, during the breeding season, insects.

DISTRIBUTION AND MOVEMENTS Breeds in the Cape Verde Islands, the Canary Islands, the Iberian peninsula, northwest Africa, Sardinia and the Balkan peninsula east to Asia Minor, the Near East, the northern Caucasus, Iran, Afghanistan and China. It is predominantly resident in Europe but migrant in Asia Minor and the Near East, where local populations winter in Egypt and Sinai. In Britain it is an exceptionally rare vagrant.

SUB-SPECIES *P.h. transcaspicus* (paler): the Near East, southwest Asia and possibly also present in parts of Asia Minor.

(Below) Wintering areas (magenta) and areas where the Spanish Sparrow may be seen all year round (orange)

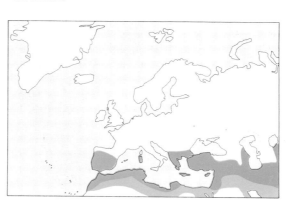

French: MOINEAU DU DESERT
Italian: PASSERA DEL DESERTO
Spanish: GORRIÓN DE DESIERTO

Dead Sea Sparrow
Passer moabiticus

HABITAT Scrub and trees by water including poplar and tamarisk.

IDENTIFICATION Length: 12 cm. Smaller than the House Sparrow from which it differs in a number of ways which are not always easy to detect in the field. The yellow patch on the side of the male's throat is the feature which best distinguishes this species from the House Sparrow. Male has a grey head with an off-white fairly prominent supercilium. Chin and throat are black. The female's plumage is much paler, and she resembles a pale female House Sparrow. Like the male she has a yellow marking on the side of the base of the throat though it is less conspicuous than the male's. Congregates in small flocks like other sparrows, often associating with Spanish Sparrows.

CALL The male utters a rhythmic chirping call note like that of the House Sparrow.

REPRODUCTION From late April. Breeds in trees and scrub in arid areas by water courses. Nest is a large cone-shaped or rounded structure with a side entrance. The male alone constructs it of twigs and needles and it is thickly lined with feathers, down and other soft debris. Eggs: four to six, white or buff spotted and speckled purple-brown or grey. Often so heavily speckled as to obscure the ground colour. Further information is lacking.

DISTRIBUTION AND MOVEMENTS Breeds in the extreme southeast of Turkey, the Dead Sea region, southwest Iran, Iraq and the Seistan region of Iran and Afghanistan.

SUB-SPECIES Sub-species are present in Asia.

(Below) Male Dead Sea Sparrow (foreground) and female

Snow Finch
Montifringilla nivalis

HABITAT Rocky and stony mountainous areas. Descends to lower levels in winter when it may be found in inhabited areas.

IDENTIFICATION Length: 18 cm. Deep brown upper parts; black rump and upper-tail coverts with some white at the sides. Off-white throat and black bib with traces of white; brownish-grey head. Creamy-white underparts. Bill: slate-black in summer and yellow with a dark tip in winter; black legs; brown iris. Female: like the male but with a browner head and more reddish coloration on the sides of its neck; smaller, less black bib. Juvenile resemble the female but with brownish rump, ash-grey throat and duller underparts with reddish coloration on the breast and flanks.
 Snow Finches perch in an upright position, nervously flicking their wings and tails. Rapid wingbeats in flight: strikingly black and white wings and tail are very noticeable in flight. Sociable and not very wild.

CALL A harsh 'tsoo-eek'. The song consists of a repeated 'siticher'.

REPRODUCTION From late April onwards. Breeds in large crevices in rocks. The nest is built by the female and consists of a heap of small roots, stalks, dry leaves and moss lined with hair and feathers. There are four or five (occasionally six) pure white or dull white eggs without markings. Incubation takes thirteen or fourteen days and is carried out by the female alone. The young are fed by both parents and leave the nest after twenty or twenty-one days. Probably double brooded.

FOOD Insects and seeds.

DISTRIBUTION AND MOVEMENTS Breeds in the Alps, Pyrenees, mountains of southeast Europe east to the Caucasus and Asia. Vagrant elsewhere.

SUB-SPECIES *M.n. nivalis:* Europe. *M.n. apicola:* the Caucasus and southwest and central Asia. Other sub-species are present in Asia.

(Facing page, near left) Snow Finch. (Below) Wintering areas (magenta) and areas where the Snow Finch may be seen all year round (orange)

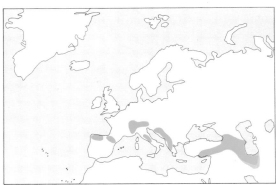

Rock Sparrow
Petronia petronia

HABITAT Rocky areas, desert edges, cultivated land and also inhabited areas.

IDENTIFICATION Length: 14 cm. Light brown with a conspicuous long, pale eyestripe. Dark stripe above, and pale stripe down the crown. Yellow upper breast patch and white spots on the tips of the tail feathers are sometimes difficult to distinguish in the field. Back is streaked although rump is almost uniform. Juveniles similar to adults but lack the yellow patch on the breast.

CALL Emits a 'tuut' and a wheezing 'chwee'.

REPRODUCTION From April onwards. Nests in a rock crevice, in a hollow tree or in a ruined building or wall. Sometimes will nest in a rodent's burrow. The nest is a domed structure of plant stalks and roots which is lined with feathers and down. Eggs: five or six, rarely four to eight, white or greenish-white with brown, dark brown or greyish markings. Details about incubation are lacking. Both parents tend the young which remain in the nest for twenty-one days.

FOOD Its varied diet consists of seeds, grain and insects.

DISTRIBUTION AND MOVEMENTS Breeds in southern Europe from Iberia east through southern France, Italy, the Balkan peninsula and Asia Minor east into Asia. Also breeds in northern Africa, Madeira and the Canary Islands.

SUB-SPECIES Sub-species are present in Madeira, the Canary Islands, Africa and Asia.

French: MOINEAU SOULCIE
Italian: PASSERA LAGIA
Spanish: GORRIÓN CHILLÓN
German: STEINSPERLING

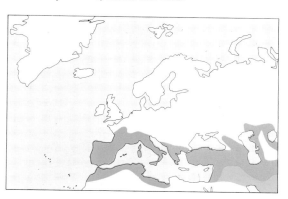

(Below) Rock Sparrow. (Left) Wintering areas (magenta) and areas where the Rock Sparrow may be seen all year round (orange)

French: PINSON DES NEIGES
Italian: FRINGUELLO ALPINO
Spanish: GORRIÓN ALPINO
German: SCHNEESPERLING

A. Christiansen

210

J. Burton/Bruce Coleman

T. Suominen

J. Carpenter/Bruce Coleman

Starlings are a comparatively homogeneous group of medium-sized passerines. They are all fairly stocky, and have strong legs, a robust bill and short tail. Starlings are highly gregarious, and may be seen in massive flocks. Their flight is direct and fast. Many species have glossy, very dark or black plumage, often with a metallic sheen. The sexes are alike.

There are one hundred and three species in the family Sturnidae. Starlings are omnivorous, but tend to prefer cultivated fruits and seeds. They are accomplished whistlers, and can often imitate other birds' songs. An Indian species, the Hill Myna *Gracula religiosa* is possibly the world's best mimic of a human voice.

Many species of this family are colonial nesters: others congregate in immense flocks, but only outside the breeding season. As a rule starlings nest in holes in trees, but some species also nest on houses or in nest boxes. They lay four or five pale bluish eggs which may sometimes have brown speckles. The female incubates the eggs although both parents tend the young.

Starlings are distributed exclusively in the Old World, mainly in the tropics, although some species are found in Europe, China and Japan. The greatest differentiation between species is found in the Indian subcontinent. One genus, *Aplonis*, is widely distributed in Polynesia, although some endemic island races are now extinct. The Lord Howe Island Starling *Aplonis fusca* and the Colonial Starling *A. metallicus* are among the few species of the family Sturnidae present in the Australian region.

The most well known and typical member of the family is the Starling *Sturnus vulgaris* which was introduced from Eurasia into the United States, and has now virtually invaded the North American continent. It has successfully ousted many local species with which it competes for nesting sites. The Starling's high-pitched squealing is familiar in town and city centres where thousands swarm to their roosting sites at dusk. In areas such as Trafalgar Square in the centre of London, starlings are considered a pest, along with the pigeons, as their droppings foul masonry and pavements. Various methods have been tried in order to drive them away, such as amplified recordings of their distress calls and the placing of a sticky jelly-like substance on the window ledges which causes them

(Above) Starling *Sturnus vulgaris* (top and bottom). (Above left) Superb Starlings *Spreo superbus* from Africa. (Facing page) Starlings *S. vulgaris:* flocks numbering thousands of birds are not uncommon. This highly gregarious species is equally at home in open woodland and city centres

A. Christiansen

(Right) Red-billed Oxpecker *Buphagus erythrorhynchus*. As its English name indicates, it feeds mainly on the parasites which infest the coats of large mammals. (Below) World distribution of the family Sturnidae

to feel uneasy when alighting. However starlings also assist humans in some ways: they feed on many insects in the soil of farmland which we consider pests.

One of the most beautiful and characteristic members of the family is the already mentioned Colonial Starling. It builds a hanging, flask-shaped nest like that of certain weavers. Among the most interesting species is the Wattled Starling *Creatophora cinerea*. It has no fixed area for breeding, but roams in huge flocks across the African savannahs in pursuit of locusts. It stops to nest where the insects breed, and feeds its young upon these insects. The conspicuous wattles on the head of the Wattled Starling disappear after the breeding season and are replaced by ordinary feathers. Another interesting species is the Rose-coloured Starling *Sturnus roseus*: it is the only medium-sized pink and black land bird. From time to time its population expansion is such that it erupts from the Middle East into Europe. It nests and then returns to its original area. This species is also a voracious consumer of insects, particularly locusts.

The two species of oxpecker of the genus *Buphagus* are usually allocated to the separate subfamily Buphaginae. The Yellow-billed Oxpecker *Buphagus africanus* and Red-billed Oxpecker *B. erythrorhynchus* are often seen on the backs of large wild and domestic mammals of the African plains, and feed mainly on the parasites which infest these mammals.

Starling
Sturnus vulgaris

French: ÉTOURNEAU SANSONNET
Italian: STORNO
Spanish: ESTORNINO PINTO
German: STAR

HABITAT Areas with scattered trees including parks and gardens. Also frequents cultivated areas and moorland, and is frequently seen in city centres roosting on buildings and in trees.

IDENTIFICATION Length: 21 cm. Compactly built with a short tail and long, pointed bill: pointed wings, triangular in shape, are noticeable in flight and help to distinguish it from the Blackbird. Adults have a green and purplish metallic sheen on the black plumage. Breast spangled with small, pale spots, more heavily marked in the winter. Juveniles are dull grey-brown with a paler throat than the male and an unspotted breast. In winter adults's bills are grey-brown or greenish-brown but in spring and summer the bill is a conspicuous lemon yellow.

The Starling may be confused with the Blackbird but the shape of the wings and shorter tail help to distinguish it. Flight is direct and fast with rapid wingbeats. It is a highly gregarious species and is often seen in huge flocks.

CALL Its usual call is a harsh 'tcheer'. Song is whistling and chattering. Also frequently mimics other birds.

REPRODUCTION From mid-April. Nests in loose colonies and isolated pairs. The nest is situated in holes in trees, buildings, in nest boxes and sometimes in holes in the ground. The nest is a loose cup-shaped accumulation of stems, leaves and other plant material. It is lined with feathers and moss. The male begins the construction of the nest before pairing has occurred: the female then completes it. Both sexes incubate for twelve or thirteen days. Both also tend the young which leave the nest after about twenty days.

FOOD Insects, worms, fruit and seeds.

DISTRIBUTION AND MOVEMENTS Breeds in Iceland, the Faeroes, Britain and Ireland east across Eurasia to Siberia. Breeds south to Italy, Asia Minor and northwest India. Winters in the breeding range and beyond to Iberia, northern Africa, Iran and India. Introduced to North America, southern Africa, Australia, New Zealand and Polynesia. In Britain and Ireland it is a widespread and numerous resident breeder, although only sparsely distributed in western Ireland. British and Irish populations are mainly sedentary. Winter and passage visitors are recorded from continental Europe.

SUB-SPECIES *S.v. faroensis:* the Faeroes. *S.v. zetlandicus:* Shetland Islands and the Outer Hebrides. *S.v. vulgaris:* the Azores and most of Europe. *S.v. tauricus:* Crimea and Asia Minor. *S.v. caucasicus:* northern Caucasus and southwest Asia. There are other sub-species in Asia.

(Above) Starling in winter plumage (top) and summer plumage. (Right) Breeding areas (yellow), wintering areas (magenta) and areas where the Starling may be seen all year round (orange)

French: MARTIN ROSELIN
Italian: STORNO ROSEO
Spanish: ESTORNINO ROSADO
German: ROSENSTAR

Rose-coloured Starling
Sturnus roseus

HABITAT Mainly open steppes and rocky areas: also cultivated land.

IDENTIFICATION Length: 21 cm. Pink breast and back: head, tail and wings black. Easily distinguished as it is the only pink and black medium-sized land bird. Crest is also conspicuous. Pink legs: bill orange-yellow in the summer and brown in the winter. Sociable at all times. Juveniles are brownish although paler than immature Starlings.

CALL Like the Starling's, but its song is more musical.

REPRODUCTION From early May. Nests in a hole in rocks or walls or on the ground. Nest is an untidy cup of plant material and is lined with feathers and hair. Breeds in large colonies. Eggs: five or six, rarely three to nine, glossy light blue. The female alone incubates for eleven to fourteen days. The young are tended by both parents and leave the nest after fourteen to nineteen days.

(Below) Adult Rose-coloured Starling (right) and juvenile (left). (Right) Breeding areas of the Rose-coloured Starling (yellow)

FOOD Mainly insects and fruit.

DISTRIBUTION AND MOVEMENTS Breeds from eastern Europe east through Asia Minor and the southern USSR to central Asia. Winters mainly in western India. It is a vagrant to western and northern Europe, and also in Iceland. In Britain and Ireland over two hundred have been recorded, but some may be escapes from captivity. Occurs in widely scattered areas, but chiefly on or near coasts.

Spotless Starling
Sturnus unicolor

HABITAT Found in habitats similar to the Starling's, although not as frequently in towns and cities.

IDENTIFICATION Length: 21 cm. Uniformly black plumage with metallic highlights: lack of spotting in breeding plumage distinguishes this species from the Starling. In winter grey-black with only slight pale spotting. Bill yellow. Juveniles darker than juvenile common Starlings.

CALL Like that of Starling, but louder and shriller.

REPRODUCTION From mid-April. Breeds both in colonies and in isolated pairs in holes in trees, ruined buildings or among rocks. Lays four to six uniform light blue eggs. The female alone incubates for thirteen days. The young are tended by both parents and leave the nest after twenty-one to twenty-three days.

FOOD Mainly insects, fruit and seeds.

DISTRIBUTION AND MOVEMENTS Breeds in the Iberian peninsula, eastern and southern Corsica, Sardinia, Sicily and northern Africa. Accidental in central and southern France, Italy, Malta and the Canaries.

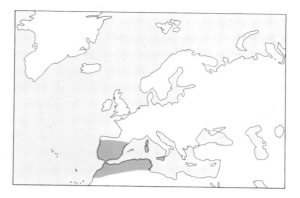

French : ÉTOURNEAU UNICOLORE
Italian : STORNO NERO
Spanish : ESTORNINO NEGRO
German : EINFARBSTAR

(Left) Areas where the Spotless Starling may be seen all year round (orange)

(Above) A flock of Starlings
S. vulgaris and (right) Starlings
drinking. (Facing page)
Starling in flight: its shorter
tail and triangular-shaped
wings distinguish it from the
Blackbird

J. S. Wightman/Ardea

ORIOLIDAE: Orioles

(Right and facing page)
Golden Orioles *Oriolus oriolus*
at the nest. (Below) World
distribution of the family
Oriolidae

This is a homogeneous family which consists of twenty-eight species. The orioles are found in Africa, Asia, Malaysia, New Guinea and Australia although they are absent from New Zealand. One species, the Golden Oriole *Oriolus oriolus*, is found throughout the southern Palearctic region, including much of continental Europe, and in India.

Orioles resemble both starlings and crows. Similar in size to a Blackbird, they have robust bills with a decurved culmen and fairly long, pointed wings especially in the migratory species. They are all arboreal in habit, feeding on insects and fruit in woods and forests. Usually found alone, they are wary and their flight is rapid and undulating.

Like the Golden Oriole, males of the species found in Africa and the Oriental region have bright yellow and black plumage, while the females have less striking greenish-yellow coloration with varying degrees of streaking. Some Malaysian species are basically black with crimson areas and one, the Black Oriole *Oriolus hosii* found in Borneo, is entirely black except for the under-tail coverts which are chestnut.

The nest is a finely woven and stitched together cup, placed on horizontal branches of trees, often at a considerable height from the ground.

Besides the resident species of the tropical forests there are also some highly migratory species such as the Golden Oriole which, originating from the Palearctic region, winters south of the Sahara. The Golden Oriole breeds in Britain only at irregular intervals.

French: LORIOT D'EUROPE
Italian: RIGOGOLO
Spanish: OROPÉNDOLA
German: PIROL

Golden Oriole
Oriolus oriolus

HABITAT Mixed and deciduous forests, less commonly in coniferous forests. Also fairly common in parks and gardens.

IDENTIFICATION Length: 24 cm. The male is bright yellow with black wings and tail. Female and juveniles yellowish-green, with darker wings and tail. Females and juveniles may be confused with the Green Woodpecker, but the bill is shorter and less stout, and unlike the Green Woodpecker, does not crouch on branches. Undulating flight. A skulking species which remains hidden in foliage.

CALL The male utters a characteristic musical whistle: 'weela-wee'. Both male and female emit a cat-like squalling cry.

REPRODUCTION From May onwards. The nest, built almost entirely by the female, is constructed in the fork of two horizontal branches. The rim of the cup-shaped nest is bound to the twigs. Usually three or four eggs are laid (rarely up to six), white or cream with a few blackish-purplish spots. Both sexes incubate for fourteen to fifteen days. Both tend the young which leave the nest after fourteen days. Possibly double brooded.

FOOD Insects and fruit.

DISTRIBUTION AND MOVEMENTS Breeds from southern Scandinavia, the Netherlands, France and Iberia east across Asia to Siberia and south to northern Africa, Asia Minor and India. Winters in tropical and southern Africa and in India. Breeds in very small numbers in Britain and also occurs as a scarce migrant in Britain and Ireland.

SUB-SPECIES Sub-species are present in Asia.

(Below) Male Golden Oriole (bottom) and female. (Right) Breeding areas (yellow) and areas where the Golden Oriole may be seen on passage (pink)

220

FAMILY CORVIDAE: Crows

The family Corvidae consists of just over a hundred species which vary in size from eighteen to seventy centimetres, thus including the largest birds in the order Passeriformes. The plumage may be black, black and white, or brilliantly coloured with various combinations of green, yellow, blue, purple and brown. The sexes are usually alike. The head may be ornamented with a crest or tufts of varying shape, size and structure. The tail varies from quite short to very long and is somewhat graduated in some species of magpie. The wings may be pointed or rounded, depending on migratory status: however most species are resident. The shape of the bill depends on the feeding habits, but it is always robust, often hooked and covered at the base with feathers. The legs are strong, with robust claws, adapted both for perching and for walking on the ground.

The family Corvidae undoubtedly represents one of the more developed stages, if not actually the most developed stage, in the evolution of birds. Extremely versatile behaviour, an often highly elaborate social structure, virtually cosmopolitan distribution and a vast number of species all testify to the success of this family. The species have achieved an extraordinary level of mental develop-

ment. This is due to their very great adaptability, in its turn rendered possible by the lack of extreme specialisation of structures which might be termed 'standard', with the exception of their mental functions which are without doubt far above average. Furthermore, the mere fact that some species, taking advantage of the habit of living alongside man, have succeeded in extending their range and increasing in numbers, is evidence of their peculiar gifts, not always found even in some of the higher mammals. Aggressive and bold, very often gregarious, all the crows are unusually able fliers.

Some sectors of the human population sometimes consider the behaviour of the crows so extremely rapacious as to justify their destruction by any means, legal or illegal. It is certainly true that the piratical habits of some species lead them to gorge themselves on the eggs of birds being reared for shoots such as pheasant and partridge, or into direct competition with farmers harvesting grain or fruit. It is however also true that, where nature has been left to its own devices, crows are among the normal predators fulfilling a necessary function.

Nesting may take place in thickly-populated colonies, but may also be isolated, even with species which are highly gregarious at other times of the

(Above) Hooded Crows *Corvus corone cornix* are easily distinguished from other crows by the grey back and underparts

I. Holmasen

J. Burton/Bruce Coleman

(Above) Siberian Jay *Perisoreus infaustus* and (above right) Jay *Garrulus glandarius:* the black and white feathers on the crown are sometimes erected to form a crest

year. The nest is usually a bulky structure of sticks and twigs, situated in trees, bushes, on buildings or cliffs. Some species build a dome-shaped nest. The number of eggs in a clutch varies with different surroundings and climatic conditions. In the tropics there is an average of two to four eggs per clutch while in other regions a clutch may contain up to nine eggs.

The level of sociability also differs, some species being highly territorial and others exclusively social. Konrad Lorenz's classical study of the Jackdaw *Corvus monedula* has revealed the way in which a sophisticated system of relationships between individuals supports a precisely-defined social hierarchy. Because of this hierarchy, needless clashes between individuals, which would only be to the detriment of the individual itself, are avoided. However at the same time it also permits far greater tolerance than is found in other forms of life. Without going into the details of Lorenz's study, it is perhaps enough to recall that among Jackdaws, if a female of low rank mates with one of the 'leaders' of the community, she herself automatically acquires higher rank and may command respect from the other birds. Furthermore, birds which respect

the social order receive in exchange aid from the community; in the Jackdaw colony studied by Lorenz, their social sense of duty led them to help one of their number which was injured.

Although many species have no true song and the call is somewhat coarse, the vocal language of crows is in fact quite rich. Although there are no real differences in voice between the sexes there may often be subtle differences of intonation between one individual and another. Another striking feature, even if not characteristic of this family, is their ability to mimic not only birds but other sounds and, at least when in captivity, the human voice.

The essentially cosmopolitan distribution of the Corvidae has been mentioned: however the family is more diversified and better represented in the northern hemisphere. New Zealand and many of the Pacific archipelagos have never been colonised by crows, for reasons which are still unclear. Typical crows of the genus *Corvus* are also absent in South America, which is however the home of several species of magpies and jays. Eight genera of jays, comprising thirty or so species, are restricted exclusively to the New World.

Taxonomists have made various attempts to

J. Burton/Bruce Coleman

separate the whole group into sub-families, a task which, despite all efforts, appears to be neither possible, nor appropriate. The most that can be said is that the nearest relatives of the crows are certain Australasian families, such as the birds of paradise of the family Paradisaeidae, the Old World orioles or Oriolidae, and the drongos or Dicruridae.

There are eight genera of American jays: the best-known species are those of the genera *Cyanocitta*, which includes the Blue Jay of North America *C. cristata* and *Cyanocorax*, with ten species in tropical America. Members of the latter genus are characterized by crests, or rather tufts, and patches of velvety plumage as in for instance the Plush-crested Jay *C. chrysops* and the Green Jay *C. yncas*. The Green Jay is perhaps one of the most beautiful of American species. Typical jays are represented by the common Eurasian Jay *Garrulus glandarius* and the Eurasian Black-throated Jay *G. lanceolatus* of the Himalayas and Lidth's Jay *G. lidthi* of the Ryukyu islands. The genus *Perisoreus* is Holarctic and comprises three species with soft plumage and delicate brown and grey coloration: the Siberian Jay *P. infaustus* found westwards as far as Lapland; the Szechwan Grey Jay *P. internigrans*; and lastly

the Grey Jay *P. canadensis*. The Grey Jay is also known as the Canada Jay.

The generic name 'magpie' is used for a group of corvids typified by the Magpie *Pica pica*. Many brilliantly-coloured species come from southeast Asia: for example the Yellow-tailed Blue Magpie *Urocissa flavirostris*, the Green Magpie *Cissa chinensis* and the Azure-winged Magpie *Cyanopica cyanus*. This last species is interesting in that it occurs discontinuously as two localised populations at either extreme of the Eurasian region, one population present in the Iberian peninsula and the other in China and Japan. The reasons for this apparent isolation are unclear but may well be related to the climatic factors of the glacial and post-glacial eras. The Magpie also occurs in North America as does the Yellow-billed Magpie *Pica nuttalli*. These two species are virtually identical except for the coloration of the bill, and some authorities consider them conspecific.

Four species found in the semi-arid plateaus of central Asia, belonging to the genus *Podoces*, as well as Hume's Ground Jay *Pseudopodoces humilis*, are known as 'ground jays' because of their terrestrial habits. They prefer to run on the ground rather

(Above) Raven *Corvus corax* with young at its cliff ledge nest

I. Holmasen

(Above) The Jackdaw *C. monedula* is the smallest of the European crows and frequents towns and villages

than fly. The two species of nutcracker are similar in shape but different in coloration. One, the common Nutcracker *Nucifraga caryocatactes* is Palearctic and is nut-brown in colour with white tear-shaped markings. Clark's Nutcracker *N. columbianus*, lives in the North American taiga and is grey with black and white wings and tail. Choughs of the genus *Pyrrhocorax* comprise two cliff-dwelling species, one of which, the Alpine Chough *P. graculus*, is found mainly in mountains.

Crows, rooks, ravens and jackdaws are grouped together in the genus *Corvus*. The most widespread of the Palearctic species is probably the Rook *Corvus*

frugilegus; in this species the adults have an area of bare skin on the face at the base of the bill. Similar, but lacking the bare skin, are the Carrion and Hooded Crow *Corvus corone*. The two distinct races, the Carrion Crow *Corvus corone corone* and Hooded Crow *C.c. cornix* are considered of a single species which, where their ranges overlap both in Europe and in Asia, form relatively stable hybrid populations. The largest species is without doubt the Raven *C. corax* which is found in the Palearctic region and also in parts of the Nearctic region, penetrating southwards as far as Central America.

Among the smaller species are the common Jackdaw *C. monedula*, typical of rocky regions inland or along the coast, where it competes for nesting with the Rock Dove *Columba livia*. The Daurian Jackdaw *C. dauricus*, the Jungle Crow *C. macrorhynchos* and the Collared Crow *C. torquatus* are other species of the genus *Corvus*. There are many American species, of which one of the most common is the Common Crow *C. brachyrhynchos* which in North America replaces, ecologically speaking, the Carrion and Hooded Crow.

Other species are present in the Ethiopian and Malagasy regions, for example the very widespread Pied Crow *C. albus* and Brown-necked Raven *C. ruficollis* which occurs as far as southeast Asia and is treated by some authorities as conspecific with the Raven. The Fan-tailed Raven *C. rhipidurus*, of northeastern Africa and the Near East, is a species with a short, fan-shaped tail. In the Oriental region, as well as the species already mentioned, the House Crow *C. splendens* is present. It is a typical representative of the Indian avifauna.

Other species inhabit Australia, New Guinea and Oceania, typified by the Australian Raven *C. coronoides*. The Moluccas, the Solomon Islands, New Caledonia and the Loyalty Islands are each the home of an endemic species. In the Pacific the only other archipelago where crows are found is Hawaii, where the Hawaiian Crow *C. tropicus* occurs.

This leaves two monotypic genera, whose real affinities are still unclear. The Piapiac *Ptilostomus afer* is found in western Africa and as far east as Uganda. It is smaller than a magpie but with an equally long and graduated tail, glossy black plumage tinged brown on tail and wings and a reddish bill in juveniles, black in the adult. It is a confiding species, and roams through villages, often among flocks of sheep and goats. The second species was only discovered in 1938, when the Italian ornithologist Edgardo Moltoni described it, from examples taken in southern Ethiopia, giving it the name Stresemann's Bush-Crow *Zavattariornis stresemanni*. It is a small corvid, with grey upper parts, bluish-black wings and tail, white underparts and a patch of bare blue skin around the eye. Its habits are still not well known, but anatomical observations indicate that it belongs to the family Corvidae.

(Left) World distribution of the family Corvidae

Jay
Garrulus glandarius

French: GEAI DES CHÊNES
Italian: GHIANDAIA
Spanish: ARRENDAJO
German: EICHELHÄHER

HABITAT Woods and areas with scattered trees such as orchards, parks and large gardens.

IDENTIFICATION Length: 34 cm. Plumage coloration variable, but white rump, blue and white wing patches combined with large size make it easily identifiable. Adults: under-tail coverts and belly white; rest of body and part of wing coverts brownish. Primaries brown-black spotted bluish, fringed whitish on outer ones; secondaries black, the base partly white with blue markings; innermost ones chestnut-brown tipped black. Bill black; iris bluish-white. Black and white feathers on the head may be erected to form a crest. Flight is slow although markedly undulating. Often seen hopping on the ground. See also page 238.

CALL Most characteristic call is a harsh 'skaak' although there are many variations. Has no true song but may emit, sometimes collectively, crooning notes interspersed with other harsher sounds.

REPRODUCTION From late April. The nest is built by both sexes and is usually situated over two metres off the ground, usually in the fork of a tree or against the trunk. It is a cup made of twigs and stems with a little mud mixed in, and is lined with grasses and hair. Eggs: generally five or seven, rarely three to ten, pale bluish or greenish very finely speckled with olive-green or buff. Speckling may be concentrated at the larger end. Both parents incubate for about sixteen days. Both tend the young which leave the nest after nineteen or twenty days.

FOOD Mainly vegetable matter such as berries and nuts: also molluscs, insects, small mammals and young birds.

DISTRIBUTION AND MOVEMENTS Breeds in Britain, Ireland and most of Europe east across southern Siberia to China and Japan. Also breeds in northwest Africa and Asia Minor east to southern Burma. Northern populations are partially migratory. In Britain and Ireland it is a widespread species breeding throughout England and Wales, in southern Scotland and in Ireland except the north and west. Also occurs as a winter visitor.

SUB-SPECIES *G.g. rufitergum:* breeds Britain and Brittany. *G.g. hibernicus:* Ireland. *G.g. glandarius:* northern Europe and the western USSR south to the Pyrenees, Alps and northern Balkans.

(Below) Jay (left) and the Asiatic form (right). (Left) Areas where the Jay may be seen all year round (orange)

225

French: MÉSANGEAI IMITATEUR
Italian: GHIANDAIA SIBERIANA
Spanish: ARRENDAJO FUNESTO
German: UNGLÜCKSHÄHER

Siberian Jay
Perisoreus infaustus

HABITAT Coniferous and birch forests in the far north. In winter it is also found on the fringes of inhabited areas.

IDENTIFICATION Length: 30 cm. Smaller than Jay with grey-brown coloration and darker head. However rufous in wing, rump and tail is conspicuous in flight. Primary coverts and base of primaries rufous, as are outer tail feathers: central tail feathers grey. Bill and legs dark. Tail is longer and bill less stout than the Jay's. A shy and retiring bird, not easily observed. See also page 238.

CALL The usual calls are a loud harsh 'chaar' and a disyllabic 'whisse'.

REPRODUCTION From early April. The nest is a loose cup of twigs and stalks, built in pine or fir, at a height of four to fifteen metres, and lined with lichens and feathers. Eggs: usually four, bluish, with olive brown or greyish spotting. The female alone incubates for eighteen to twenty days. Both tend the young which leave the nest after about twenty-four days. However the family remains together through the following winter.

FOOD Insects, berries and fruits.

DISTRIBUTION AND MOVEMENTS Resident in the coniferous belt from Scandinavia east through the USSR to the Pacific coast. Also found south as far as southern Urals, Mongolia and Manchuria.

SUB-SPECIES Sub-species are present in Asia.

Azure-winged Magpie
Cyanopica cyanus

HABITAT Open woodland and areas with scattered trees such as cork and olive groves and large gardens.

IDENTIFICATION Length: 34 cm. Distinguished by jet-black head and nape. Wings blue, fringed black on primaries; distinctive long, blue, graduated tail. Upper parts grey-brown, underparts pale, almost white, with grey-brown flanks. A gregarious and noisy species. Flight, like the Magpie's, is weaker than that of the typical crows and both species appear almost unbalanced by the long tail. See also page 238.

CALL A characteristic peevish 'sreee' which is repeated.

REPRODUCTION From late April. Nest is a bulky cup of twigs, roots, moss with some mud mixed in. It is lined with plant fibres, hair and fur and is situated in a fork or on large branches of a tree from three to four metres off the ground. Eggs: five to seven, rarely nine, pale creamy-buff with sparse but bold brownish or grey markings. The female alone incubates but both parents tend the young.

FOOD Insects, seeds and some animal matter.

DISTRIBUTION AND MOVEMENTS There are three isolated breeding populations: one in Portugal and southern Spain, the second in Transbaikalia and northern Mongolia, the third from eastern Siberia to China and Japan. Resident although, especially in the east of the range, performs erratic movements.

SUB-SPECIES Sub-species are present in Asia.

(Below) Siberian Jay. (Right) Wintering areas (magenta) and areas where the Siberian Jay may be seen all year round (orange)

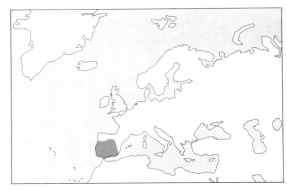

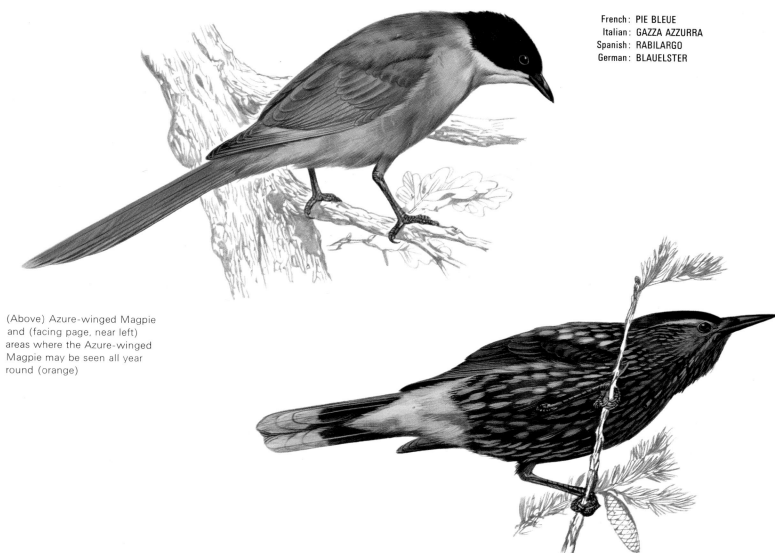

French: PIE BLEUE
Italian: GAZZA AZZURRA
Spanish: RABILARGO
German: BLAUELSTER

(Above) Azure-winged Magpie and (facing page, near left) areas where the Azure-winged Magpie may be seen all year round (orange)

French: CASSENOIX MOUCHETÉ
Italian: NOCCIOLAIA
Spanish: CASCANUECES
German: TANNENHÄHER

Nutcracker
Nucifraga caryocatactes

HABITAT Coniferous and mixed forests.

IDENTIFICATION Length: 32 cm. Only large bird with dark brown plumage covered with large white spots. Under-tail coverts white and sides of shortish tail also white: this white coloration is very noticeable in flight. Bill long and pointed. Hops on the ground, but is frequently seen perching on the top of a tree. Flight is markedly undulating. In Scandinavia, like the Jay, it collects and stores nuts by burying them. See also page 238.

CALL Usual cry is a harsh 'kraak'. Like the Jay does not have a true song.

REPRODUCTION From mid-March. Nest is a cup of twigs, moss and lichens with some mud mixed in. It is lined with grass and lichens. The nest is built in conifers, usually fairly high up against the trunk. Eggs: three or sometimes two to five, bluish-green eggs with fine olive-brown specklings. The female alone incubates for about eighteen days. Both parents tend the young which leave the nest after about twenty-one days.

FOOD Chiefly seeds of conifers, but also berries, insects and small mammals.

DISTRIBUTION AND MOVEMENTS Breeds in northern and mountainous areas of Europe from Scandinavia, the Alps and southeast Europe east across Eurasia to China and Japan. Occasionally irrupts southwards and westwards into temperate Europe including Britain. Generally rare in Britain, but a major invasion in 1968 brought several hundred to the country.

SUB-SPECIES Sub-species are present in Asia.

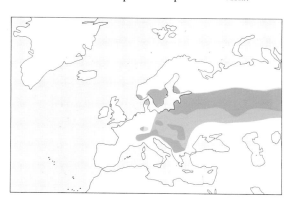

(Above) Nutcracker. (Left) Wintering areas (magenta) and areas where the Nutcracker may be seen all year round (orange)

French: PIE BAVARDE
Italian: GAZZA
Spanish: URRACA
German: ELSTER

Magpie
Pica pica

HABITAT Areas with scattered trees and scrub, including cultivated land and suburban areas.

IDENTIFICATION Length: 46 cm. One of the most distinctive and easily recognised birds in Europe due to its very long graduated tail and black and white coloration. Purple-blue gloss on body feathers and green gloss on tail are only apparent when seen at close quarters. Juvenile is duller than the adult and has a much shorter tail. Flight is weaker than that of other crows and appears unbalanced due to the long tail. On the ground hops or walks sideways. Usually seen in small flocks except at roosts and in spring when it gathers in greater numbers. See also page 238.

CALL The usual call is a rapid 'chat-chat-chat-chat'.

REPRODUCTION From early April onwards. The nest is a bulky cup of sticks, mud, plant fibre and hair. An open dome of twigs, leaving an opening at the edge of the cup, is usually present. Both male and female build the nest which is situated in bushes or trees or rarely on buildings. Eggs: five to eight, rarely up to ten, bluish greenish or buff, heavily spotted with olive brown and grey. The female alone incubates for seventeen or eighteen days. Both parents tend the young.

FOOD Chiefly insects, but also small mammals, birds (and their eggs and young), worms, molluscs and vegetable matter such as nuts.

DISTRIBUTION AND MOVEMENTS Breeds throughout much of Eurasia from Scandinavia, Britain, Ireland and Iberia east to Siberia and south through Asia Minor to Indochina. Also breeds in northwest Africa and North America. Sedentary. In Britain and Ireland it is a numerous and widespread resident breeder, becoming, however, rather thinly spread in the north of Scotland.

SUB-SPECIES *P.p. pica*: southern Scandinavia, central and southeastern Europe, Asia Minor, Near East and Cyprus. *P.p. galliae*: Belgium. France, Switzerland, Italy and the Balkan peninsula. *P.p. melanotos*: Iberia. Other sub-species are present throughout the range.

(Below) Areas where the Magpie may be seen all year round (orange)

Chough
Pyrrhocorax pyrrhocorax

HABITAT Cliffs both in mountains and on coasts.

IDENTIFICATION Length: 40 cm. Black plumage glossed greenish-blue; bill and legs bright red. Easily distinguished from Jackdaw by absence of grey in plumage and from Alpine Chough by longer, red bill. Juveniles less glossy than adults, with wings and tail tinged brown, bill tinged yellowish to orange, and orange-red legs. Flight more buoyant than that of other black corvids: also performs aerobatics like the Raven. Both hops and walks.

Sociable, roosts in colonies. Flocks are usually small. During courtship the male flaps his wings, 'caresses' the female with his bill and offers her food. See also page 238.

CALL Emits a 'kyow' and a 'k-chuff' from which its English name is derived. Also rarely emits a Starling-like chattering but no true song.

REPRODUCTION From late April. Nests in crevices or on cliff ledges: occasionally on old buildings. The nest is a bulky cup of twigs and grasses and is thickly lined with wool and hair. Eggs: three to five sometimes two to seven, creamy-white or pale greenish, with profuse brown, yellowish-brown and grey spotting. The female alone incubates for seventeen to twenty-one days.

FOOD Mostly insects: also small molluscs, crustaceans and worms.

DISTRIBUTION AND MOVEMENTS Breeds in Ireland, Britain, France and Iberia eastwards locally across southern Europe to the Himalayas and China. Basically sedentary. In Britain and Ireland it has decreased as a resident breeder over the past two centuries and is now present only in coastal Ireland, southwest Scotland, the Isle of Man and west and north Wales. The breeding population numbers under a thousand pairs.

SUB-SPECIES *P.p. erythrorhamphus:* Iberia, France, Switzerland and Italy. Other sub-species are present in Asia.

French: CRAVE À BEC ROUGE
Italian: GRACCHIO CORALLINO
Spanish: CHOVA PIQUIRROJA
German: ALPENKRÄHE

(Left) Areas where the Chough may be seen all year round (orange)

French: CHOCARD DES ALPES
Italian: GRACCHIO
Spanish: CHOVA PIQUIGUALDA
German: ALPENDOHLE

Alpine Chough
Pyrrhocorax graculus

HABITAT High mountainous country.

IDENTIFICATION Length: 38 cm. Distinguished from Chough by shorter, less decurved and yellow not red bill. Seen at close quarters, the black plumage has more greenish, less bluish, gloss. Juveniles have more brownish plumage with blackish legs. Flight and behaviour very similar to the Chough. See also page 238.

CALL Emits a musical 'cherrish' and a short 't-chuiup'.

REPRODUCTION From April onwards. The nest is built in crevices in rocks. It is a bulky cup of sticks and roots and is lined with finer grasses. Eggs: usually four, sometimes three to six, whitish with brown and greyish speckles and spots.

FOOD Insects, molluscs, fruit and seeds; also carrion and refuse.

DISTRIBUTION AND MOVEMENTS Breeds in the Alps and Pyrenees, and mountainous areas in Morocco, central and southeastern Europe. Breeds eastwards through Asia Minor, the Near East, Caucasus and Iranian region as far as the Himalayas.

SUB-SPECIES A sub-species is present in Asia.

Daurian Jackdaw
Corvus dauricus

HABITAT Prefers cultivated, open country like the Jackdaw; also frequents river valleys and rocky mountain areas.

IDENTIFICATION Length: 32 cm. Slightly smaller than Jackdaw, but otherwise very similar. The black upper parts have somewhat less metallic gloss and the underparts are either whitish (in the light phase) or black (in the dark phase). Has a distinct white collar at the base of the neck. The wings are shorter than those of the Jackdaw. Considered by some authorities to be conspecific with the Jackdaw. See also page 236.

CALL Similar to that of Jackdaw.

REPRODUCTION From May onwards. Nests in colonies in trees or among rocks. However further information is lacking.

FOOD Insects and plant material.

DISTRIBUTION AND MOVEMENTS An Asiatic species, breeding from central Siberia east to Japan, China and south to the Altai mountains. Winters in the south of the breeding range. Accidental in Europe in Finland.

(Below) Alpine Chough. (Right) Areas where the Alpine Chough may be seen all year round (orange)

French: CHOUCAS ORIENTAL
Italian: TACCOLA DI DAURIA
Spanish: GRAJILLA DÁURICA
German: WEISSBAUCHDOHLE

French: CHOUCAS DES TOURS
Italian: TACCOLA
Spanish: GRAJILLA
German: DOHLE

(Above) Daurian Jackdaw

Jackdaw
Corvus monedula

HABITAT Open countryside and cultivated areas: frequently seen on coasts. Common in towns and villages.

IDENTIFICATION Length: 33 cm. Smallest black crow and the only black bird with a grey nape. Adult: has nape and ear coverts grey, remaining plumage black above and dark grey below. Juveniles browner. Scandinavian sub-species *C.m. monedula* has light grey collar and paler underparts. Flight and gait quicker and jerkier than those of other black crows. See also page 236.

CALL A short 'chack' and 'kyow'.

REPRODUCTION From late April. Nests on a rocky outcrop on cliffs, in a crevice in a tree, a hole in the ground or on a building. Often breeds in colonies. In open sites builds a stick nest which is lined with wool, hair and plant materials. In holes the sticks may be absent or only scanty. In vertical holes sticks may be lodged into position. Eggs: four to six, sometimes two to nine, pale blue with black-brown and blue-grey markings. The female alone incubates for about seventeen days. Both tend the young which leave the nest after twenty-eight to thirty-two days.

FOOD Insects and plant material.

DISTRIBUTION AND MOVEMENTS Breeds from Scandinavia, Britain, Ireland and Iberia east across Eurasia to Kashmir and China. Also breeds in northwest Africa and the Middle East. Generally sedentary although northern populations winter in the south of the breeding range or just beyond. In Britain and Ireland it is an abundant breeding bird and a numerous winter visitor.

SUB-SPECIES *C.m. monedula*: Scandinavia. *C.m. spermologus*: western Europe and Morocco. Other sub-species are present in Asia.

(Above) Jackdaw. (Below) Breeding areas (yellow), wintering areas (magenta) and areas where the Jackdaw may be seen all year round (orange)

French: CORBEAU BRUN
Italian: CORVO COLLOROSSO
German: BRAUNNACKENRABE

Brown-necked Raven
Corvus ruficollis

HABITAT Desert areas; also on rocks near sea coasts.

IDENTIFICATION Length: 50 cm. Similar in appearance to Raven but less bulky: bill is also less stout and wings are more pointed. The brown coloration of nape and neck, is difficult to observe in the field except when observed close to. Reliable distinguishing feature is its desert habitat. In some cases may co-exist with Raven, but does not interbreed with it.

CALL Higher-pitched and clearer than that of Raven: emits a bell-like note. Also has a cawing which resembles the Rook's or Carrion Crow's.

REPRODUCTION From mid-March. Builds a bulky nest of sticks which is lined with grass, hair and wool. It is situated in a tree, bush or on a rock ledge or old building. Eggs: usually five, smooth glossy blue with olive-brown or blue-grey speckles and scribbles. The female incubates, occasionally assisted by the male for about twenty days.

DISTRIBUTION AND MOVEMENTS Breeds in northern Africa and the Middle East south to Kenya and Nigeria and east to Iraq and Turkestan.

SUB-SPECIES *C.r. edithae:* Somalia.

(Right) Areas where the Brown-necked Raven may be seen all year round (orange)

Rook
Corvus frugilegus

French: CORBEAU FREUX
Italian: CORVO
Spanish: GRAJA
German: SAATKRÄHE

HABITAT Open country and cultivated areas. Less frequent, although present, in swampy or well-wooded areas. Also present in inhabited areas although avoids dense habitations.

IDENTIFICATION Length: 46 cm. Adult has bare, grey-white face: remaining plumage black. The Rook is the only large black land bird with a bare face patch. Bill blackish-grey. Purple gloss to the head and back feathers and 'bushy' thigh feathers distinguish it from the Carrion Crow. Juvenile has completely feathered face and may be confused with the Carrion Crow, but has a more slender bill.

Highly gregarious; gathers in groups in rookeries. Flight sustained and rather heavy. Walks slowly and sedately. Frequently seen in company with Jackdaws.

CALL The usual note is a 'caw' or 'caaah', less raucous and more prolonged than the call of the Carrion Crow. However has a highly varied vocabulary including a Raven-like croak.

REPRODUCTION From late March. Nests in colonies in the top of large trees: nests may be very close together. The nest is a bulky cup of sticks with mud built into it, and is lined with grass, roots, leaves and hair. It contains three to five eggs which vary in colour from bluish-green to grey-green: the markings range in intensity from heavy blotching to fine speckling, and are usually pale blue to brown-green in colour. The female alone incubates for sixteen to twenty days. Normally single brooded.

FOOD Its varied diet includes roots, seeds, insects, molluscs, small birds and their eggs.

DISTRIBUTION AND MOVEMENTS Breeds from Scandinavia, Britain, Ireland and France east across Europe and central Asia. Also breeds locally south to Spain, Greece and Iran. Northern populations winter south in the breeding range and beyond to northern Africa, the Persian Gulf, northwest India and southern China. In Britain and Ireland is an abundant and widely distributed resident breeder, although only locally in northwest Scotland. Basically sedentary although there is some post-breeding wandering. Also occurs as a winter visitor from the continent.

SUB-SPECIES Sub-species are present in Asia.

(Above) Adult Rook (right) and juvenile (left). (Below) Breeding areas (yellow), wintering areas (magenta) and areas where the Rook may be seen all year round (orange)

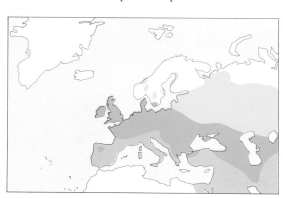

233

French: CORNEILLE
Italian: CORNACCHIA
Spanish: CORNEJA
German: KRÄHE

Carrion Crow and Hooded Crow
Corvus corone

HABITAT All types of country including arid areas, coasts, cultivated and wooded land and city centres.

IDENTIFICATION Length: 46 cm. The Carrion Crow *C.c. corone* has completely black plumage and is distinguished from the adult Rook by the feathered, not bare, base of the bill and from the juvenile Rook by the more robust and decurved bill. It also has a greenish gloss and 'non-bushy' thigh feathers. The Hooded Crow *C.c. cornix* is similar in shape and size to the Carrion Crow, but its grey back and underparts make it immediately distinguishable. However many hybrids, intermediate in coloration between the Hooded and Carrion, do occur.

Like other crows, feeds mainly on the ground. Flight appears rather ponderous. Walks and sidles in a somewhat awkward, hopping manner. Generally seen singly or in pairs, sometimes in flocks especially to roost.

CALL Both the Carrion and Hooded Crow emit a rasping 'kaah' which is usually repeated three times.

REPRODUCTION From late March. Nest is a bulky cup of sticks and moss bound together with earth. It is lined with wool, hair and sometimes feathers and is usually situated high up in a tree but may also be in a bush or on a rock ledge. Eggs: four to six, blue or bluish-green spotted and streaked to varying degrees with olive-green, brownish, or blue-grey. The eggs may be almost unmarked or completely obscured. The female alone incubates for eighteen or twenty days.

FOOD Consumes a wide variety of food including small mammals, young birds and eggs, frogs, molluscs, insects and vegetable matter.

DISTRIBUTION AND MOVEMENTS Breeds from the Faeroes, Britain and Ireland across most of Eurasia to China and south to Egypt, the Persian Gulf and the Himalayas. Northern populations are partially or wholly migratory and winter in the south of the breeding range or beyond to northern Africa and northwest India. In Britain and Ireland it is a widespread and resident breeder. The Hooded Crow *C.c. cornix* is found north of a line across the Scottish lowlands and in the Isle of Man and Ireland. The Carrion Crow *C.c. corone* breeds in the rest of Britain.

SUB-SPECIES *C.c. corone* (entirely black plumage): western Europe including Britain except for northern Scotland east to the Elbe and south to Iberia and the Alps. *C.c. cornix* (grey back and underparts): Ireland, Isle of Man, northern Scotland, Scandinavia and from the Elbe and northern Italy eastwards. Other sub-species are present in Asia.

(Below) Carrion Crow (left) and Hooded Crow (right). Breeding areas (yellow), wintering areas (magenta) and areas where the Carrion and Hooded Crow may be seen all year round (orange)

Raven
Corvus corax

HABITAT Inhabits a wide variety of open and hilly areas from tundra to coasts. Also common in arid areas and wooded areas.

IDENTIFICATION Length: 64 cm. Largest all-black bird of Europe: almost the size of a Buzzard. Distinguished from other crows by large size, heavy bill and distinctive voice. Even the juvenile has a long bill. Flight is heavy, with regular, powerful wingbeats, often soars, and in spring performs acrobatics, nosediving and flying upside down. Lives in pairs throughout the year and gathers in flocks to roost. See also page 236.

CALL Chief call is a repeated 'pruk-pruk'. Also emits a high-pitched 'tok-tok-tok'.

REPRODUCTION From February. Nest is a large mass of twigs, sticks and plant material, bound together with earth and moss. It is lined with grass, moss and hair, and is built by both sexes. The nest is situated on a rock ledge or in the fork of a large tree. Eggs: four to six, rarely three to seven, glossy bluish or greenish with olive, grey or brownish scribblings and blotches. Extent of marking on eggs may vary within a clutch. The female alone incubates for about twenty days. Both tend the young.

DISTRIBUTION AND MOVEMENTS Breeds from Greenland, Iceland, the Faeroes, Scandinavia, Ireland, Britain and Iberia east across Eurasia to the Pacific and south to northwest Africa, the Near East, Iran and India. Also breeds in North and Central America. Mainly sedentary. In Britain it is a widely distributed resident breeder in western coastal and upland areas.

SUB-SPECIES *C.c. varius:* Ireland and Faeroes.

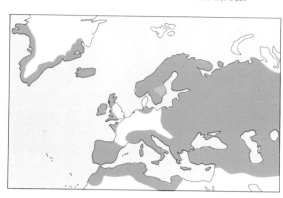

French: GRAND CORBEAU
Italian: CORVO IMPERIALE
Spanish: CUERVO
German: KOLKRABE

(Left) Wintering areas (magenta) and areas where the Raven may be seen all year round (orange)

Crows in flight

1: **RAVEN** *(Corvus corax)* Larger in size than any other member of the family. Head rather elongated, tail wedge-shaped, wings long and pointed (a). In profile (b) the long neck is particularly conspicuous. When soaring (c) the tail is spread and appears rounded. Seen from in front (d), the wingtips curve slightly upwards.

2: **ROOK** *(Corvus frugilegus)* Adult (a) is distinguished by bare, whitish face patch. The long narrow wings and long tail are also noticeable (b).

3: **DAURIAN JACKDAW** *(Corvus dauricus)* From above (a) grey collar is a distinguishing feature. From below (b) differs from Hooded Crow by having grey only on belly and not on undertail coverts and wings. In profile (c) distinguished by pale collar.

4: **JACKDAW** *(Corvus monedula)* Wings fairly short and broad (a). Illustrated in flight (b) and when soaring (c). In profile (d) wingtips appear fairly compact.

5: **CARRION AND HOODED CROW** *(Corvus corone)* Carrion Crow (a) is distinguished from Rook by shorter head and tail and squarer wings. Hooded Crow (b) distinguished from all other crows by grey on underparts and back. Shown in profile in (c) and (d).

(Below) Rook *C. frugilegus*

A. & E. Bomford/Ardea

6: CHOUGH (*Pyrrhocorax pyrrhocorax*) From beneath (a) distinguished by red bill and legs and rounded wings. From front (b) wingtips are upturned. Various phases of flight are illustrated (c, d, e). For comparison the Jackdaw is also illustrated (f, g). Flight of the Chough is much more buoyant than that of other black crows: also performs aerobatics like the Raven.

7: ALPINE CHOUGH (*Pyrrhocorax graculus*) Has yellow bill and red legs; tail is more rounded than that of Chough and wings narrower.

8: NUTCRACKER (*Nucifraga caryocatactes*) From beneath (a) shows dense pale spotting, also present on upper parts. Under-tail coverts and tip of tail white. Sometimes 'dives' (b) from tops of trees.

9: SIBERIAN JAY (*Perisoreus infaustus*) From above (a) crown is dark and wings, rump and tail rufous. From beneath (b) rufous on wings and tail conspicuous.

10: JAY (*Garrulus glandarius*) From above (a) tail is black, rump white, distinctive pattern on wings black, white and blue. Beneath (b) under-tail coverts are white, belly and wing coverts brownish. Illustrated in profile (c).

11: AZURE-WINGED MAGPIE (*Cyanopica cyanus*) From above (a) predominantly blue coloration and long tail are conspicuous. From below (b) is brownish-grey.

12: MAGPIE (*Pica pica*) From above (a) scapulars and part of wings are white. From beneath (b), is black and white. Tail long and graduated.

(Below) Choughs *P. pyrrhocorax*

R. F. Porter/Ardea

L. Nostrom

(Right) Alpine Chough *P. graculus* and (below) Magpie *P. pica*

J. & S. Bottomley/Ardea

FINCHES AND FOOD
Feeding habits and adaptations

To most people, the word 'finch' implies a small seed-eating bird with a stout bill. But in one part of the world or another, the same word has been applied to at least eleven different groups of birds of varying degrees of affinity. All these birds have the same specialisations for dealing with hard seeds: heavy conical bills, strong skulls, large jaw muscles and powerful gizzards. Yet they differ so much in the other details of their anatomy and behaviour that they are without doubt derived from several ancestral stocks. They provide an example of convergent evolution, that is, of unrelated animals growing to look like one another because they have the same way of life.

In this article two well-known groups are discussed: the Fringillinae (Old World seedeaters) and the Carduelinae (goldfinches and allies). They are joined into a single family Fringillidae. These finches are distinguished from other seed-eating birds by certain details of skull-structure, the presence of nine instead of ten large primary feathers in each wing, twelve large tail feathers, and the fact that the female is responsible for building the cup-shaped nest and for incubating the eggs. Here the eighteen European representatives of this family are discussed, in regard to their feeding behaviour and the way that their diets influence their particular lifestyles.

Feeding habits of different species

Each of the European finches has fairly distinct feeding habits, which helps to reduce competition for food between them. The species differ from one another in three main ways. The first is in the size of seeds taken, and in general, the larger the bill, the larger the seeds in the diet. This is illustrated, for example, by the Redpoll *Acanthis*

(Above) Male Linnet *Acanthis cannabina* feeding chicks: Linnets feed mainly on the seeds of farmland weeds

A. Fatras/Ardea

(Above) Greenfinch *Carduelis chloris*: its bill is larger than the Linnet's, and it feeds on larger seeds of trees and cereal crops. (Below) Crossbill *Loxia curvirostra*

H. Reinhard/Bruce Coleman

flammea, Linnet *A. cannabina*, Greenfinch *Carduelis chloris* and Hawfinch *Coccothraustes coccothraustes* which have bills of roughly similar shape, but of different size, from small to large. Thus, the Redpoll specialises on tiny seeds of plants such as birch and willowherb, the Linnet on slightly larger seeds of various farmland weeds, the Greenfinch on larger seeds of cereals and trees, and the Hawfinch on large, hard tree-fruits, including cherries.

The second main way in which species differ is in the shape of the bill, which influences the types of seed-heads they can best feed upon. The species just mentioned have blunt, conical bills and feed largely from the ground, or from plants which have fairly exposed seeds along a stem, such as grasses. The Goldfinch *Carduelis carduelis* and Siskin *C. spinus* have narrow, tweezer-like bills, which are well-suited for extracting the seeds that are deeply embedded in cones or in the heads of thistles. The bill of the Goldfinch is slightly longer than that of the Siskin, and this is reflected in the kinds of plants these birds favour. Also, the bill of the male Goldfinch is slightly longer than that of the female, and this enables the male to reach the seeds of teasels which lie at the bottom of long spiked tubes. The Bullfinch *Pyrrhula pyrrhula* has a short, rounded bill, which enables it to nip off tree-buds, as well as various kinds of seeds and fruits. Lastly, the three species of crossbills, as their name implies, have specialised bills which are curved and crossed at the tip. These are used to prise apart the bracts of conifer cones to release the seeds which form almost their entire food. The three species differ in size of bill and in size of cone preferred. The small Two-barred or White-

winged Crossbill *Loxia leucoptera* has the smallest bill and feeds largely from the small, soft cones of larch; the medium-sized Crossbill *L. curvirostra* has a medium-sized bill, and feeds chiefly from the larger, harder cones of spruce; and the largest Parrot Crossbill *L. pytyopsittacus* has a very heavy bill, and specialises on the large, hard cones of pine. Sub-species of these various crossbills, which live in areas with other conifers, have bills which are adapted accordingly. Thus, in these various ways, the shape of a finch's bill influences the kinds of plants it can best exploit. For much of the year there is considerable overlap in diet between the various species, and the differences are most marked in winter when food is scarcest and competition most intense.

The third factor influencing feeding habits is the positions in which the birds are able to feed. Some species, such as the Chaffinch *Fringilla coelebs*, can only feed in a standing position, and obtain most of their food from the ground or from firm horizontal twigs. Others, such as the Greenfinch and Linnet, can cling to vertical stems with ease and can also hang upside down; these species obtain almost all their food directly from the plant. They also use their feet in feeding, clamping a plant-head against a branch while it is worked with the bill: thereby they tackle seed-heads that would otherwise be difficult for them. The positions in which finches feed are in turn influenced by their anatomy – the most agile species are either light in weight (Redpoll and Siskin) or have unusually short, strong legs (crossbills).

Finches also differ in habitat, and, because of the different kinds of plants available, this tends to accentuate the food differences. The Hawfinch, Bullfinch, Siskin, Redpoll and the crossbills are generally associated with woodland or scrub, while the Linnet, Goldfinch and Greenfinch are associated with more open areas with scattered trees and bushes. However, some of these species in their foraging move freely between wooded and open country. Only about four species breed freely in gardens, although others come in for food in winter. The latest to begin feeding in gardens is the Siskin which has recently taken to feeding on peanuts placed in hanging nut-bags.

To summarise, the bill and body structure of different species of finch lead them to differ in the size of seeds they prefer, the kinds of seed-heads they can best exploit, and the proportion of food they obtain directly from plants, as opposed to the ground. Together with differences in habitat this all results in no two species of finch having the same feeding habits.

Bullfinches and fruit buds

The natural feeding habits of finches inevitably lead some of them to damage crops. In Britain the Bullfinch is most important in this respect as it is a major pest in fruit orchards, removing the fruit buds and reducing the subsequent crop. The damage is indisputable: to confirm it visit the

J. Markham/Bruce Coleman

orchards in the winter of a bad year and watch the birds in action. Then make another visit in spring and note the shortage of blossom. If you examine the trees closely, you will see that the blossom buds have been nipped off neatly at the base and that their remains litter the ground below. And the damage is greater on some fruit varieties than on others, being greater on trees near to woods and hedgerows than on those near the middle of the orchards.

The damage varies greatly from year to year depending on when the birds start eating buds. In some years they begin as early as November, in others not until March: however once begun the attacks continue until the blossom is finished around mid-May. The birds usually start near woods and hedgerows and move gradually nearer the middle of the orchard, stripping the trees in turn. They generally prefer dessert apples to cooking varieties, and among pears the 'Conference' variety is especially favoured. Recent research has shown that it is those varieties whose buds have a high protein content that the birds like most of all.

The Bullfinch had a price on its head for this damage as long ago as the sixteenth century, when one penny was offered in reward for 'everie Bulfynch or other Byrde that devoureth the blowthe of fruit'. Recently the damage increased greatly in the 1960's following the increase and spread of the Bullfinch outside woodland. In those years, in extreme cases, whole orchards of trees were almost denuded of buds and gave only a few pounds of fruit instead of several tons. In comparison the damage to buds by other birds is negligible,

although that caused by House Sparrows *Passer domesticus* can be severe around human habitation.

The Bullfinch might have been expected to become a major pest in orchards, for in its natural habitat it takes a greater proportion and variety of buds, and for a longer period each year, than does any other small European bird. Indeed, it is well adapted to do so in bill structure, feeding technique and digestive system, having a shorter and broader bill and a relatively longer gut than other finches. All cultivated fruit trees, moreover, have buds of the size most acceptable to Bullfinches. Furthermore the cultivated fruit trees are derived from tree species, whose buds the Bullfinch prefers under natural conditions. Various ornamental shrubs are also attacked in spring, partly because their early flowering is preceded by an early bud-swell.

The main factor influencing the date at which Bullfinches turn to buds is the natural winter seed supply, particularly the crop of ash seeds. If ash seeds are scarce the birds are forced to shift earlier to a diet of buds. In southern England the ashes tend to crop heavily every second year, so damage by Bullfinches in orchards tends to be most severe in the alternate years when little or no ash seed is available. Other common winter foods include the seeds of nettle, dock, bramble and birch.

The fruit-growers' solution to the problem is to trap and remove Bullfinches, not so much in the spring when the damage is actually occurring but in the preceding autumn, especially in years of poor seed crops. By removing birds then, the natural winter seed-stocks are conserved and last longer into winter, thus delaying the date at which the remaining birds turn to buds.

(Above) Juvenile Bullfinch *Pyrrhula pyrrhula* eating honeysuckle berries. The natural feeding habits of the Bullfinch lead it to damage fruit orchards, and it has been considered a pest and persecuted for centuries

243

David Hosking

(Above) Chaffinch *Fringilla coelebs*: one of the fringilline finches, the Chaffinch holds insect food in its bill and carries it to its young

Breeding

Food influences the breeding of finches in several ways. The Old World seedeaters or fringilline finches—Chaffinch *Fringilla coelebs* and Brambling *F. montifringilla*—feed their young on insects which are distributed fairly evenly through their woodland habitats. These birds have large feeding territories while nesting. They convey the insect food to their young in the bill, a few at a time, and visit the nestlings about every five to ten minutes.

In contrast, the cardueline finches feed their young on seeds (although some supplement the diet with a few insects in the early stages). They nest in loose colonies and fly outside the colonies to forage in flocks, wherever seeds happen to be plentiful. They can pack large quantities of seeds into their distendable gullets for later regurgitation to the young. This enables them to forage at long distances from the nest, and feed their young at long intervals of twenty to sixty minutes. They may raise successive broods in the same season at

places long distances apart. The extreme is shown by Redpolls in Sweden, some of which raise one brood in the south of the country in spring when the spruce cones are opening, and another brood the same year in the north of the country when the birch seeds are forming. Thus the different dispersion patterns of the two groups of finches—territories and colonies—are suited to their different foods, that is, insects and seeds respectively.

Like other birds, finches breed only when their particular foods are plentiful, and this leads to differences in breeding seasons between species. The Chaffinch, which depends mainly on caterpillars when breeding, has a short, fairly early breeding season and normally raises only one brood in a year. Some cardueline finches, such as the Linnet and Greenfinch, feed chiefly from weeds and other herbaceous plants. They have an extended breeding season, more or less corresponding with the growing season of plants, in which each pair can raise two or three successive broods. The Goldfinch, which specialises on Compositae (one of the largest

families of flowering plants), begins rather later, and its breeding reaches a peak in late summer, when thistles are seeding. Even more extreme is the American Goldfinch *carduelis tristis* which breeds almost entirely on the thistle crop, and starts later than any other bird in North America. The Siskin and Redpoll, when feeding on conifers, can extract seeds only from open cones and, when the spruce crop is good, they start breeding in March or April when the cones begin to open but often when snow still lies on the ground. Later broods are raised after the growing season has begun, and are fed on fresh seeds of other plants. In years when the spruce crop is poor these species raise only the later broods.

The crossbills can extract seeds from closed cones and can breed in any month of the year, depending on the availability of appropriate seeds. In larch areas they breed mainly in autumn, in pine areas mainly in spring, while in spruce areas they begin in late summer when the seeds are forming, and continue through the winter to the following

spring when the seeds fall. In areas where a mixture of conifer species is available, their breeding is lengthened accordingly. This is true of the population as a whole, but individual pairs do not necessarily breed this long. In the USSR nests of the Crossbill have been found in six-hour winter days when temperatures were down to minus thirty-five degrees Celsius and snow lay thick on the ground: however the all-important spruce seeds were abundant. In conclusion it is apparent that finches vary in their breeding times, and in each case breeding coincides with the period when their respective foods are most available.

Moult

After breeding, finches replace their feathers in an annual moult. Normally each individual starts to moult at about the time its last young leave the nest and, if breeding is prolonged, moult is delayed accordingly. As in other birds, the feathers are replaced a few at a time, in regular sequence, so that

(Above) American Goldfinch *Carduelis tristis* feeding its young: this species subsists almost entirely on thistle seeds

D. D. Burgess/Ardea

the bird is never left without effective insulation or powers of flight. The process takes several weeks, somewhat longer in resident than migrant species: twelve weeks for the Greenfinch in Britain and eight weeks for the Redpoll. But whereas the adult birds replace all their feathers, the young of the year replace only their body feathers, retaining the large flight and tail feathers for another year. The moult is a demanding process, particularly in terms of the protein required for feather growth, so it is important for it to be completed as soon as possible after breeding and before food becomes scarce.

Migration

After the moult, the next major event in the annual cycle for many birds is migration and here again food plays an overriding role. The main distinction is between species that feed on low herbaceous plants and those species that feed high in trees. Herbaceous plants produce an abundance of seeds every year but at times of snow these seeds may be unavailable. Most finches that depend on such seeds migrate towards southwest Europe for the winter, and many thousands winter in the Mediterranean region. They have fairly fixed migration routes and show strong homing tendencies, returning to the same areas for breeding and wintering in successive years. Included in this category are such species as Goldfinch and Linnet, in which most individuals leave the northern climes for the winter.

The tree-feeders have a different problem because although their food is generally available above the snow (enabling them to winter much further north in Europe), at any one locality the seed-crops vary enormously from one year to the next. As every country-dweller knows, in some years the trees and bushes are laden with fruits but in other years are barren. In different parts of Europe, however, the crops are not necessarily in phase with one another, so while in any particular year the crops may fail in some regions, they may be good in others. With such a fluctuating food-supply, there would be little point in individuals migrating to the same places every year. In consequence, the migrations are highly variable from year to year, both in direction and distance travelled. When seed-crops are good in the north of Europe most of the birds stay there. However when northern crops fail most of the birds move further south, accumulating wherever the crops are good. As ring recoveries testify, individuals of such species may breed or winter in widely separated regions in different years—wherever the crops are good at the time. Enormous year-to-year fluctuations of populations may be seen at any one locality, but the continental population as a whole probably does not fluctuate to such a large degree. This system applies particularly to the Siskin and Redpoll, but also to some extent to the Bullfinch *Pyrrhula pyrrhula* and Pine Grosbeak *Pinicola enucleator*.

All these irruptive species eat different foods in summer and winter, and have two main migrations each year—in spring and autumn—like most other birds. Crossbills, on the other hand, eat the same type of food all the time, and in Europe show one main period of movement each year in mid-summer; they move from areas where one crop is finishing to other areas where a new crop is forming. Movement is usually necessary because it is rare for crops to be good in the same area in successive years. Crossbills are therefore somewhat nomadic, spending up to a year in any one area before moving on again to another. Mostly the birds remain in their regular range, that is, the conifer forests of northern and montane regions. But when the crop failure is widespread and the population is high, enormous numbers of crossbills move outside their regular range to areas where they are not often seen. Such invasions have been documented in England on and off since the thirteenth century. They often take the birds to regions devoid of conifers, so that unusual foods are eaten: as one early account testified: 'in the course of this year, about the fruit season, there appeared, in the orchards chiefly, some remarkable birds which have never before been seen in England, somewhat larger than larks, which ate the kernel of the fruit and nothing else, whereby the trees were fruitless to the loss of many. The beaks of these birds were crossed, so that by this means they opened the fruit as if with pincers'.

Irruptions of crossbills have been recorded from all their main centres, including parts of North America, Japan and the Himalayas, but have been best documented in Europe. On this continent, between 1800 and 1965 Crossbills *L. curvirostra* irrupted at least sixty-seven times. Sometimes they came in several successive years (probably from different areas), and at other times at intervals of up to eleven years. The two other species, despite their different foods, often came in the same years as the Crossbills although less frequently. This was true of at least thirty-six out of forty-seven invasions of the Two-barred Crossbill, and of twenty-two out of twenty-seven invasions of the Parrot Crossbill. This is partly because different conifer species tend to crop heavily in the same years as one another (except for pine whose cones take two years to mature, so it is always a year behind the others), and partly because the different crossbill species are not restricted to one kind of food, so are all affected by major crop failure. Only recently have ring recoveries confirmed that some birds return to their regular range in a later year. From a batch of birds ringed in Switzerland on migration, some were recorded the following autumn and winter in southwest Europe, having continued their journey. And others were recorded in later years up to four thousand kilometres to the northeast in northern USSR.

From the foregoing it will be seen that although all finches eat seeds, they differ widely in their adaptations to different kinds of plants. Their diets have a considerable influence on their breeding and movements, and indeed on their whole lifestyles. Most of these finches are common in the countryside of Britain and Europe, and there is plenty of scope for further study.

Dr Ian Newton, author of this section, works at the Institute of Terrestrial Ecology in Edinburgh. He has spent many years studying finches, particularly the problems caused by Bullfinches in fruit orchards and has published many scientific papers and popular articles on this group of birds

SPECIATION OF BIRDS
Adaptation and specialisation

C. Haagner/Ardea

Some species of birds are very common and others are extremely rare. Some like the queleas of Africa are so numerous that, like locusts, the flocks devastate cultivated crops, causing untold damage. Yet other species become progressively scarcer until perhaps they become extinct. These two categories are probably the most well-known: the first because they have frequently threatened our livelihood, the second because people have become more and more aware of the detrimental effect our highly industrialised society has on the environment. The majority of species fall somewhere between these two extremes and while their numbers may fluctuate, and often substantially, they never seem to reach plague proportions or to decrease to anything approaching the danger of extinction.

Another aspect of bird populations which is readily apparent is that different species are numerous or scarce in different areas. The reasons for some of these differences seem obvious; for example at certain places, such as an English lakeside with reed fringes, one expects to find species like Reed Warblers *Acrocephalus scirpaceus* or in open arable farmland areas, Skylarks *Alauda arvensis*. These are differences associated with habitat type, but this is an over-similification since, if we visited similar habitats in southern Europe, the equivalent species might be Great Reed Warbler *Acrocephalus arundinaceus* and Crested Lark *Galerida cristata*. Clearly the importance is similar habitat, not identical habitat. Taking the situation a stage further and considering similar habitats in North America, the equivalent species may not be a warbler and a lark but may belong to entirely different families of birds.

All the above goes to show that different species occupy different habitats, and also in different parts of the world the species making up the bird community in similar or equivalent habitats may

(Above) Red-billed Queleas *Quelea quelea*: this African species may be seen in huge flocks

247

(Above) Reed Warbler *Acrocephalus scirpaceus* trying to brood a young Cuckoo *Cuculus canorus*. The Reed Warbler is a typical inhabitant of lakesides with reed fringes. (Above right) Skylark *Alauda arvensis* at its nest in a ploughed field

be, and usually are, entirely different. Each species occupies, in the whole community structure of plants and animals, its own particular ecological 'niche'. This is particularly noticeable on travelling to different countries: what appear to be identical ecological niches are occupied by different species, thus showing them in truth to be different niches. It is widely held that two species occurring in the same area cannot have identical niches, as one species would inevitably oust the other and force it to change niche, move from the area or die. Thus the Reed Warbler and Great Reed Warbler are not occupying the same niche in the two areas but only superficially similar ones.

Sometimes there are ecological niches which are not occupied by a species. This is usually because some aspect of the environment has changed and created new niches, and the existing species in the area have had insufficient time to adapt to the new opportunities or to change genetically into new forms. Perhaps the simplest example of this is the formation of marine islands by volcanic eruptions. These islands are usually used quite quickly as nesting grounds by sea-birds. They leave droppings to provide nutriment for plants: later insects become established and so soon there is scope for land birds. As the island 'develops', there are niches for more and more species and the community structure becomes more complex.

Just how rich the ecology becomes will depend largely where in the world the island is but also on the variety of topography: for example if there are hollows in which rainwater collects and lakes form,

which in turn overflow to form streams and waterfalls. Eventually, it is likely that most niches will be filled. However, on the mainland areas certain niches may be occupied by birds which are weak fliers or non-migratory, highly sedentary species and these are most unlikely to reach marine islands. Even so, in this sort of situation it is improbable that the niches will remain unoccupied for long; competition for food and nest-sites is usually so intense that opportunities do not often go unexploited for long. Some of the species arriving, either because they are blown off course during migration or because the island has appeared on their regular migration route, will find some aspect of the new environment such as the insect life sufficiently similar to their normal habitat so they not only survive but indeed thrive. These could be described as species which are simply occupying new habitat and expanding their range.

In some cases, on moving to a new area, individuals of a species may find that they are able to colonise a new habitat or to enter a new niche. They may eat an entirely new type of food because their bill shape, adapted originally for something else, can also cope well with the new; this is termed pre-adaptation and is not an infrequent occurrence.

How does the original adaptation come about? The subject is intricately tied up with evolutionary concepts based on the original theory of evolution by natural selection as expounded by Charles Darwin. This, in simple terms, states firstly that within a group of living things, be they plants or animals, there is an inherent variability, sometimes marked and sometimes very slight, but always there. And secondly, the environment which a group of living things occupies is not uniform but varies greatly from place to place. In the constant striving for living space, food, water and a means to reproduce, and as a result of the intense competition existing in the natural world, some of these individuals will not survive while others in certain circumstances will be at a distinct advantage. In other circumstances different individuals will be at an advantage so that in different parts of a species' range conditions will favour different types or sub-groups of individuals within the populations. These individuals will survive and reproduce and come to dominate the others. In breeding, they will pass on to their offspring their genetically governed characters which have given them their advantage. In this way there is an 'automatic' improvement by selection of those best fitted to survive and a weeding-out of those not so fitted. The result is that populations of individual animals or plants become ever better adapted to their environment. Eventually, the sub-groups drift further and further apart in appearance, behaviour, diet, voice and so on; in short they are so genetically changed that they become distinct species.

If the separation is to become complete one further event appears to be necessary: the differing populations, which are perhaps already geographically separated, must become in some way physically separated to prevent continued mixing and interbreeding, for it is by this means that the hereditary material governing the physical and behavioural characteristics remains mixed and the population relatively uniform. An example may serve to illustrate the point. Suppose that a population has a variation in bill length, related to the size of food taken, from one end of its range to the other. Anything tending to prevent a thorough mixing and interbreeding of individuals from these extremes will favour development of races and eventually species. The agent of separation can be a natural disaster, a change in the habitat such as the formation of a desert area dividing two parts of a forest, or a pre-existing feature such as expanses of sea separating the islands of an archipelago which is colonised by a species. In one part of the range the bill length could be small to medium and in the other medium to large. In general most individuals will have a bill-length near the middle of the range. These individuals with average length bills feeding on average size prey will have stiffest competition from within their own species; this is known as intra-specific competition. Those near the edges of the range of bill length, namely those with smallest and largest bills, will have less competition from their own species but will be in danger of competing with other species (inter-specific competition). There is a fine balance between intra-specific and inter-specific competition. Each species tends to be squashed into its niche by neighbouring species with similar diets, but must avoid being too restricted because this leads to extremely high competition between individuals of the same species.

To return to the example of bill length, the average bill length for the small to medium group will drop and that of the medium to large group will rise. If there were an eventual re-meeting of the populations, a remixing and interbreeding might occur if the two groups had not diverged too far but otherwise the separation would be accelerated. The larger billed members of the small-billed group would come into competition with the smaller billed members of the large-billed group and these 'edge' members of the two groups would not be so successful. The result would be that the range of bill lengths on each side of the average would be less, which is another way of saying that the two groups would be more clearly defined with fewer and perhaps eventually no intermediates. So, the result of lengthy separation followed by re-meeting is two (or more) clearly defined species. The important criterion seems to be physical separation for a period during which the changes in the sub-groups can take place.

Work on the process of speciation has thrown a great deal of light on the subject of adaptation, specialisation and ecological niches. Species which have well marked races or sub-species are particularly valuable in this field. The dividing lines between different geographical sub-species nearly always coincide with physical barriers such as stretches of water, mountain ranges or broad stretches of unfavourable habitat. It is not surprising therefore to find excellent examples of speciation on such marine archipelagos as the Galapagos Islands and Hawaii. The groups of species concerned are respectively Darwin's finches (sub-family Geospizinae of the family Fringillidae) and the Hawaiian Honeycreepers (family Drepanididae). The process by which a range of species evolve from one species so that a whole range of specialist niches are occupied, where very few were exploited before, is called adaptive radiation. The fact that it has occurred so repeatedly in all forms of life suggests that specialisation has considerable advantages for the survival of a species. Certainly for a species to concentrate on one type of life style, with one type of food for example, does mean an advantage over others which are not so specialised. Unnecessary competition and fighting is also avoided and full use is made of available resources.

Thus on superficial observation, it would appear that the secret of success for a bird (or any other form of life) is to specialise in order to avoid competition from other species. Clearly, to specialise, for example, in only one kind of food is to court disaster. If the food or prey item become scarce because it is over-predated or for some other reason, the result is starvation. Perhaps the answer would be to eat almost anything available in opportunist fashion? However, then the result is that no matter what food is chosen, another species could be better adapted to feed on it: the result—always at a disadvantage.

Since so many thousands of species are still in spite of the havoc caused by our industrialised society, surviving and thriving, the answer must lie in a compromise somewhere between complete

G. Ziesler/Bruce Coleman

(Above) Snail Kite *Rostrhamus sociabilis*. This species is one of the best examples of a specialist feeder: it feeds only on fresh-water snails and the upper mandible is shaped to help it extract the snails from their shells

specialisation and complete generalisation. The degree of compromise, or the extent to which each species is specialised, varies enormously from species to species. Examples serve to best illustrate the point: the Snail Kite *Rostrhamus sociabilis* is one of the most outstanding examples of a specialist feeder. It survives exclusively on fresh-water snails, and its upper mandible is long, curved and pointed, being adapted to 'winkling' the snails from their shells. It should be pointed out that this does not mean a lack of competition: many birds, particularly members of the heron family, feed on water snails which they usually swallow whole. The Snail Kite is, of course, restricted to areas with shallow vegetated water where snails are plentiful. And since these are just the areas the developer loves to claim for agriculture or building, the suitable habitat is shrinking and the future of the Snail Kite is somewhat uncertain. It is interesting to consider to what extent the species, which has at present a very limited distribution in the Americas could be successful in other parts of the world if introduced there, for there are many areas of apparently suitable habitat throughout the world. Interestingly, but that is not to say surprisingly, in spite of its atypical diet for a diurnal raptorial bird, the Snail Kite retains the curved talons and many other anatomical features of the family Accipitridae.

By contrast, the Herring Gull *Larus argentatus* has become, although it is not known just how recently, almost omnivorous. With such a wide range of dietary options open to it, it is not surprising to find that the Herring Gull is extremely successful with the population steadily increasing, new breeding colonies being established and existing ones growing. To what cause, the increase, which is incidentally shared by a number of other gull species, can be attributed is not known; it seems probable that it is directly related to human activities: the large rubbish dumps with food remains in plenty; the large freshwater reservoirs which provide washing, bathing and drinking and safe roosting facilities and the fishing fleets which produce large quantities of fish offal. Whatever the cause, the Herring Gull is now a problem species in many areas. This is particularly so on nature reserves where much scarcer and more attractive species such as terns have been progressively ousted from their breeding colonies.

Such eruptions are not infrequent in nature, as populations of living things are dynamic and constantly changing and re-adapting. Occasionally such changes are very rapid as instanced by the Collared Dove *Streptopelia decaocto*. Exactly what caused the sudden spread in distribution from southeast Europe right across the continent to the western islands of Britain, Iceland and beyond is unknown. Perhaps it was a sudden genetic change! The spread of the Cattle Egret *Ardeola ibis* from Africa and southern Europe across the Atlantic Ocean and subsequently throughout parts of central and North America is a similar success story. Whether it is due to some genetic change, causing a change in feeding for example, enabling the species to occupy new niches is not known.

On the other hand, some species are retracting their range: this includes the Wryneck *Jynx torquilla* in Europe. Again the causes are not known as the Wryneck's ecology has not been sufficiently studied. Climatic changes are often blamed, but this simply replaces one question with another. Whatever the underlying cause it does appear that the niche for the Wryneck is ceasing to exist in large areas of its former range; perhaps the niche has been taken over by one or more other enterprising species.

Certain types of major population change are not natural, at least in the early stages, but are at least as spectacular. These are those resulting from changes brought about by human activities and in particular the introductions of species into parts of the world where they do not occur naturally. Two species which have been particularly favoured in this direction are the House Sparrow *Passer domesticus* and the Starling *Sturnus vulgaris*. Highly successful in their ancestral range, they have also become extremely successful in many of the countries to which they have been introduced.

The House Sparrow, a member of the weaver family (Ploceidae), is generally adapted to a seed diet. The bill is short and conical with hard and sharp cutting edges for cracking open seed husks. The nest is an untidy woven structure of grasses and other stems lined with feathers. The young are fed on insects and also on soft developing seeds. So, what is remarkable about the House Sparrow and why is it so successful in new areas? The answer seems to be in its adaptability and the fact that it has learned to live side by side with humans. In character it is a born winner: pugnacious, industrious, inquisitive (yet wary) and able to learn 'new tricks'. New food supplies are investigated and exploited; far from being merely a seed eater, the House Sparrow is thoroughly opportunist and takes a wide variety of foods as and when they become available. Thus, aphids are taken from the garden roses, the polyanthus petals are stripped, and almost any type of food scraps put out in the garden are accepted. Add to this feast, the provision of plentiful roosting accommodation in the form of ornamental shrubs, nest sites galore under house roofs and in gutters, fresh drinking-water in pools and bird baths: the House Sparrow is obviously quite well provided for! Once the adaptation to living alongside humans had been perfected, the way is open to colonising any area where humans are found. And that means a large proportion of the world could be available.

Of course the garden scraps provided by the housewife are insignificant at some times of the year when vast areas of grain become available. This is a second important reason for the success story. As soon as the variety of species found in an area is reduced—as happens when cereal growing areas which become a monoculture—the opportunity for exploitation by specialising in that food item becomes enormous. A similar phenomenon has occurred with the queleas of the weaver family in Africa. In fact the House Sparrow has not merely taken over a new ecological niche, it has also, by vigour in its populations and in some cases sheer weight of numbers partly taken over the niches of other species. These species, if small or timid enough are driven away from food supplies and roosting and nesting sites such as tree-holes. The nesting holes of smaller woodpeckers and the suspended mud nests of House Martins *Delichon urbica* are taken over, as are nest boxes provided for various species of tits.

The success of the Starling is similar; the key criterion seems to be an ability to cohabit with humans. The starling can be seen probing for invertebrates in lawns, playing fields, and pastures provided for cattle. You can also spot it eating the grubs in animal dung, taking berries from ornamental shrubs in gardens as well as food scraps left out in the garden. Warm, cosy, roosting sites on convenient ledges of city buildings are also much used by Starlings as are ample nest sites in houses, factories and barns. Orchards are also much appreciated by starlings!

Both species, in learning to live with humans, have in fact entered into competition with use for food. Millions of pounds worth of damage are done annually throughout the world. The secret of success in both species is adaptability, and this is really connected with the 'personality' of the birds. The House Sparrow and Starling are the 'spivs' of the bird world: they quickly seize good opportunities, and in a very competitive world that spells success. To specialise in a narrow field of requisites means being restricted in distribution. A species that has a broad spectrum of ecological requirements can fit in almost anywhere. A good example of this type of adaptability, but a less unwelcome one than the House Sparrow or Starling, is the Ring-necked Pheasant *Phasianus colchicus*. A native of eastern Asia, it has been introduced by man to a large number of countries around the world as a sporting bird. At the present the Ring-necked Pheasant occurs from sea-level to altitudes of nearly four thousand metres, from subtropical temperatures to freezing point on occasion. It seems equally at home in areas with twenty-five or seven hundred and fifty centimetres of annual rainfall, and in any habitat from forests, through grassland and cultivated farms to deserts. It would be difficult to determine exactly what aspect of the Ring-necked Pheasant's make-up enables it to succeed in such a wide variety of niches where other species fail to adapt.

The very worrying aspect of this is that when introductions are made, the entire ecosystem is frequently upset, immense economic damage is done and native species often suffer. Sadly, we have not learned by our mistakes, and introductions still continue. The spread of the Rose-ringed Parakeet *Psittacula krameri* in southern England in the 1970's is an example: considerable damage to fruit crops is already being sustained.

Howard Ginn, author of this article and of 'Passerine Classification', is a Research Officer at the British Trust for Ornithology and has specialised in the study of the moulting habits of birds. He has contributed to several books on ornithology and has written a number of scientific papers

(Below) Rose-ringed Parakeet *Psittacula krameri*. Having escaped from captivity it has established a successful feral population in southern England and is becoming quite widespread in London suburbs

GARDENING FOR BIRDS
Plants, food and nest sites

(Above) A trellis on a wall provides a home for a Song Thrush *Turdus philomelos* and its young

Birds are adaptable animals and have been quick to exploit a relatively new habitat—the garden. Most garden birds were originally woodland edge species and some, such as the Blackbird, have found this man-made environment even more suitable than their traditional woodland haunts. However, the potential of a garden for birds is entirely dependent on the owner's attitude. A more casual gardener will have a far richer bird population than the local trophy-winner who sprays his or her immaculate plants with every conceivable chemical. But a happy compromise between the two can easily be achieved. With a little effort and thought for the birds gardening can take on an entirely new dimension.

Planning and planting

When planting a bird garden there are three basic requirements that must be provided: food, shelter and nest-sites. The greater the diversity of these essentials, the more varied the bird population will be. Whether the garden is large or small, new or well-established, there are a few important points to consider when planning for birds. If possible, shelter the garden from the cold north and east winds with a good thick hedge. Always think in three dimensions and choose flowers, shrubs and trees that give a range of heights. Natural areas are seldom flat, and straight lines rarely occur in nature, so a small, south-facing bank or rockery adds variety and provides a sheltered spot in snowy weather. Plants are seasonal, so choose a selection that provides food and shelter throughout the year. While species that provide seeds and berries are important, if insectivorous birds are to be encouraged, plants that are attractive to insects must also be included. Try to choose native species as these support a greater variety of invertebrates and are better suited to our climate.

By far the most productive of our native trees is the oak; it supports so many insects and other wildlife that it is almost a habitat in itself. Few gardens, however, are large enough to support a full grown oak and it may be preferable to plant smaller and quicker-growing species. A rowan is an attractive tree to grow in the front garden with its cascades of white flowers and clusters of orange-red berries in the autumn; the berries never last long as they are avidly fed on by the thrushes. Birches, with their attractive silver bark, yield many small

J. A. Bailey/Ardea

Eric Hosking

seeds from their catkins and attract numerous small insects on which many bird species feed. Willow is quick-growing, especially if planted in a damp area, and Robins, tits, Wrens and Dunnocks feed on the caterpillars that are found on the leaves. Ash and poplars also support a good caterpillar population, and the poplars provide elevated song-posts for thrushes. An old apple or pear tree, perhaps past its best for fruit, provides perfect nest-sites for Goldfinches and the rough bark will house a large selection of insects and grubs.

Evergreen trees offer nesting and roosting sites, and some species also produce berries. Yew and holly are both good food sources for thrushes but there are drawbacks; both these plants are slow-growing and dioecious (separate male and female plants). It is, therefore, important to grow mainly female plants which bear the fruit, but have a male nearby to provide the pollen. These trees also offer nesting sites for Blackbirds, Robins, Dunnocks, Greenfinches and Wrens, and a Goldcrest may hang its tiny nest from the tips of the yew branches. A clump of laurels provides an ideal roosting site and early nesters, such as Blackbirds, often choose these bushes for their first brood as the evergreen

leaves offer a well-concealed site before the deciduous trees have developed their foliage. Rhododendrons also provide useful nesting sites but as they are a non-native shrub they support a poor insect fauna. However, in snowy weather, the bare earth beneath them may provide one of the few places where birds can hunt for insects and spiders. After Christmas always plant the Christmas trees in the garden—if it grows, birds will roost in it and the seeds in the cones will add to their winter diet.

If possible, a hedge is a great asset to a bird garden. Hawthorn is an ideal hedge shrub because of its rapid growth and abundant crop of berries: it also forms an excellent cat-proof barrier. Spindle and blackthorn are also suitable. Elder often self-seeds in a hedge and is rather unruly as it tends to smother other species. But its flowers attract insects and its dark purple berries are favourites with many birds. Privet is another suitable berry-bearing hedge plant, but it is disliked by many gardeners as it impoverishes the soil. All hedges should be trimmed so that they are about two metres high and at least sixty centimetres thick. It is important not to rigorously trim back all the new growth or the hedge will soon become too thick and woody for

(Above left) Like many other passerines, the Tree Sparrow *Passer montanus* finds an old shed an attractive nesting site. (Above) A Great Spotted Woodpecker *Dendrocopos major* can be attracted to your garden by food such as fat

Eric Hosking

(Above) Great Tits *Parus major* and Blue Tits *P. caeruleus* at a peanut feeder. Although most of the time birds are able to feed themselves well, in the hard weather of winter feeding helps them to survive and is also one of the easiest ways to attract birds to a garden

nesting. Occasionally it may be necessary to thin out the centre so the birds can easily fly in and out.

There are also a number of attractive non-native species that can be planted in a bird garden. Barberry with its numerous red berries can either be grown as a shrub or as a hedge. If it is allowed to grow to about two metres Dunnocks, finches and thrushes may use it for nesting. The numerous varieties of cotoneaster can either be trained back as neat wall-climbers or trimmed into three-dimensional bushes. A well-berried bush will not only feed local thrushes and finches but may well attract that handsome winter visitor—the Waxwing. Firethorns are good shrubs to train against the house: Blackbirds and Song Thrushes take the berries in late winter when other fruits are in short supply, and the dense foliage may house a Spotted Flycatcher in the spring.

Leave old dying trees to rot; a multitude of insects burrow in the rotting bark and their larvae may attract Great Spotted Woodpeckers. The dead stump can be made more aesthetically pleasing, and attract yet more insects, by planting a honeysuckle or clematis around it. Ivy, another climber, is often accused of strangling trees, but in fact does not harm them at all. A large ivy-covered tree may house a Collared Dove or Stock Dove, and a cluster of ivy on a post is an ideal site for Dunnocks or Wrens. Ivy-clad trees are also popular roosting sites, as the birds can change their positions according to the prevailing wind. However, do not encourage ivy to grow up main supporting walls as it will damage the mortar.

There are many smaller plants that a gardener can grow for the benefit of birds as well as for his or her own pleasure. The oil-rich seeds of sunflowers are favourites with finches, tits and Nuthatches. Roses, poppies, evening primrose, antirrhinum, phlox and most of the daisy-type flowers, such as cosmos and michaelmas daisies, supply good seed crops. Late flowering plants, such as buddleia and veronica, will also attract butterflies.

Many weeds yield tasty seeds for birds, and some thistles, plantains, teasels or fat-hen left in a far corner of the garden may well provide some excellent views of Goldfinches or Linnets swaying precariously to and fro as they deftly extract the seeds. A well-grown patch of brambles is a popular roosting site for sparrows and finches, as well as providing berries in the winter and in rural gardens perhaps attracting a nesting Blackcap or Garden Warbler. Stinging nettles are a host for many insects and at the bottom of an overgrown hedge they may conceal a Whitethroat's nest. However, beware of certain weeds listed in the Weeds Act 1959; the occupier of the land can be ordered by the Ministry of Agriculture, Food and Fisheries to prevent them from spreading.

Remember that birds abhor tidiness of any sort. A pile of twigs and brushings in a corner is ideal for nesting Dunnocks, Blackbirds and Song Thrushes. A tumble-down wall need not be completely repointed—the hole left by a missing brick may encourage nesting Pied Wagtails, Spotted Flycatchers or Wrens. A shed door left slightly ajar, or perhaps a small entrance in one of the sides, will

Eric Hosking

provide winter hunting grounds for Wrens when the snow is thick on the ground. In spring Song Thrushes, Blackbirds, Robins and perhaps a Swallow can find suitable ledges or crannies for nesting.

A lawn, no matter how small, is a great asset to a bird garden. Although grass itself is not a bird food, the seeds are taken by Dunnocks, finches and sparrows. The worms and insect larvae in the soil attract thrushes and Robins, and a Green Woodpecker may visit a secluded patch of grass in search of ants. On a hot, dry summer's day a fine lawn spray will not only water the grass but will attract birds which like to bathe and feed on the worms which come to the surface. In autumn do not be too quick to sweep up the leaves as they too encourage worms.

Water is of course essential for all wildlife and therefore is a great attraction to birds throughout the year. In built-up areas it is particularly important as there may be few natural pools. Birds need water for both drinking and bathing, and unless there is a stream or pond in the garden, it will have to be provided artificially. Bird-baths are the obvious answer. They can be purchased from most garden centres, but are often expensive and so badly designed that they do not fulfill their primary purpose. Almost any shallow container will make an adequate bird-bath, providing the birds can reach the water without slipping. An upturned dustbin lid supported on three bricks is easy to set up and serves the purpose. In winter a small night-light covered with a flower pot can be placed beneath the lid to prevent the water freez-

ing; a thermostatically-controlled aquarium heater is a slightly more sophisticated method. Never add glycerine or anti-freeze to the water as these chemicals damage the birds' plumage.

If a garden is large enough, the ideal solution to the water problem is a small pond, and even elusive birds such as the Grey Heron or Kingfisher may be tempted to pay a visit. A pond can be easily made by digging a shallow hole and lining it first with newspaper and then with heavy gauge polythene sheeting. After a few weeks water plants can be added and the pond will soon become a considerable asset to any wildlife garden.

Feeding birds

For most of the time birds can obtain sufficient food for themselves, but in hard weather feeding the birds can be an important way of helping them to survive. It is also one of the easiest ways to attract birds to the garden.

The best place to feed birds is on a bird-table. A simple, flat tray with square battens round the edge, to prevent food rolling off, is quite adequate. Complex rustic designs sometimes seen on sale are more likely to frighten off the more timid species. Always mount a bird-table on a smooth pole, as this is more difficult for cats and squirrels to climb; an upturned biscuit tin below the feeding platform can be added as an additional deterrent. The ideal bird-table should be about one-and-a-half metres off the ground in a sheltered position. It should be fairly close to a hedge or tree so that the birds can

(Above) Robin *Erithacus rubecula* at its nest in an old jug. One of the best known and well-loved birds of Britain, it is closely associated with humans and is a frequent visitor to parks and gardens

H. Kinloch/Aquila

(Above) Starlings *Sturnus vulgaris* at a bird bath

There are a few foods that are harmful to birds. White bread should be soaked in water before being put out as it tends to swell up inside the crop. Dessicated coconut should be avoided. Never put out salty foods such as salted peanuts—garden birds lack the special salt excreting gland found above the eye in seabirds, and therefore have difficulty in getting rid of excessive amounts of salt.

Garden birds can be divided into three groups requiring different sorts of foods. The true seed-eater, such as the Greenfinch; the insect-eater, for example the Wren, and the omnivorous feeders which will eat almost anything available such as the Starling. The type of food put out in the garden must be varied to meet the needs of all three groups.

Specially prepared commercial bird foods have a carefully balanced composition and cater for all birds' tastes, but they can become extremely expensive when devoured by hoards of hungry House Sparrows. A mixture of natural seeds, fruits and berries is just as nourishing and far cheaper. Bunches of teasels, thistles, redleg, campion, plantain and knapweed can be collected once they have seeded. Dry them in the sun before storing in a dry, airy place. Later in the winter these can be hung from branches or stood in the ground for finches. Hazel nuts, acorns, conkers, sweet chestnuts and beech mast are well worth gathering and in the cold weather they can put on the bird-table or mixed with suet into a bird pudding. Pine cones can be collected when they are still tightly closed, and if they are put in a warm place they will slowly open and the seeds can be shaken out. Hips, haws, elder, holly, ivy, rowan and yew berries are the natural foods for thrushes. Once again dry them in a warm room and store the berries in a cool, dry place where mice cannot get at them. Crab apples are also worth gathering. Alternatively 'tired' apples or pears from the local greengrocer are a treat for Song Thrushes and Blackbirds; scattered at the far end of the garden, they may even entice a Redwing or Fieldfare.

If spare time is at a premium, the birds' diets can be supplemented with a variety of artificial foods. During cold weather birds need energy-giving foods—large marrow bones, bacon rinds, ham skins and suet, which can be obtained cheaply from the local butcher, all fall into this category. These foods can be placed in convenient scrap baskets or hung up on strings for the more acrobatic species, or put on the bird-table. Suet is also very useful for binding together easily blown-away foods such as stale cake and small seeds. The basic recipe for bird pudding is a seed mixture which can include cake, oatmeal, porridge oats, maize, corn, cooked rice, nuts, dried fruit, cooked spaghetti etc, plus twice the amount of melted fat. Mix everything well together and pour the ingredients into a flower pot, half a coconut shell or other container. Once it has set, the pudding can be placed on the bird-table or hung from a branch and is an ideal food for insect and seed-eating birds.

Baked potatoes and wholemeal bread are other

make an inconspicuous approach or beat a hasty retreat, but this cover must not be within easy pouncing range of marauding cats. Remember that some birds are reluctant to feed at such elevated heights, so always sprinkle some food on the ground nearby for birds such as wagtails and Dunnocks.

Before putting out any food for the birds, there are a few simple rules to observe:

Do not feed between April and September. This may encourage birds to feed unnatural foods to their nestlings which could kill them.

In cold weather food should be put out at least twice a day: in the early morning so that the birds can build up their fat reserves and in the afternoons to allow them to fill their crops before they go to roost. In hard weather a bird such as a Bullfinch loses about half its fat reserves each night, so it must replenish these each day to survive the following night. In milder weather it is adequate to feed the birds once a day.

Do not put out a surfeit of food as the birds will cease to forage for natural items, and this can lead to dietary deficiencies and reduce their resistance to disease. The aim should be to attract dozens rather than hundreds of birds.

Move the table at least once during the winter. This will avoid an accumulation of droppings and the risk of disease such as salmonella.

useful foods. Crumbled up cheese and bacon rinds are favourites of Wrens, Robins and Goldcrests, and the leftovers from the dog's or cat's plate are good items for attracting insectivorous birds. A sure way to a Robin's heart is with mealworms, but these are expensive to buy from pet shops and to breed them requires a certain amount of enthusiasm. As well as attracting the Robins, the larvae will bring in Blackbirds, and possibly Wrens and woodpeckers. Maggots, which can be obtained from angling shops, are also a delicacy, but place both types of larvae in a straight-sided container before putting them on the bird-table.

Half a fresh coconut adds variety to the menu for the tit species. Peanuts are also definite winners with all members of that family as well as with Nuthatches; peanuts are packed full of protein and therefore excellent cold weather foods. There are a variety of special hanging food baskets for all types of nuts, but these must be suspended on at least a metre of string so that they swing and spin in the breeze, otherwise the nuts will be devoured by flocks of hungry House Sparrows.

Larger birds, such as Moorhens, Mallards, Jackdaws and gulls have insatiable appetites and if they are regular garden visitors, it is quantity rather than quality that is required. Boiled potatoes peel and other food scraps are good stomach fillers.

Nesting birds

Many gardens, particularly newly established ones where plants and shrubs have not had time to mature, have a shortage of nest-sites. The problem can be solved for most species by offering artificial alternatives.

Birds are discriminating in their requirements and suitable nesting boxes must be within a particular size and shape range. Tits, sparrows and Starlings are the most common hole-nesting species. An entrance hole of not more than 2.8 centimetres in diameter will admit the tits and Tree Sparrows, but exclude the less desirable House Sparrows and Starlings. Other species such as Robins, Wrens, Spotted Flycatchers and wagtails prefer open-fronted boxes, and some birds, such as the Swallow, only require a small ledge or even a couple of fairly large nails hammered into the inside wall of a shed. By studying the nesting requirements of other species, for example, owls, Treecreepers and Swifts, various custom-built boxes can be devised.

Hole-fronted nest-boxes are very easy to make, and the small gaps where the wood has not been cut at right-angles provide essential drainage and ventilation. There are a few important design features. First, the roof needs to be sloping to allow drainage. Second the floor area of the box needs to be at least twelve centimetres square—a growing brood of at least twelve young Blue Tits requires ample space. And third, the entrance hole needs to be about two and a half centimetres from the top and there is no need for a perch under the hole: tits are agile enough to fly straight into the box, and it

O.S.F./Bruce Coleman

will only give House Sparrows the chance to sit near the entrance and antagonise the occupants.

The siting of a box needs care. It must be sheltered from the wet, westerly winds and the full blaze of the sun from the south. A northerly or easterly facing hole is the most suitable. Always remember to tilt the box forward slightly to improve drainage, and a branch nearby may serve as a convenient staging post and encourage occupation. Try to put up new boxes in the autumn or early winter so that the birds become accustomed to them and perhaps use them for roosting.

It is difficult to state categorically how many boxes are needed in a garden, as it will depend on the availability of natural nest-sites round about. Start with two or three boxes and slowly add more until some remain unoccupied. Always put up more hole-fronted nest-boxes than open-fronted ones. If birds do nest in the garden, remember to try to cause as little disturbance as possible. It is unlikely that any fledglings in the garden have been abandoned. They should be left alone as the adults are probably nearby waiting to feed them.

By careful planning the bird gardener can produce an attractive garden which is also a haven for birds. And he or she will also be helping to offset the habitat lost as our countryside disappears under bricks and mortar.

(Above) Interior view of Blue Tits *Parus caeruleus* inside a hole-fronted nest box

Linda Bennet, author of this section, is an ornithologist and writer. She has also worked with the Royal Society for the Protection of Birds

PASSERINE CLASSIFICATION
Sub-dividing the largest order of birds

One of the most fundamental and continually recurring problems in the study of birds is their classification. Without some form of order, the 8,600 or so species of birds in the world would be a very unwieldy group to study and it is difficult nowadays, with our up-to-date system, to imagine what it would be like to study birds without some form of grouping. The aim of taxonomists is to arrive at the most natural classification, that is, a grouping of the various species according to their 'true' relationships.

There has always been a tendency for a species to vary in different parts of its range. Since those individuals best-suited to survive in any place will be the ones to breed most frequently or successfully, the stage is reached in which different populations are ideally adapted to their particular habitat or way of life. Inter-breeding tends to keep the characteristics mixed up in the population. However if groups of birds of a particular species in different areas become isolated by physical barriers like rivers or mountains, the separated units may drift apart so that inter-breeding does not occur and the eventual result is two separate but similar species. The effect of this process over the one hundred and fifty million years of avian evolution has been rather like the constant branching of a tree, each twig representing a species. The more closely related two species are (the closer together their points of attachment on the tree), the more recently they have become separate species. The problem is that at the present time, we have only the twigs to work on with no apparent points of attachment! The only exception to this is the fossil record, the fossilised remains of species usually long since extinct, often provide intermediates between different modern groups and thus suggest true affinities. Sadly, the fossil record is meagre and extremely incomplete.

The baseline on which all modern classification systems are founded is the species, the smallest grouping of birds which contains all those capable of inter-breeding and producing fertile young. Individuals within a species do vary, sometimes substantially and particularly in widespread species where different populations are widely separated geographically but they are always capable of inter-breeding and producing fertile young; individuals of two different species are, in general, not capable of inter-breeding. This sounds a very clear-cut basis for the classification system but in fact there is always much debate about whether geographically isolated races (sub-species) should be considered as separate species. However, the problems really arise when the species are grouped into larger groups of genera and particularly into families. The larger-still groupings, the 'orders' are generally much less of a problem. Orders are frequently

recognisable by the non-biologist: for example the penguins (order Sphenisciformes), the hawks, eagles and vultures and their relatives (order Falconiformes) and the owls (order Strigiformes) Even so, experts disagree on the number of orders that should be recognised. For example, Wetmore has divided birds into twenty-seven orders while Stresemann using a similar system arrived at fifty orders. The size of orders varies enormously from only one species, the Ostrich, *Struthio camelus* in the order Struthioniformes to more than half of the world's species grouped into sixty or so families of the order Passeriformes.

It is evident that taxonomy is complex and subject to much revision and debate: some of the more puzzling species are constantly shuffled from genus to genus, and species and families are quite frequently being re-grouped. With several thousand species in the order Passeriformes, and with so many families, it is not surprising that problems have arisen. There are two main types of taxonomist; the 'lumper' who prefers to amalgamate into as large a conglomeration as possible, and the 'splitter' who prefers to subdivide into as many separate categories as possible. But in order to be able to work with the passerines, which includes nearly half of the world's bird species, it is necessary to break them down into some sort of smaller division. The order Passeriformes, often referred to as the 'perching' birds, falls into two major subdivisions: the oscines often referred to as the songbirds and the sub-oscines. As far as Europe and northern Asia are concerned, the terms perching bird and song-bird are synonymous as the sub-oscines do not occur there.

The sub-oscines consist of three sub-orders: the Eurylaimi, Tyranni and Menurae. The Eurylaimi contains one family—the fourteen species of broadbills of Africa and southeast Asia. The Menurae, entirely restricted to Australia, contains two families: the lyrebirds (family Menuridae) and the scrubbirds (family Atrichornithidae). The remaining sub-family contains twelve families in two groups, the super-families Furnarioidea and Tyrannoidea. The first contains the woodcreepers, ovenbirds, antbirds and tapaculos, all from central and southern America. The second is more widespread and consists of, among others, the pittas, tyrant flycatchers, plantcutters and manakins.

The second major division of the order Passeriformes, the oscines, consists of some forty families, varying in form from the small graceful swallow family (Hirundinidae) to the crows (Corvidae).

The passerine birds as a group have the following characters in common: they all have what might be referred to as the typical 'bird's-foot' with three toes directed forwards and one, the hallux, homologous with the human big-toe, backwards. This is

Howard Ginn is the author of this section and of 'Speciation of Birds'

an ideal adaptation for gripping a branch, twig or reed-stem or even a wire. The muscles of the upper leg and the tendons in the legs and toes which they operate, are so arranged that any hint of the bird falling from its perching position immediately tightens the grip. No passerine species ever has webbing on the feet, and this applies even to species with remarkably aquatic life-styles, like the Dippers.

A second common feature is the degree of development of the "voice-box' or syrinx (plural syringes). Passerines are the most accomplished songsters, and in most species it consists of a development of the junction of the main windpipe or trachea and the smaller paired branches, the bronchi.

Other physical characters of the passerines are the wing feathering with nine or ten distinct primaries and the tail usually with twelve feathers. The bill shape varies greatly and is not necessarily a good criterion for a natural classification as it has become adapted to different diets. Thus there is the rather unspecialised type of bill for a mixed animal and/or vegetable diet such as the Blackbird's: the short, hardened, conical bill of the finches for cracking or shelling seeds and fruits: the short bill with an enormous, wide gape for capturing flying insects in the swallows: and the short, stout, hooked bill for large insect and small bird or mammal prey as found in the shrikes.

In overall size passerines range from the tiny Goldcrest *Regulus regulus* to the medium-sized Raven *Corvus corax* and in colour from the exceedingly drab to the most brilliantly plumaged of birds. The entire order are strictly land birds; many are highly migratory and the variety of habitats occupied is considerable. As a group they have been especially successful in making use of man-made situations, frequenting artificial nest-sites, roosting-sites, food and so on. In breeding

biology they are also highly variable, but usually build fairly substantial and often elaborate woven nests. Among this assemblage of features few are restricted exclusively to the passerines; only taken together do they provide a means of defining the order Passeriformes and also a basis on which to sub-divide this huge order.

However, many of the subdivisions within the order are somewhat tentative or speculative. This is because the general overall degree of similarity between different species is very high and it is very difficult to distinguish the features of true relationship from those resulting from convergent evolution. One of the most important structures in this context is the syrinx or voice-box and its muscles. Only the passerines have from five to nine pairs of syringeal muscles; it serves to separate the oscines and sub-oscines and is also taken into account in the further subdivisions.

Although some major groups stand out, there are always borderline families within the order Passeriformes which could be lumped with any of two or three other families. Dr Ernst Mayr, the distinguished taxonomist, once said that with only a few exceptions, none of the other families could be defined with certainty on anatomical characters alone: there is always at least a hint that the features might be similar because of adaptation or convergent evolution rather than because they are ancestrally similar.

Generally, in most lists, three main groups of families have been recognised, the Old World insect-eaters and related forms, the New World insect-eaters and finches (the group with nine-primaries) and thirdly the crows, birds of paradise and their relatives. Though different authors have recognised these groups of families they have placed them in different sequences. Mayr and Greenway placed the groups in the order given above with the crow group last; the American

(Above) Goldcrest *Regulus regulus* (left) and Raven *Corvus corax*: these two species show the tremendous variation in size and coloration between the passerines. The Raven, Britain's largest crow, has been closely associated with humans and was once a common scavenger on the streets of London but has gradually declined and is more confined to the north and west of Britain. However, like the bird in the photograph above, it is still present in the city at the Tower of London and legend has it that the safety of the kingdom depends upon the presence of the Ravens there.
(Below) Dipper *Cinclus cinclus*: despite its aquatic life style, its feet are typically passerine and not webbed

David Hosking

(Above) Rooks *Corvus frugilegus* and Jackdaws *C. monedula*. Like other crows they are usually regarded as the most advanced species, being the most intelligent and adaptable of all birds

school, including Wetmore placed the crow group first followed by the first group with the second group last. The subject has not been simplified by the moving of the shrikes (Laniidae) and starlings (Sturnidae) between the first and third groups. Storer and Voous place the crow group between the other two. Voous believes that the nine-primaried group are the most recently evolved and that the starlings and weavers and their relatives are the most advanced of the remaining songbird families. He relates the finch and bunting development of seed-crushing or shelling to the evolution of the monocotyledonous plants, particularly the grasses and cereals which is from other evidence a fairly recent event in evolutionary terms.

This, then, leaves a consideration of the crows; why do some authors place them last suggesting that they are the most highly developed or specialised of birds? The main reason for such an opinion seems to be that they are 'intelligent' as birds go. In spite of the difficulties of assessing or even defining what is meant by intelligence in animals, it does appear that there is evidence for considerable development in corvids. Just how much of the 'intelligence' is in fact intelligence, in the sense that human beings use the word, is still a subject for investigation. There is in any case good evidence to suggest that the crow group have retained many of the characteristics of the supposed passerine ancestors from whom the near-passerines —the bee-eaters, kingfishers, rollers and their relatives—are also believed to have arisen. Many of the corvid features are non-specialised; they are

generally fairly omnivorous, partially arboreal, not particularly specialised in any of their structures and perhaps for these reasons able to exploit a wider range of opportunities than the more specialised groups. Fossil evidence also suggests that some of the earliest known passerines were 'crow-like'. Some ornithologists therefore argue that there is good reason to place the crows at the beginning of the sequence.

There is indeed rarely any good reason for the order in which the passerine families are placed. Every species is in its way extremely well adapted to its particular habitat and way of life and is in that sense highly specialised. The parrots (Psittacidae) are in some ways apparently as intelligent as crows and also endowed with the ability of vocal mimicry in many species. For almost any family, some aspect of morphology or behaviour could be cited as a reason for regarding them as advanced, and the endless discussion seems in many ways purely academic. What most ornithologists need above all is some sort of stability; a halt to the constant changing of groupings and sequences. At the outset, it was mentioned that in order to study the large number of species, some form of order to classification is necessary. Once a reasonably acceptable structure is achieved, the frequent changing of groupings becomes counter-productive. This is not to say that when really good new evidence for relationships is discovered, the groupings should be changed, but the sequence of families within a large order like the Passeriformes is of much less importance.

FURTHER READING
General Works

Cramp, S. and Simmons, K. E. L. *Handbook of the Birds of Europe, the Middle East and North Africa*, Vol. I, 1977, Oxford University Press, Oxford.

Dementiev, G. P. *et al. The Birds of the Soviet Union*, 1966, Israel Program for Scientific Translations, Jerusalem.

Etchécopar, R. D. and Hüe, F. *Birds of North Africa*, 1967, Oliver & Boyd, Edinburgh.

Gooders, John *Birds—An Illustrated Survey of the Bird Families of the World*, 1975, Hamlyn, London.

Hüe, F. and Etchécopar, R. D. *Les Oiseaux du Proche et du Moyen Orient*, 1970, Boubée, Paris.

Landsborough Thomson, Sir A. (Ed.) *A New Dictionary of Birds*, 1964, Nelson, London.

Vaurie, Charles *The Birds of the Palearctic Fauna*, 2 vols., 1959 and 1965, Witherby, London.

Voous, K. H. *Atlas of European Birds*, 1960, Nelson, London.

Witherby, H. F. *et al. The Handbook of British Birds*, 5 vols., 1938–1941, Witherby, London.

Specialist Works

Grey, Viscount, of Fallodon *The Charm of Birds*, 1927, Hodder & Stoughton, London.

Howard, Eliot *Territory in Bird Life*, 1920, Murray, London.

Hudson, W. H. *Birds in London*, 1898, Longman, London.

Lack, David *Population Studies of Birds*, 1969, Oxford University Press, Oxford.

Mountfort, Guy *The Hawfinch*, 1957, Collins, London.

Murton, R. K. *The Wood Pigeon*, 1965, Collins, London.

Murton, R. K. *Man and Birds*, 1971, Collins, London.

Newton, Ian *Finches*, 1972, Collins, London.

Index

The main reference for each bird is printed in bold type; picture references are in italics.

THE ENCYCLOPEDIA OF
Birds

Index   Volumes 1–5

This is the general index to the encyclopedia. Bold type indicates volume number. Italic page references indicate illustrations.

X

Y

Z